AF262867

THE GATHERERS

MoMA PS1

FOREWORD
Connie Butler

The most urgent exhibitions put forth speculative inquiries in real time. Bringing together artists from around the world under the same roof, and within shared theoretical frameworks, can shape critical discourse, and artistic practices in turn. MoMA PS1 is committed to taking risks that foster dialogues on contemporary art through curatorial approaches that allow us to think alongside artists. Considering the broader social management of excess, the fourteen artists in this exhibition make visible the tangible and more latent methods of circulation, from gas lines to data management, surfacing the thresholds between surplus and waste. I'm thrilled that *The Gatherers* offers an opportunity to take the temperature of a moment wrought with accumulation, as contradictions between digital advancement and crumbling infrastructures come to the fore.

This project is a captivating addition to MoMA PS1's rich history of thematic shows that concretize critical moments in contemporary art and introduce global practices to wider audiences. Such exhibitions include *Afro-American Abstraction* (1980), *The Knot: Arte Povera* (1985), *Inside Out: New Chinese Art* (1998), *Wack! Art and the Feminist Revolution* (2008), and *Theatre of Operations: The Gulf Wars 1991–2011* (2019). Yet, where many of these shows identified artistic currents across national identities and their diasporas, *The Gatherers* distinguishes itself by drawing methodological parallels across four continents. The exhibition features over a dozen artists—working in painting, sculpture, assemblage, video, and performance—whose practices materialize the spatialized politics of memory. In an age where the accumulation of refuse seems insurmountable, I am particularly struck by how these artists have activated intersecting conversations around labor, agency, and the built environment.

An exhibition like this one—featuring ambitious new works, many of which are large-scale installations—can only be accomplished by a collective force with a multitude of skill sets. I thank Ruba Katrib, Chief Curator and Director of Curatorial Affairs, for her steadfast commitment to this project. Her rigorous research has taken her across the globe and culminated in both a clever exhibition and an imaginative publication. I also commend the MoMA PS1 staff for their collaborative spirit and collective passion.

I am exceedingly grateful to the Board of MoMA PS1, led by the undaunted Robert Soros, for their unwavering support of artistic experimentation. We also thank our municipal partners: Laurie Cumbo and the New York City Department of Cultural Affairs; Donovan Richards, Queens Borough President; Julie Won, New York City Council Member; and the New York City Council overall. I deeply appreciate Glenn D. Lowry, The David Rockefeller Director of The Museum of Modern Art, for his wisdom, camaraderie, and support of this exhibition.

This exhibition would not have been possible without major support from the Contemporary Arts Council of The Museum of Modern Art, the International Council of The Museum of Modern Art, and Jamie and Robert Soros. We also thank The Deborah Buck Foundation for their significant support, as well as George Petrocheilos and Diamantis Xylas and Eleanor Heyman Propp for additional support. Furthermore, MoMA PS1 offers our gratitude for funding from the Royal Norwegian Consulate General in New York, Marieluise Hessel, the Lithuanian Culture Institute, the Consulate General of Sweden in New York, Vicky Chen, and Webber Huang.

This publication was made possible with additional support from the MoMA PS1 Publication Fund, with special thanks to Philip Aarons and Shelley Fox Aarons, Elyse Benenson, and Kathy Fuld.

We are very thankful to the lenders to the exhibition: Thomas Alexander; David Galperin; private collection; Sammlung von Storch, Cologne; TAO ART Collection, Taipei; and X Museum, Beijing.

Finally, we thank the artists of the exhibition: Karimah Ashadu; Tolia Astakhishvili; Miho Dohi; Andro Eradze; He Xiangyu; Samuel Hindolo; Geumhyung Jeong; Klara Liden; Jean Katambayi Mukendi; Nick Relph; Selma Selman; Ser Serpas; Emilija Škarnulytė; and Zhou Tao, whose incisive practices attend to the resonance of history in our current moment. Seen together, their work draws our attention to the forces—architectural, institutional, and psychological—that structure life across the globe.

Connie Butler
The Agnes Gund Director
MoMA PS1

ACKNOWLEDGMENTS
Ruba Katrib

This exhibition developed at the wane of the COVID-19 pandemic, a major global crisis that has rendered a new normal of seemingly constant change and chaos acutely felt. As contemporary art exhibitions around the world opened after lockdowns, many asked how artists would respond to such a catastrophe, and seemed to want those responses to be literal, prescriptive, or at least legible. Artists, however, are not journalists. The world creeps into artistic production in myriad ways, often surreptitiously. Because of this, I wanted to look more deeply at artworks to understand the nuances of the moment, to be receptive to what was arising instead of seeking answers to questions I had already formed.

I encountered the work of several of the artists included in this exhibition in a resumed itinerary of international travels over the past few years. During those very first trips, when we were able to more safely step out of our locales, the art I saw didn't yet feel like it had fully entered into the moment. We were still getting our bearings, and many artists tarried to produce new works while occasions to publicly exhibit them would still take time to arise. It took a minute for the shared conversations, concerns, and approaches to come into focus. Within the aftermath, I noticed that many artists were processing the idea of the past in relation to the end of the future. Of course, time continues to move, but in my discussions with many of them, and with others, the forward thrust of the clock felt more like a loss, an uncertain disappearance of the world we thought we once knew. As Franco "Bifo" Berardi argues, the conviction that the futures holds potentiality, a concept dear to the twentieth century, has all but eroded in the twenty-first.[1]

Thus, *The Gatherers* developed as a way to consider how artists pick up the pieces—how they process, retain, and remake what the force of the world might jettison. I think that, increasingly, artists will be the keepers of details that might otherwise be squeezed out of the churn of time. More and more, they are the ones working in "zones," interstitial or abandoned spaces outside of established territories, which have changed meaning or have not yet been defined. This project gives equal consideration to how these areas emerge within physical terrains, in cities, on the outskirts, and in architectures, as well as in conceptual realms. Their positions will inform how we think of what came before.

While this exhibition could have included dozens of artists with kindred inquiries into excess and its effects, I brought together this group of fourteen to understand qualities of this moment emerging from particular geopolitical situations and events. The show underscores a generation who came to maturity in a post-1989 moment, who hold an expanded idea of the former East, and whose adulthood so far has been impacted by the promises and failures of global neoliberalism. I also wanted to bring together a group of related practitioners—including artists who know each other, or are familiar with each other's work—and whose practices share a belief in the potential for liberation, at least from the disillusionment of past world orders. They also realize that offerings of salvation from challenging subjects and situations can deny human aptitudes for waste, destruction, and violence. Instead, their artistic approaches offer an analysis that comes from deep observation. I am eternally grateful for these artists and their perspectives onto the world. I want to thank them each for their collaboration and their incredible work: Karimah Ashadu, Tolia Astakhishvili (with Dylan Peirce, and contributions by Maka Sanadze and Zurab Astakhishvili), Miho Dohi, Andro Eradze, He Xiangyu, Samuel Hindolo, Geumhyung Jeong, Klara Liden, Jean Katambayi Mukendi, Nick Relph, Selma Selman, Ser Serpas, Emilija Škarnulytė, and Zhou Tao. I additionally want to acknowledge the assistants and managers of some of the artists who have also been critical facilitators: Marie Becker, Annie Hägg, Ebi Han, Erik Vojevodin, and Petar Vranjković.

The structure of this book offers each artist a focused text, and I am grateful to the brilliant contributors, who expand our understanding of these artists' practices with diligent attention to their work, its context, and broader cultural conversations. I thank Kirsty Bell, Amber Esseiva, Anette Freudenberger, Sheldon Gooch, Summer Guthery, Estelle Hoy, Quinn Latimer, Laura McLean-Ferris, Camila Palomino, Filipa Ramos, Nadim Samman, Fabian Schöneich, and Jeppe Ugelvig.

Additionally, I want to extend gratitude to Annie Godfrey Larmon, a talented editor who shaped all of the texts in this book and brought excellent cohesion to this collective writing endeavor. I also want to recognize Alec Mapes-Frances for his design, which brought a distinct form and feel to this ambitious publication. I thank Sheldon Gooch, MoMA PS1 Curatorial Assistant, for essential support on the project and for keeping all of the moving parts in order; Serena Moscardelli, NYU Curatorial Fellow, who offered critical assistance on the book production; and Audrey Min, CCS Bard Curatorial Fellow for her research support. I extend my gratitude to Polly Watson, proofreader, and Jack Radley, MoMA PS1 Editor. I would also like to thank the rest of my colleagues on the MoMA PS1 Curatorial team: Andrea Sánchez, Coordinator of Curatorial Affairs; Jody Graf, Assistant Curator; Elena Ketelson González, Assistant Curator; and Kari Rittenbach, Assistant Curator.

The Gatherers would not be possible without the incredible work of the entire MoMA PS1 staff, who have each contributed to the realization of this project. I would like to thank the entire production team, and in particular Lilly Hern-Fondation, Senior Project Manager, who supported this exhibition, as well as Lauren DiLoreto, Director of Program Production; Richard Wilson, Exhibition and Production Designer; Diana Matuszak, Senior Registrar; Jetaime Pizzaro, Assistant Registrar; Zachary Taube, Assistant Manager of Installation; and Dylan Newlon, Program Production Fellow. I appreciate the contributions of Nick Scavo, Senior Project Manager, to realizing the performance program.

Furthermore, we value the installation team for their stellar work mounting the exhibition. Additionally, Jose Ortiz, Deputy Director; Molly Kurzius, Director of External Affairs; Daniel Schaeffer, Director of Development; Catherine Schreiber, Major Gifts Officer; Teresa Lillis, Manager of Individual Giving; Philip Brand, Manager of Institutional Giving; and Julia Fesser, Publicity Coordinator, have each been essential in the critical fundraising and administration needed to mount an exhibition of this complexity.

The Gatherers would not have been possible without the support of the Board of Trustees of MoMA PS1, led by Robert Soros, who—along with Glenn D. Lowry, The David Rockefeller Director, The Museum of Modern Art—gave critical support to the development of this exhibition and the artists it brought together. I would also like to extend my sincere appreciation to Connie Butler, the Agnes Gund Director, for her encouragement and guidance as I embarked on this endeavor, as well as for her enthusiasm for the artists in the exhibition.

This exploratory exhibition would not be possible without the essential support of the generous lenders and donors to the exhibition. Here, I would like to thank the artists' galleries who have lent works and offered logistical support: 15 Orient, acb Gallery, Andrew Kreps Gallery, Galerie Buchholz, ChertLüdde, Galerie Crèvecœur, Gordon Robichaux, Hagiwara Projects, Herald St, Karma International, LC Queisser, Maxwell Graham Gallery, Micki Meng, Nonaka-Hill, Galerie Neu, Ramiken, Sadie Coles HQ, and Vitamin Creative Space.

I would also like to thank MoMA's International Council and Jay A. Levenson, Director of the International Program at MoMA, and his team for the important travel support specific to this project and that has been granted over the years. As I mentioned, these trips and encounters with artists and artworks have been critical to the relationships forged, which ultimately made this show possible.

Further, friends, family, and colleagues have offered guidance, feedback, and insights. I would like to express my sincere appreciation to Lawrence Kumpf, Lauren Cornell, Kyle Dancewicz, Chris Aque, Donald Ryan, Robert Snowden, Irena Popiashvili, Lisa Offermann, Nika Lelashvili, Jordan Carter, Sarah Suzuki, Stuart Comer, Sophie Cavoulacos, Niels Olsen, Rochelle Goldberg, Veit Laurent, and Win McCarthy.

Ruba Katrib
Chief Curator and Director of Curatorial Affairs
MoMA PS1

1   See Franco "Bifo" Berardi, *Futurablity: The Age of Importance and the Horizon of Possibility* (London: Verso Press, 2019).

THE GATHERERS:
CONTENDING WITH ACCUMULATION IN THE TWENTY-FIRST CENTURY
Ruba Katrib

And we did not age. The things around us didn't last long enough to grow old, replaced and rehabilitated at lightning speed. Our memory didn't have time to associate them with moments of existence.
—Annie Ernaux, *The Years*

Waste is the defining character of the twenty-first century. Endless cycles of production, consumption, and destruction drive our sustenance and labor, our social lives and politics, our violence and aesthetic paradigms. We acquire objects, clothes, electronics, and food, with all of their packaging, and we use them up and toss them out. Consumer participation is just one step in the resource-intensive process that propels each plastic bottle and takeout container into a landfill or the ocean, where it forever haunts our consciousness and carbon footprint. Most of us are aware of this insidious cycle, but its magnitude and our complicity embroiled therein make it abstract; in turn, our daily activities can become anxieties. Today, our sheer existence generates waste in such extremes that we've overwhelmed the parameters of environmental discourses. The problem is only intensifying.

The production of our commodities often involves some kind of violence toward the earth and its people—natural minerals are ruthlessly extracted, pollutive factories are sequestered in particular regions (and among vulnerable populations), and goods are piled up in warehouses at the edges of cities to be dispatched by precarious workers. In many parts of the world, to shop is to go online, pick something out, click to pay, and voilà, a package arrives at the door. Eventually, the plastic and cardboard packaging and gadgets themselves end up in trash bins. If you live in a city, a percentage of this material ends up strewn about the streets. The rest is buried, burned, or perhaps shipped off, sold, or dumped elsewhere in the world. In this well-rehearsed sequence within the wealthier nations of the twenty-first century, there is no visible maker, no shopkeeper, no place of production; purveyors promise convenience, and this entails smoothing over any sign of the physical impact of our commodities. On the other hand, stomach-churning exposés on sweatshops, child labor, and microplastics periodically pop up as we scroll. This information momentarily returns our awareness to the physical impact of goods on the world and our bodies, briefly complicating the seamless experience of acquisition. Yet consumer behavior rarely adapts in any significant way—even the most motivated find themselves in a game of whack-a-mole. The facts of environmental devastation remain deliberately obscured from and frustratingly irreconcilable with daily life. As waste grows, so does a sense of detachment. We, humans of this century, still suffer from what Karl Marx famously identified as "alienation from the means of production," yes, but we also experience alienation from our acts of consumption and disposal. Political theorist Wendy Brown succinctly sums up this conundrum: "Just as commodities in the market do not announce the social relations that produced them, they do not carry on their surfaces the violations of earthly life through which they are constructed, transported, used, and eventually shed as 'waste.'"[1]

In the twentieth century, we believed advances in the means of production would lead to a better life; but in the twenty-first, we are learning that the means we developed junked it all. While our virtual technologies have created the misperception of a dematerialized world—effacing both the physical, carbon-guzzling infrastructure required to uphold that illusory world and the material consequences of our transactions within it—of course, this deception is a mask that serves to disguise the harm the consumer ecosystem, and the corporate interests that fuel it, has on all forms of life. The theorist Franco "Bifo" Berardi has diagnosed the suffering that has befallen "Internet natives and precarious workers" in response to these convolutions as "essentially aesthetic." He writes that any revolt in this generation stems from "a disgust at suffocating over-consumption, at the ugliness of rampant plastic, at the cynicism of those who have suffered long exposure to neoliberal domination, and also at the spectacle of politics."[2] That is, in an increasingly mediated world, ethics are ever more located in the realm of aesthetics; this phenomena stems from what we look at, what we are prevented from looking at, and how incentivized frameworks fashion what we are looking at in the first place.

In a variety of modes, the international artists in *The Gatherers* work against the forces that attempt to conceal the aftermaths of our contemporary lifestyles, not by simply portraying mountains of rubbish or toxic runoff in rivers, but by treading in the rough edges of the contradictions that accompany such dissimulation. Some draw their materials from sources and events so ubiquitous they are nearly invisible, while others explore cordoned-off zones where such byproducts are managed. These artists point to the ways in which excess not only muddles the landscape but blots out the future.[3] To analyze our contemporary condition more holistically, it is critical to address the entanglement of many factors, actors, and impacts. *The Gatherers* engages these knots, focusing on the broader psychic and aesthetic burdens that accompany the existence—whether explicit or hidden—of such extraordinary scales of waste and environmental ruin.

This exhibition takes place at a moment in which a widely documented genocide has been largely ignored, debated, and invalidated on the global stage, especially by Western powers. A recent global pandemic that took millions of lives has been all but forgotten, and a right-wing president has retaken the White House with a tech billionaire at his side. While technocrats dramatically cut what they perceive to be fiscal waste in institutions, they destroy the livelihoods of many. Slashed funding for the U.S. Agency for International Development has left to rot nearly five hundred million dollars' worth of food stores managed by the organization. As I write, multiple

12

wildfires have ravaged Los Angeles. The magnitude of destruction—the worst
in the city's history—could have been avoided, but puzzlingly, LA leadership
divested from municipal services that should battle such anticipated events
amid a historic lack of rainfall and other mounting impacts of climate change.
Conservative governments have taken hold across Europe, Georgia, and Latin
America, and a coup failed in South Korea. In so many parts of the world, the
ruins of war, itself a perverse economic engine of waste and production, meet
and fuel climate disaster. These catastrophes continue not because there is a
shortage of photos, evidence, or information, but despite them.

I would venture that these global events are symptoms of the loss of a
shared reality, caused, in part, by a widespread alienation from life's materiality. Philosopher Michel Foucault warned against the trappings of exceptionality
that are embedded in humanist constructions. Notions of man, progress, and
modernity, he evocatively speculated, are in fact recent ideas that will meet the
fate of a "face drawn in sand at the edge of the sea," swept away by waves.[4]
As this face erodes and a new order for our species is yet to emerge, what
remains is all the junk that will continue to wash up on the shore.

The artists in *The Gatherers* engage the contradictions bound up in
cultural narratives and technological effects of convenience and immediacy;
referencing, for example, the heavy material infrastructure that produces the
weightlessness of the internet. Gigantic cables stretch across the ocean floor,
and enormous data centers require constant cooling and other forms of inten-
sive maintenance. All of it contributes to our environmental impact, and all
of it seems to be operating under the cover of out of sight, out of mind.[5] This
logic attends most commodities today—objects are created without bearing
any trace of their making, freeing the consumer from guilt surrounding the
conditions of production.[6] The extent of global trade has expanded the field of
labor resources and waste deposition, making class distinctions starker. The
wealthiest among us have an entire world of "others" to dump on. Yet this
exhibition is not positioned as an exposé of specific events; rather, it intersects
with the issues that transpire between surplus and waste, use and disuse.
Here, I define excess as resources that are not necessary to sustain life and
retain potentiality, and waste as the unnecessary loss of that potentiality.[7]
These designations, marked by related and disputably visible thresholds, have
also operated as critical subjects in aesthetic realms throughout history.

Discussing the age-old fascination with what has been tossed, literary
critic David Trotter writes: "People started to drop things as soon as they
started to pick them up," and these things "did not pass entirely without
comment."[8] Indeed, visually remarking on what has been left behind is a
phenomenon that can be traced as far back as the second century BC deco-
rative theme known as *asàrotos òikos*, or "unswept floor" (Fig. 1). Attributed to
Sosos of Pergamon, these mosaics were intended for dining room floors and
featured trompe l'oeil depictions of debris from fine edibles—fruit, lobster,
walnuts.[9] More than a millennium later, Dutch still lifes would frequently take

                    THE GATHERERS   Ruba Katrib

Fig. 1   Heracleitus, after Sosos of Pergamon, *The Unswept Floor*, 2nd century BCE, Museo Gregoriano Profano/Vatican Museums. Scala/Art Resource, NY

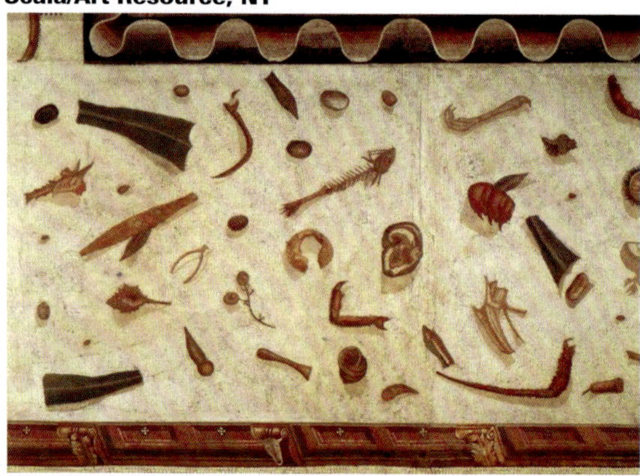

"the wreckage of a meal," as their subject.[10] Depicting the slough that accompanies a feast not only announced wealth, but warned of the rot that would follow. While this pictured waste indeed signals the transience of life and the futility of desire, it also pronounces a kind of heedlessness to these warnings.

The twentieth century offered a glut of litter to comment on. As the industrial era saw goods pile up, artists turned to the trash bins. In the 1920s, the Surrealists were fascinated by flea markets, where they could examine the types of objects that were disappearing into history while the new emerged. At mid-century, artists working with assemblage and the found object responded to a postwar exuberance around the abundance of newly available consumer goods, which were just as easy to acquire as they were to throw in the wastebasket. In 1961, The Museum of Modern Art in New York mounted *The Art of Assemblage* in response to such emergent practices. Writing on assemblage's counterbalance of poetic and realistic qualities, the exhibition's curator, William Seitz, noted that "when paper is soiled or lacerated, when cloth is worn, stained, or torn, when wood is split, weathered, or patterned with peeling coats of paint, when metal is bent or rusted, they gain connotations which unmarked materials lack."[11] For included artist Eduardo Paolozzi, and other artists associated with what Hal Foster has called "brutal aesthetics," there was

14

something particularly enticing about used, trashed goods; Paolozzi described car junkyards as "hunting grounds."[12] In these cemeteries of stuff, scraps are charged with significance, bearing markers of manufacturing ingenuity, wealth or poverty, use and disuse. And then there is the simple fact that such waste is the flip side of luxury, which also marks a sort of failure.

For other artists working at the time, the excess of already given objects made creation possible. Take Simon Rodia, who built the monumental Watts Towers (1921–54) in Los Angeles out of scavenged Seven-Up bottle fragments, scrap ironwork, and broken dishware (the work is discussed in the *Art of Assemblage* catalogue but not represented in the show). Later, at the end of the 1960s, Arte Povera artists in Italy responded to the country's industrial developments and waning "economic miracle" by working with "impoverished" materials—scraps of fabric, surplus bags from American aid shipments, bits of Styrofoam or bread—that were found, junked, or readily available and inexpensive.

Indeed, waste, creation, and destruction were central topics to art of the '60s. In Europe, critic Pierre Restany's 1960 manifesto for Nouveau Réalisme expressed the "depletion" of established forms of artmaking and called for a kind of symbolic type of social realism, claiming that "sociology comes to the rescue of consciousness and chance, whether with a choice of poster deface-ment, the look of an object, household garbage or salon scraps, the unleashing of mechanical affectivity, the diffusion of sensitivity beyond the limits of its perception."[13] That year, Nouveau Réaliste member Jean Tinguely brought *Homage to New York* to MoMA's Sculpture Garden, where the self-destructing assemblage detonated. Back in L.A., Noah Purifoy made assemblages from the charred and melted detritus of the 1965 Watts rebellion, establishing a defini-tive practice of "Junk Dada"[14] that would bring elements of site-specificity and activism to assemblage.

Of course, Robert Rauschenberg's Combines are critical to this conversation of postwar waste. In a 1961 text on Rauschenberg, John Cage associates the sticky juncture between accumulation and emptiness in his friend's work with the excesses of contemporary society. Cage writes that the world has too much food, too many people, too much art; "We've gotten to the point of burning food," he says. "When will we burn our art?"[15] He then cites Rauschenberg's ultimate sacrificial act of 1953: erasing a drawing by Willem de Kooning. In his practice, Rauschenberg moved between white (or blank) paintings and junk sculptures, continuously navigating the material residue of something, even in what seems to be an absence. These art historical examples are meant to trace not just innovations of form and concept, but reckonings with cultural issues of waste and its (mis)management. While artistic engage-ments with the found object, junk, and assemblage are now codified, the detritus from which postwar artists pulled to make their work has reached an unimaginable scale. This situation requires a reexamination of the foundations of such practices as they operate today.

 THE GATHERERS Ruba Katrib

The title of this exhibition, *The Gatherers*, nods to Jean-François Millet's 1857 painting *Des glaneuses* [The Gleaners], which features people on the fringes of society who subsisted by collecting agricultural scraps (Fig. 2). When unveiled in the Paris salons, the work provoked negative reactions due to its commentary on class, still a touchy subject after the Revolutions of 1848. In the decades prior, J. M. W. Turner included pollution in his landscape paintings, similarly addressing the social dynamics of his time by not shying away from the impact of industrialization and emergent capitalism in the city and its outskirts. Turner captured the gloom of early nineteenth-century London, where he, as art critic John Ruskin described, "devoted picture after picture to the illustration of effects of dinginess, smoke, soot, dust, and dusty texture; old sides of boats, weedy roadside vegetation, dung-hills, straw-yards, and all the soilings and stains of every common labour."[16] Both artists looked to the intended and unintended consequences of production, documenting the waste and toxins that were increasingly visible in the environment. In 2000, when Agnès Varda released her film *The Gleaners and I*, which considers modern-day gleaners of all stripes, there was nothing shocking about the subject. Varda states that she loves to film "rot, leftover, and waste" as her camera pans over scenes of detritus, and the allure of her subject is evident, even if it is complicated that the depicted litter in the margins is widespread, accepted, and even mundane.

In the face of mounting waste, the contemporary artists in *The Gatherers* ultimately reflect urgent concerns surrounding this "advanced" era's crumbling municipal infrastructures, careless social behavior, and dangerous management practices. The specificities of sociopolitical and historical context are in many ways key to understanding how these artists variously engage discard, refuse, and mess. However, already in 1961, Seitz wrote in his catalogue essay for the *Art of Assemblage* that in the art in the exhibition and of his time, "it is not hard to discern behind these vernacular subjects a striving, embittered by disenchantment," which is "in part an outcome of insecurity that is more than economic." Noting ongoing reverberations from "the failure of liberal politics during the thirties and forties," he mentions, among other conflicts, "the anguish of the scrap heap; the images of charred bodies that keep Hiroshima and Nagasaki before our eyes."[17] Sounds familiar. Perhaps the anxieties underpinning the works in Seitz's show and this one aren't so different after all. Although it is hard to deny the harrowing effect of acceleration—whether measuring the impacts of globalization or "late capitalism," new technologies in the production of life and death, climate change, or our greater awareness of all these issues and our implication within them. There are, of course, distinct causes of our disappointments and horrors, from Hiroshima to Fukushima. Today, one must also contend with the interplay of cynicism and neglect. It's ironic that the information age, with its endless documentation, has come to be defined by a kind of social amnesia, a condition of forgetting and denial.

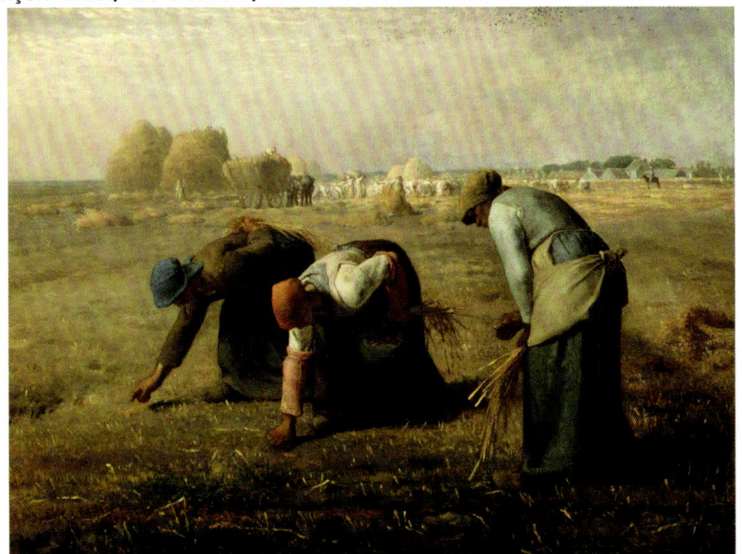

The artists participating in *The Gatherers* passed through formative life stages during the global shifts of the 1990s: the end of the Cold War; the explosion of new tech; and the acceleration of globalization and neoliberalism, with their bad-faith claims that commerce could smooth over rough edges between nations and peoples. The era promised that humanism was back, that the digital would replace the analog, and that the old regimes, conflicts, and wars would eventually be chalked up to failures of a primitive past. A major theme of this period was disarmament, as governments sought to reduce fears surrounding nuclear war. Though that particular threat seems to have taken a backseat in our contemporary psyches, there have been recent nuclear tragedies tied to human error and negligence, not to intent.[18] Emilija Škarnulytė's filmic installation *Burial* (2022) directly responds to this situation, meditating on the fate of the Ignalina Nuclear Power Plant, which was established in 1983 on Lithuania's border (Figs. 3–4). In 1999, as part of Lithuania's bid to join the European Union, the country agreed to shut down the facility due to engineering similarities to the Chernobyl plant in Prypiat, Ukraine, where a flawed Soviet reactor design led to a devastating accident in 1986. While Ignalina's main units were closed in 2004 and 2006, the full decommissioning process will take longer than the plant was ever in operation. Disposing of nuclear material is not so easy, as Škarnulytė's haunting scenes attest.

Fig. 3   Still, Emilija Škarnulytė, *Burial*, 2022.
Fig. 4   Still, Emilija Škarnulytė, *Burial*, 2022.

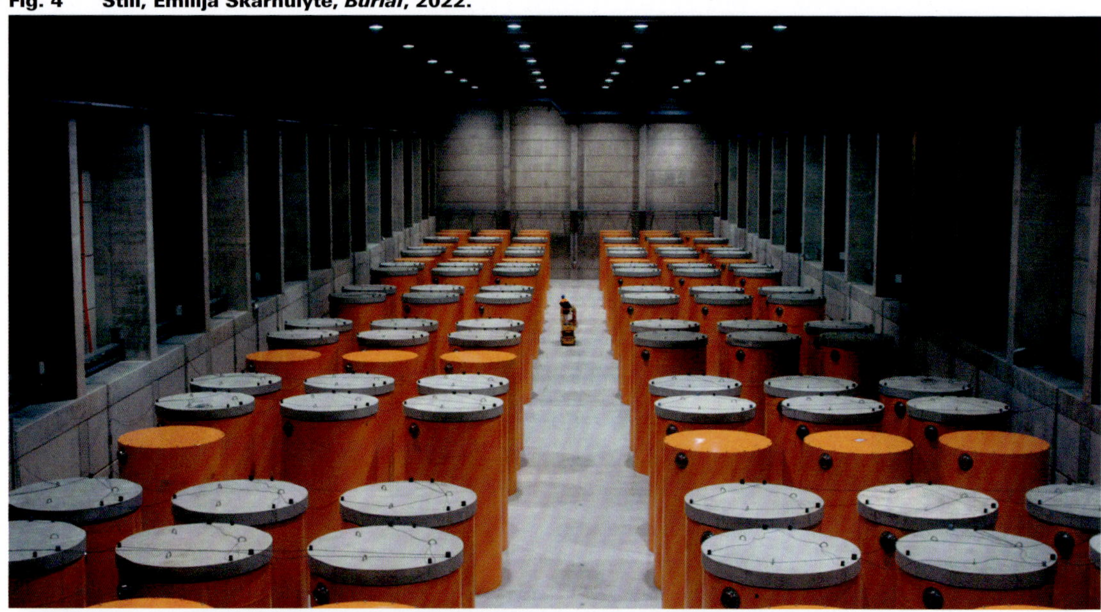

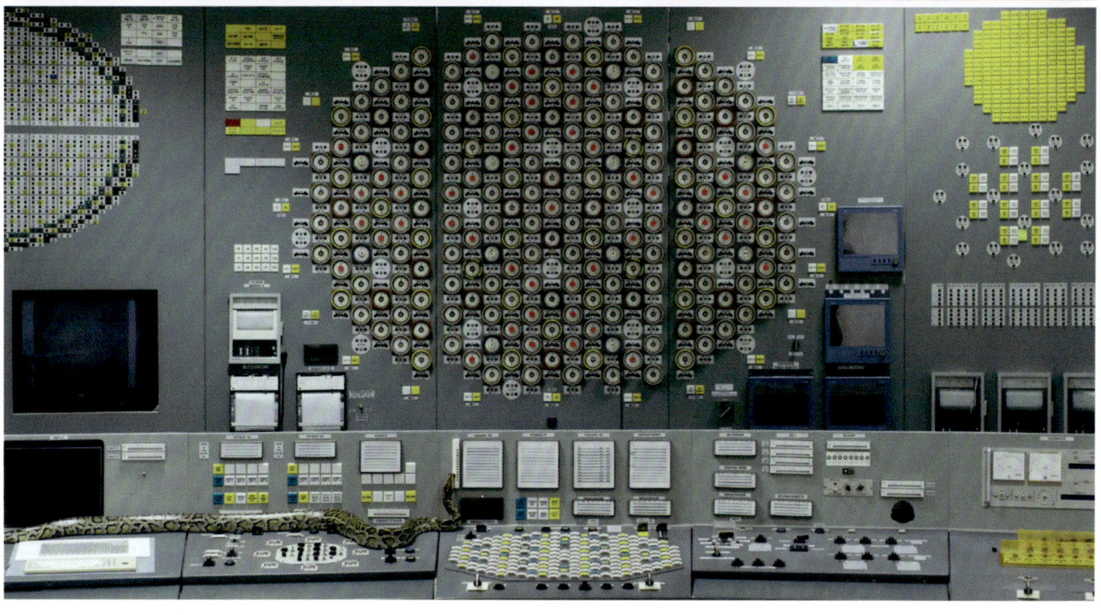

The Ignalina plant's history reflects both the explosive failures of the Soviet Union's technological prowess and the new era of neoliberal member states, tracing a global turn to capital and embodying the waste the pursuit of capital leaves behind. In Škarnulytė's film, a giant python slithers across the facility's otherwise abandoned control center, signaling a future in which humans are completely removed from the equation. While the creature seems threatening, the real danger is of course the power plant, its destructive capabilities, and the countless orange barrels of toxic sludge the artist documents. Yet with its gray-toned 1980s Soviet color scheme and impressive array of buttons, the analog control center seems strangely harmless now, coming across, however misleadingly, like a defanged relic from a simpler time.

In another part of the world, and located in a newer enterprise, Zhou Tao's film *The Axis of Big Data* (2024) offers another vantage on such colossal operations (**Figs. 5–6**). The work takes as its subject the phenomenon of data centers and the constructions that maintain the virtual cloud, focusing on the Guizhou region in rural China. Operating and cooling these centers requires enormous amounts of energy, which at this point largely comes from nuclear and other destructive forms of power—sources that were considered outmoded not long ago. Zhou documents the picturesque mountainous area that surrounds the behemoth data center, where the local potential for hydraulic power will be a critical resource to exploit in storing just a portion of the world's exponentially growing data. Škarnulytė's and Tao's works both touch on how waste is embedded in the industrial sites of the electronic age, whether decommissioned or newly constructed. Rather than dwell on depictions of the waste itself, they each incorporate visual strategies of negation. Neither artist zooms out enough to reveal the full scope of their locations, thereby highlighting the incommensurability of the portrayed structures with common understandings of the purposes they serve. Both artists document the mundane aspects of these sites without directly indicating their impact, past or future, on the environments and communities around them.

In Zhou's film, the camera starts inside a data center, picturing endless shelves of servers with cascading wires and cords. After a few short minutes, it cuts through the walls and pans out into a bright day. Bucolic scenes of everyday life featuring farmers, tourists, and natural beauty unfold around the site, circling around the "axis" of the data center before the camera eventually returns to the buzzing darkness behind its walls. By turning his back to the subject of his film, Zhou suggests that the facility's relationship with its environs is not only incongruous, but ultimately antithetical. In discussing such artistic modes of withdrawal or abandonment, it is hard not to evoke Walter Benjamin's famous allegorical interpretation of Paul Klee's 1920 painting *Angelus Novus* [New Angel], in which the "angel of history" is pictured contemplating the past; this angel "sees one single catastrophe which keeps piling wreckage upon wreckage…[a storm] propels him into the future to which his back is turned, while the pile of debris before him grows skyward.

  THE GATHERERS Ruba Katrib

Fig. 5   Still, Zhou Tao, *The Axis of Big Data*, 2024.
Fig. 6   Still, Zhou Tao, *The Axis of Big Data*, 2024.

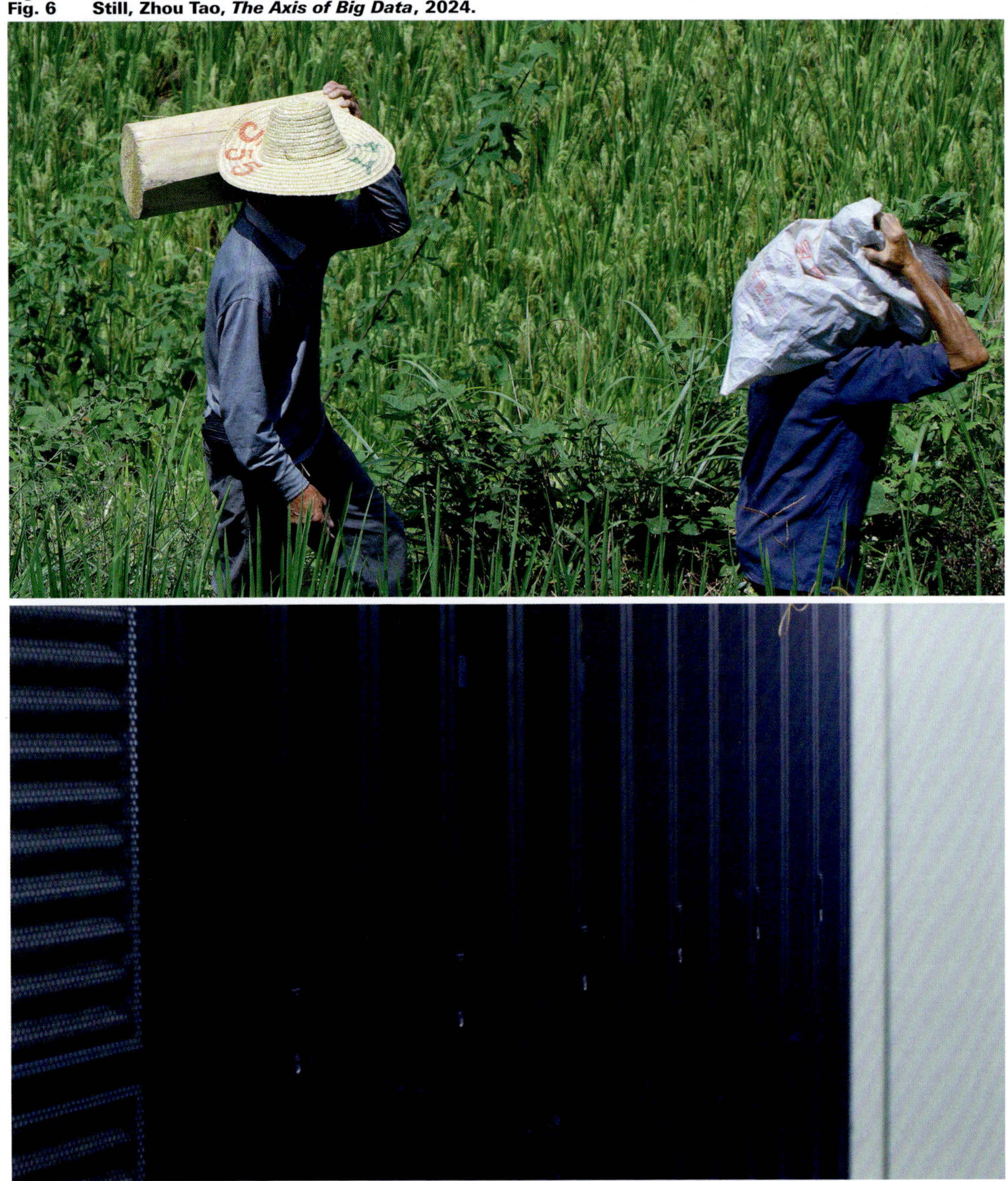

This storm is what we call progress."[19] For Benjamin, writing in 1940 amid the accumulating horrors referenced by Seitz, progress is simply an idea that distracts us from the mounting rubble we have caused. To turn one's back on such progress—the angel's lofty sky, the data center's outsourced memory, the nuclear facility's herculean power—these various works suggest, may be the only way to take stock of our material reality.

Jean Katambayi Mukendi's work directly contends with wreckage in the name of progress, responding to activity he witnessed firsthand growing up in Lubumbashi, a major mining hub in the Democratic Republic of the Congo. His sculptures and drawings feature invented machines and flowcharts that propose alternative realities to the exploitation and devastation experienced by the people and land in his region, tapped for the minerals and precious metals that run our gadgets. His kinetic sculptures and diagrammatic drawings imagine new contraptions, but they also function like afterimages, echoing the impact of wasted stuff. For example, *Trash TV* (2022) repurposes a truck windshield filled with assorted garbage: toothbrushes, string, plastic wrappers, and cassette tapes (Fig. 7). The assemblage resembles a busted television whose screen has been burned with a palimpsest of layered images. His monumental drawing *Doors* (2023) was inspired by the New York City subway and stretches nearly the length of a train car (Fig. 8). The schematic centers on a pair of sliding doors, from which real and imagined elements extend in a complex circuit that includes iconography of electricity as well as garbage, a rat, and other symbols of the metropolis. While the work speaks to Mukendi's interest in the interconnected flows between extraction, production, and destruction, it also serves as a reminder that the New York City subway system, which services one of the wealthiest cities in the world, is a notoriously unkept and dysfunctional amenity.

The end of a commodity's life is often long and complex. It may have chapters that are incomprehensible to us, as the lives of plastics, synthetics, and extracted materials are much lengthier than ours. These fates might continue the global journey that started with production and consumption; for example, precious metals mined in the Congo may be placed into devices made in China. These items might be purchased and used in Germany, only to be junked and returned, in salvaged pieces, to Africa. Selma Selman has an intimate relationship to this flow of materials. Her family has a business recycling scrap metal in Bosnia, and it was in this context that Selman learned there is gold to be found in garbage. In most of her works, she repurposes materials associated with the fringe economies of salvage yards. Embedded in the gallery wall, *Nail* (2025) is a gold-gilded nail sculpture composed of metal sourced from the scrapped circuit boards of computers (Fig. 9). In a sort of reverse extraction process, Selman reclaims the precious materials that have been stripped from the earth and repurposes them before they return to the environment in the form of waste. In another act of reversal, Selman turns the discarded claw from an industrial crane upside down in *Flower of*

　　　　THE GATHERERS　　　　Ruba Katrib

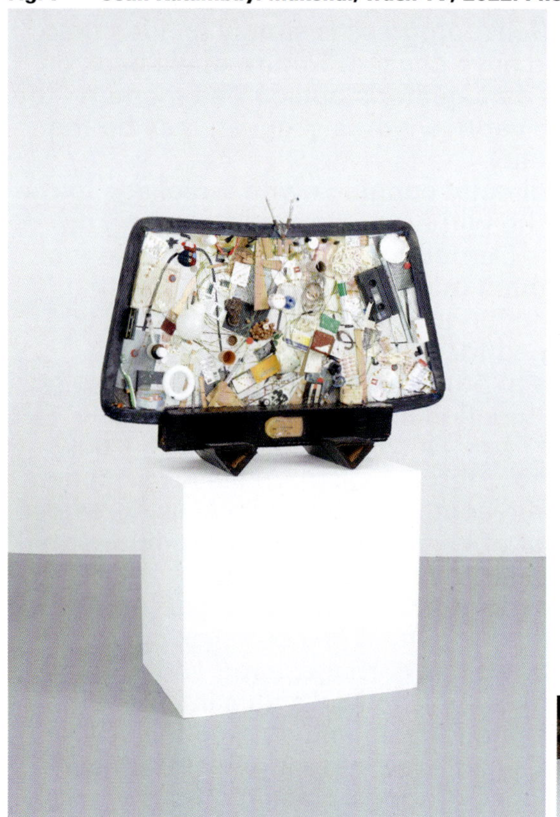

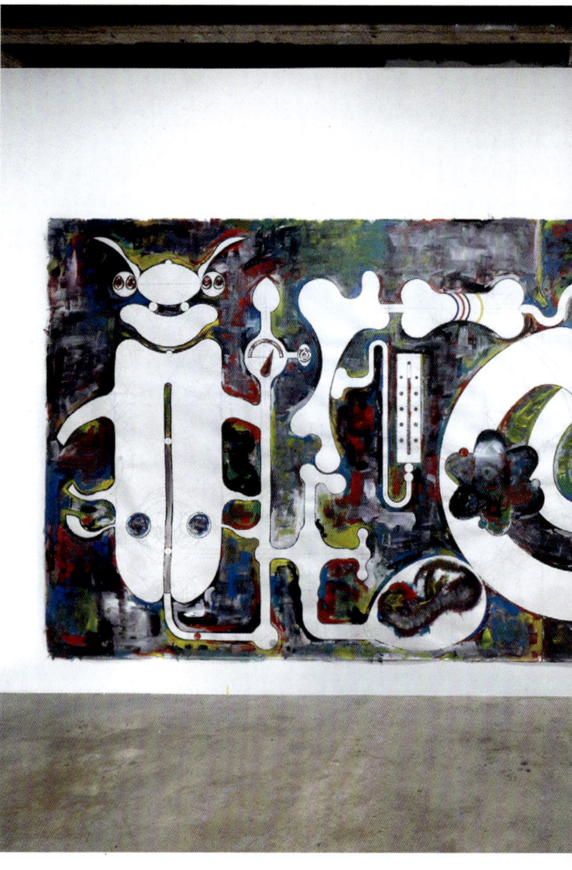

         THE GATHERERS   Ruba Katrib

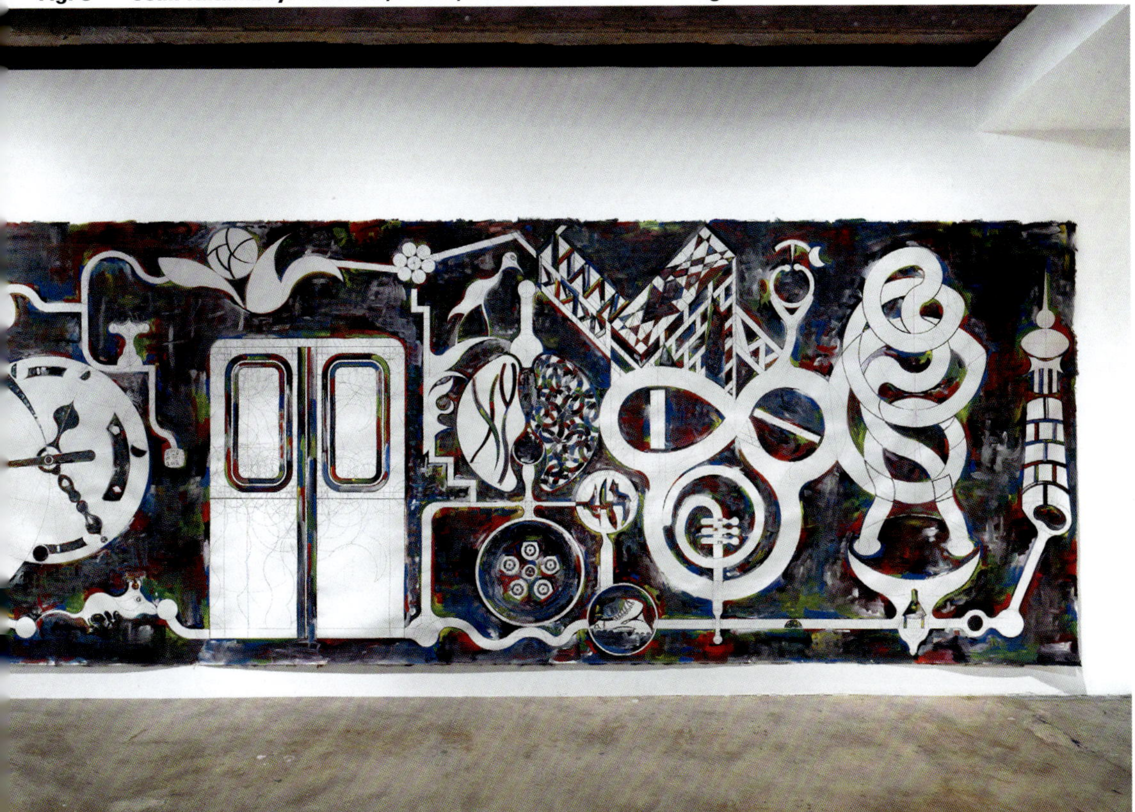

Fig. 9   Installation view, Selma Selman, *Motherboards (A Golden Nail)*, 2023, in *Sleeping Guards*, Stedelijk Museum, Amsterdam, 2025. Photo: Gert Jan Van Rooij

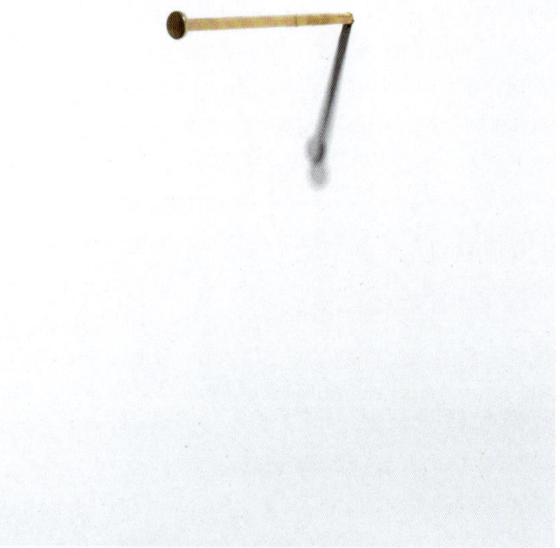

Fig. 10   Installation view, Selma Selman, *Flowers of Life*, Schirn Kunsthalle Frankfurt, 2024.

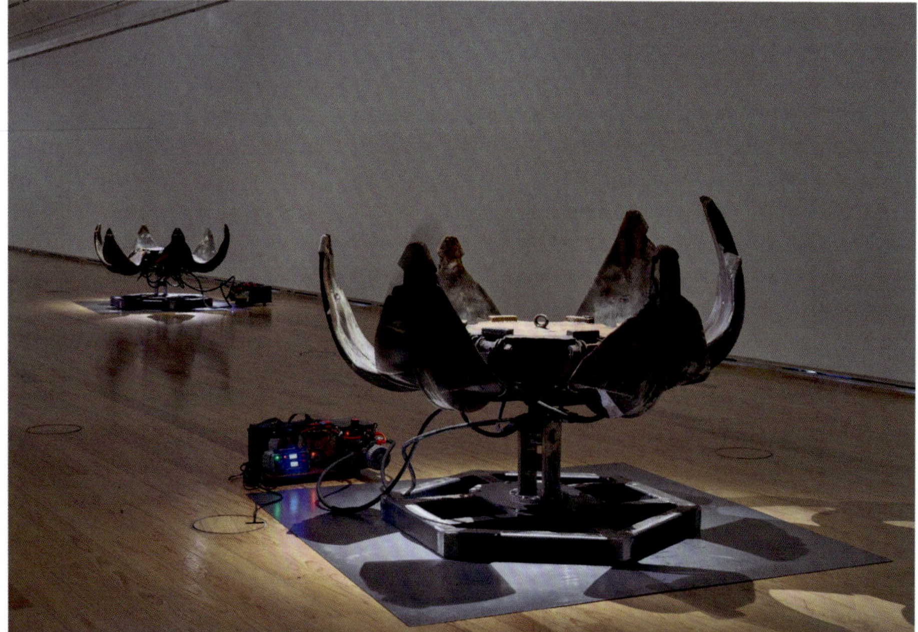

Selma Selman, *Motherboards*, 2023–ongoing, KRASS Festival, Kampnagel, Hamburg, 2023. Photo: Marko Ilić

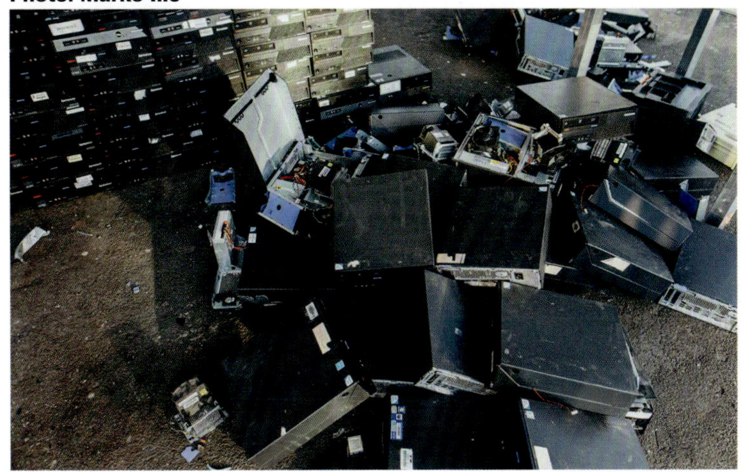

Installation view, Selma Selman, *her0*, Gropius Bau, Berlin, 2023. Photo: Eike Walkenhorst

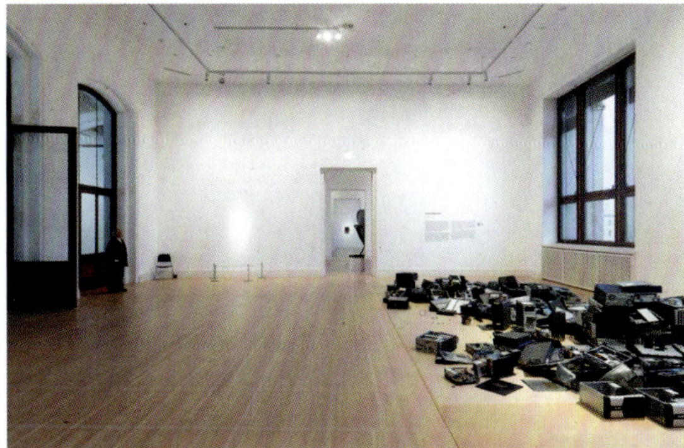

Selma Selman, *Motherboards*, 2023–ongoing, Gropius Bau, Berlin, 2023. Photo: Eike Walkenhorst

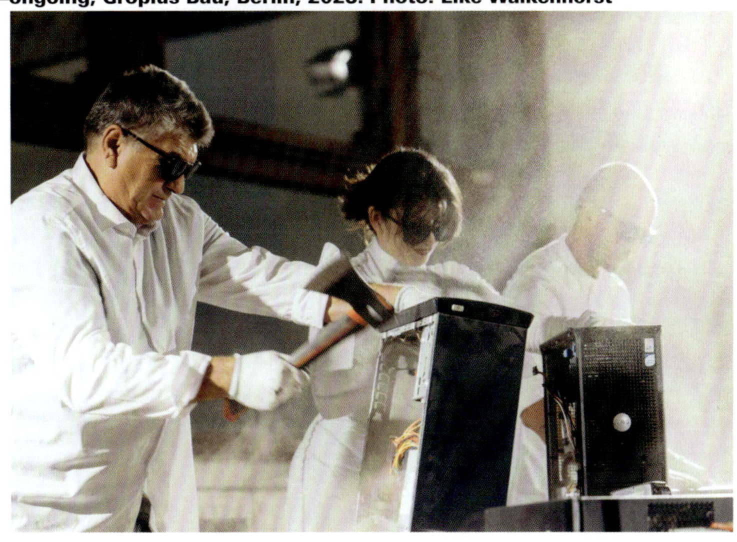

    THE GATHERERS   Ruba Katrib

Life (2024) **(Fig. 10)**. In its new orientation, the decommissioned equipment, which is typically used to move large-scale materials in junkyards, resembles the ephemeral flora of the natural world, with petals that slowly open and close.

Karimah Ashadu's video *Brown Goods* (2020) also focuses on the futures of discarded appliances, as well as on the alternative economies that center on such afterlives **(Figs. 11–12)**. Documenting the happenings of a particular street in Hamburg, Ashadu offers a glimpse of the site where cast-off household items and electronics (i.e., brown goods) end up—not their final resting place, but a stop on their journey. The work's narrator, Emeka, a Nigerian immigrant who labors on this street, explains that this "waste from the Germans"—stacks of mattresses, tires, and refrigerators—is collected, sold, and shipped to African countries. He regularly communicates with Lagos, seeking updates on the local market, while physically working in the junkyards of Hamburg, securing the items in demand. As a result, much of the money that flows into this German street is from sales made in Nigeria. While there is a global waste trade, where one country pays to send its trash to another for treatment or disposal (and hazardous waste produced by developed countries is often taken on by developing countries), the unofficial marketplace depicted in Ashadu's video almost reverses these terms: potentially useful European junk is sold in Africa. Many of the goods departing from the Hamburg port are likely powered by precious metals that originated in Africa, a subject Ashadu has addressed in other works.

The currents that take goods to the landfill do diverge, resulting in the revival of some materials and the waywardness of many others. Street garbage—stuff artist Allan Kaprow referred to in 1960 as the "nameless sludge and whirl of urban events"[20]—has become an integral part of the visual landscape and psychogeography of cities. Such materials possess evidence of their use and disuse that gestures to broader social, economic, and environmental conditions. Klara Liden, Ser Serpas, and Nick Relph each trace, or even abscond with, the refuse and future-refuse of the city through fugitive acts. Liden and Serpas remove objects from the street and recontextualize them to make their sculptures, while Relph scans urban surfaces to produce his photographs. These artists build on artistic traditions of engaging the terrain of the street as a "hunting ground," à la Paolozzi.

Closely surveying the sidewalks and rubbish bins of different cities, Serpas collects a range of materials and objects and composes them in sculptural situations. She combines heterogeneous objects that don't together suggest any kind of typology—a fence, a couch, a mattress, a shopping cart, etc.—in installations that might be described as strewn scenes bordering on mess **(Fig. 13)**. Rather than speak to broader contextual problems regarding how or why things come to be tossed on the street, her work responds to the sense of spontaneity that attends finding a dresser or drying rack on the sidewalk. The distinction between waste and mess is key in Serpas's work.

     THE GATHERERS   Ruba Katrib

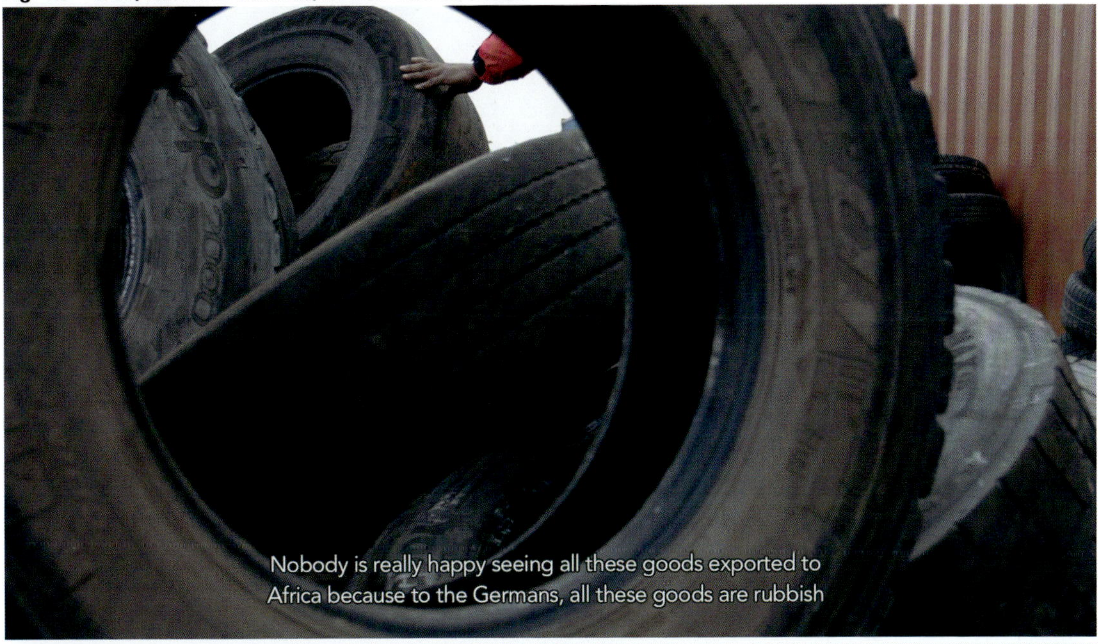

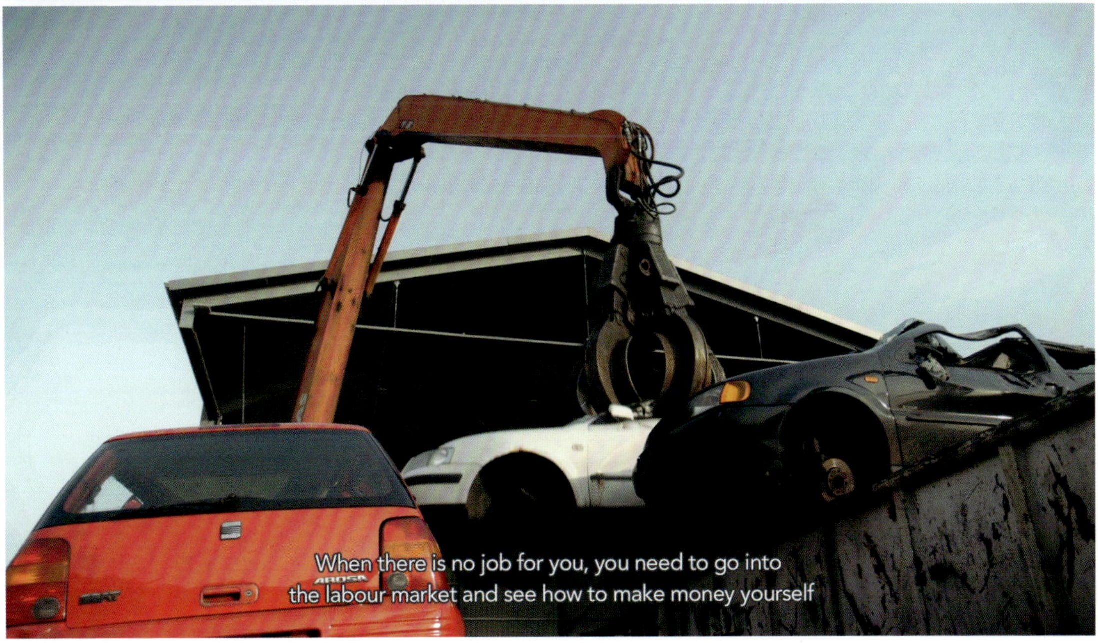

Detail, Ser Serpas, *say me and object*, 2022.

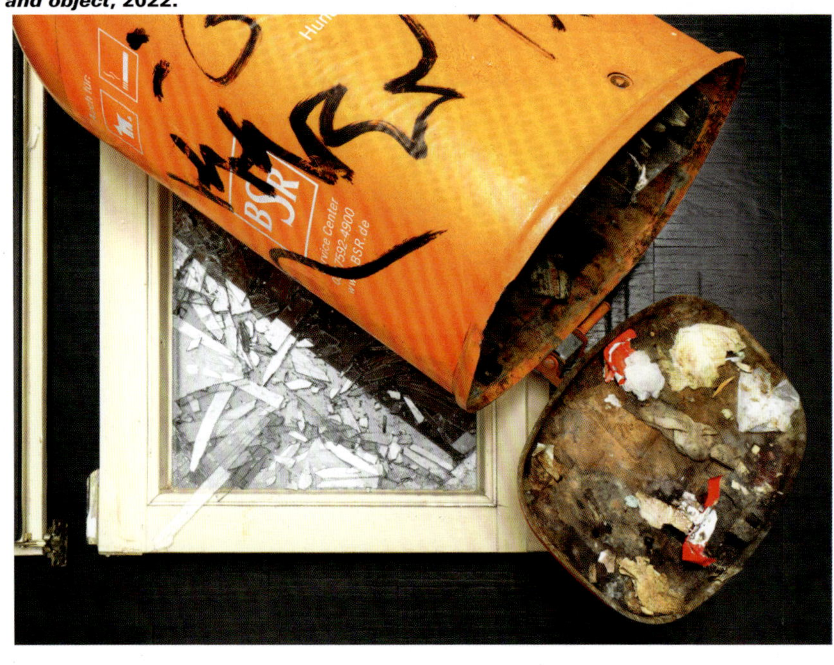

Fig. 13   Installation view, Ser Serpas, *Head banger boogie*, Galerie Barbara Weiss Trautwein & Herleth, Berlin, 2022.

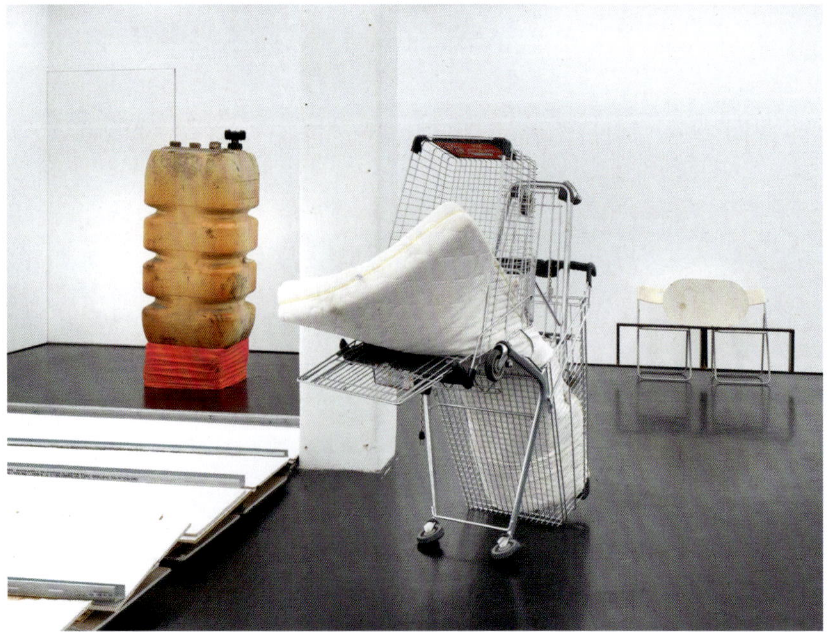

"Waste is a condition, mess is an event," David Trotter theorizes, distinguishing the symbolic and durational aspects of these interrelated states of matter.[21] Waste, he explains, is related to systems and is condemned to its defining characteristic—circulation (as in the waste organisms excrete as they process fuel), whereas mess is a temporary state, related to contingency and chance (a splash of mud on clothing, an array of papers on a desk). Transience is critical to Serpas's installations; her works seize on the moment in which a discarded object becomes other through the creative act—when waste is revealed to be, simply, mess. And it is the aleatory nature of how an object appears to Serpas on the street, its quality of mess, that indicates its potential use in her work. The artist's compositions then open up vistas onto surprising or overlooked qualities of her chosen objects, qualities that were perhaps effaced by the mask of habitual use. (This approach extends into her painting practice; *Backdrop* [2025], featured in the exhibition, is a large-scale canvas covered with the marks and outlines of other paintings made on its surface, composed of excess material.) (Fig. 14) Often, her works are characterized by tension; her objects quite literally balance on one another. Each element of her installations has its own story of use and disuse, but together in new spatial arrangements, they suggest new possibilities of relation.

The philosopher Michel Serres has written about pollution as a form of appropriation. His definition of pollution is broad, extending from garbage and toxic sludge to the billboards and signage that visually litter a place. Such contamination, he argues, is a mechanism that functions much like urine does for animals, marking the perimeters of a territory with something unpleasant to keep others out. Territorialization involves repellent: *"Appropriation takes place through dirt,"* he contends. "The spit soils the soup, the logo the object, the signature the page."[22] Serres finds that globalization has in effect "eras[ed] the borders where polluting starts and stops" in ways that make the right to property *"literally unbearable."*[23] Liden's work seems to respond to this condition, attempting to reassert such borders where there are none. Over the past two decades, she has taken disused municipal objects from the streets to make her works, leaving a particular void where these things once were. These commonplace objects are, specifically, variously used to designate or navigate space. The work *Untitled (Haltestelle)* (2024), a Berlin bus stop sign, features ghostly battle scars from life in the city, including official signage (though most of its text has faded away or been removed), bits of graffiti, and random marks made by passersby (Fig. 15). *Jean* (2021) is a pilfered junction box, once used to conceal and protect the cables that channel electricity throughout the city (Fig. 16). As a sculpture, the object can be appreciated for its surface, where layers of peeling paper—adverts paled from exposure to the elements—give texture to the box's unofficial life as a signpost. *Untitled (Dunmoore, right)* (2023), a lit sign that was once mounted at the entrance of a (now shuttered) bar, bears traces of its former existence as a site for sanctioned bulletins as well as spontaneous communication (Fig. 17). The newest work in the show

          THE GATHERERS   Ruba Katrib

Fig. 14   Ser Serpas, *Backdrop*, 2025. Photo: Carter Seddon

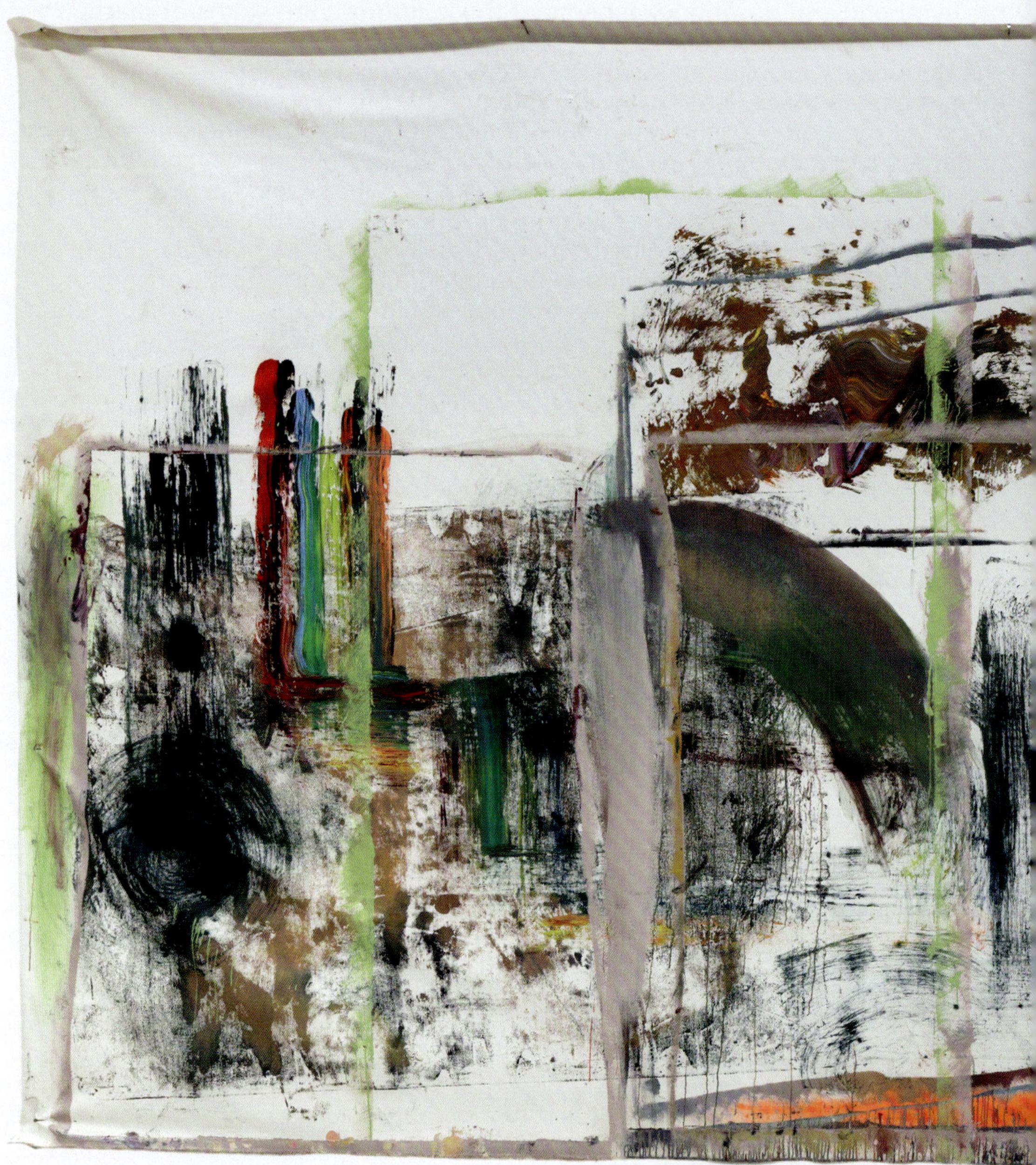

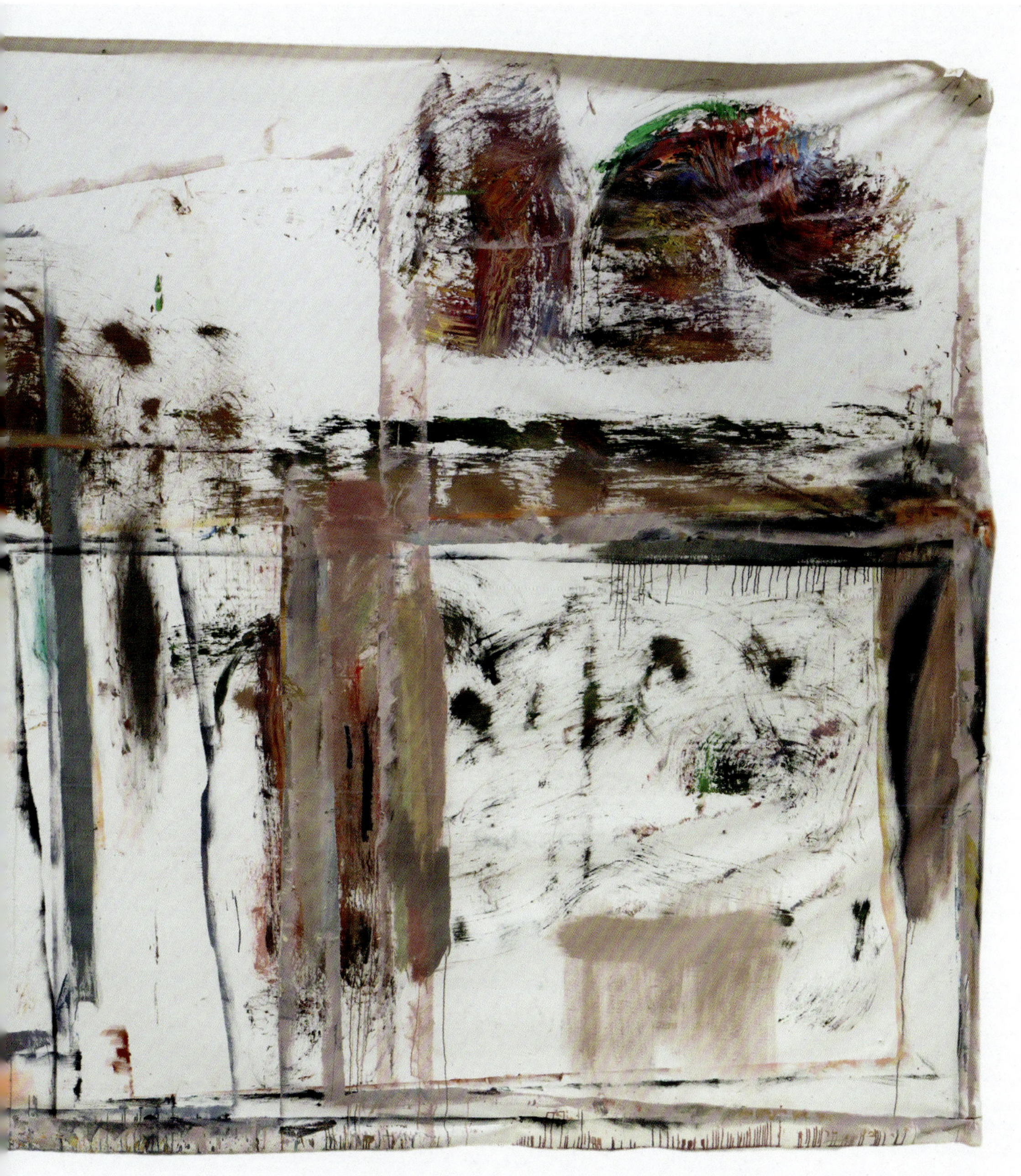

 THE GATHERERS Ruba Katrib

Fig. 15   Klara Liden, *Untitled (Haltestelle)*, 2024.

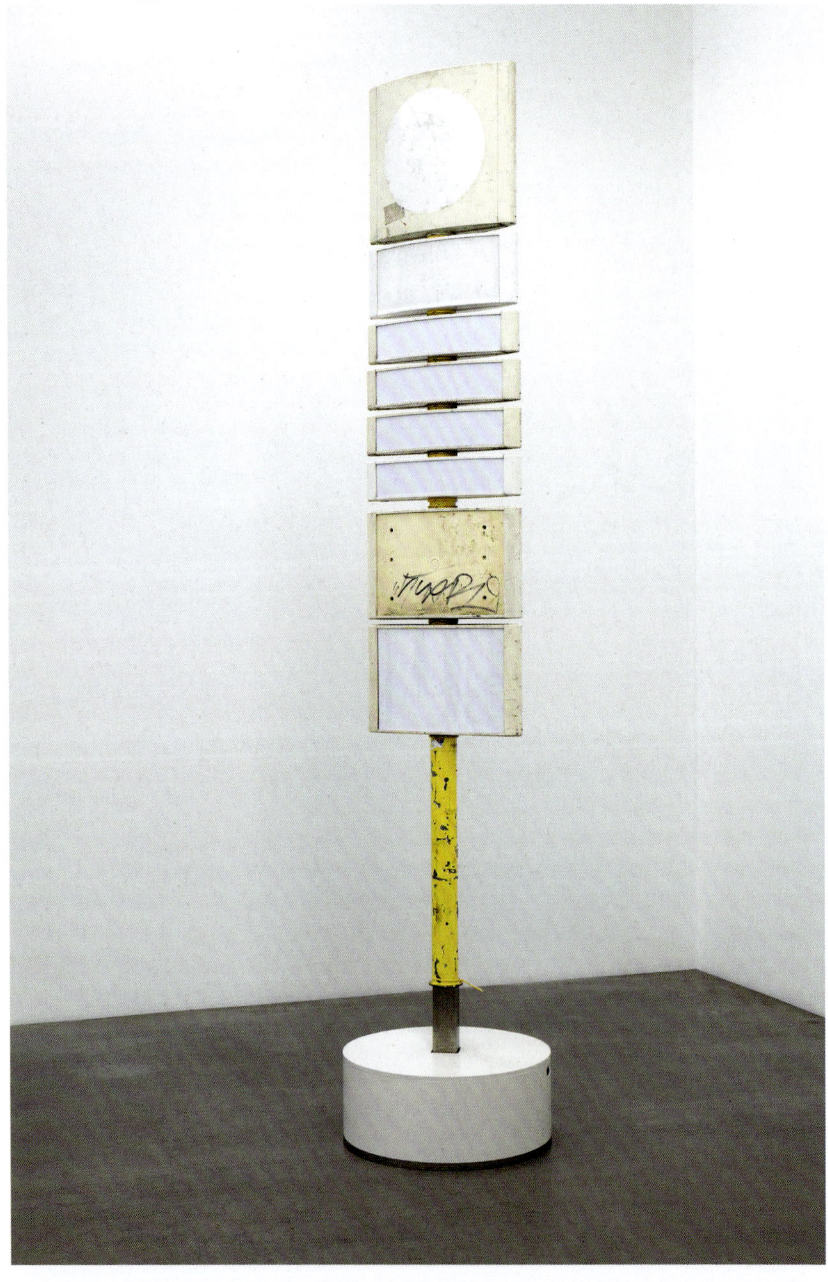

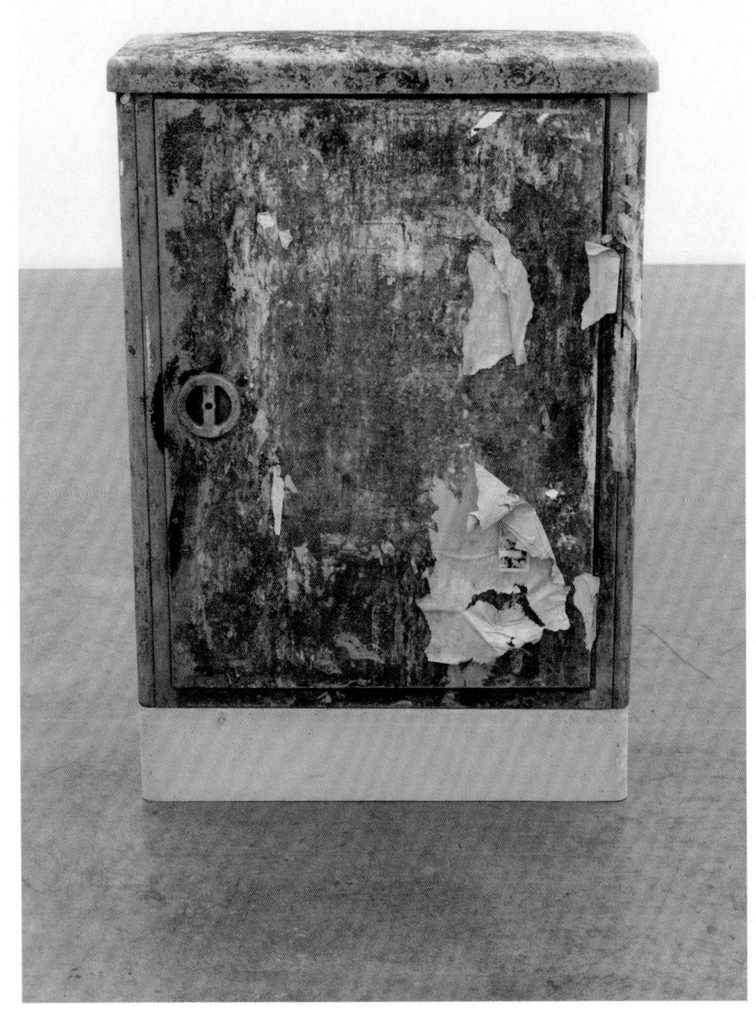

    THE GATHERERS   Ruba Katrib

Klara Liden, *Untitled (Membrane 5)*, 2024. Photo: Joerg Lohse

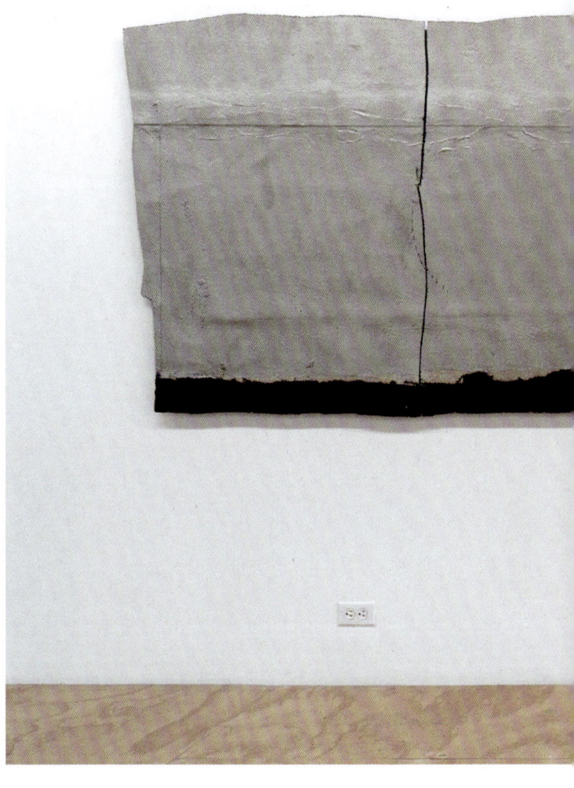

Installation view, Klara Liden, *Verdebelvedere*, Reena Spaulings, New York, 2024. Photo: Joerg Lohse

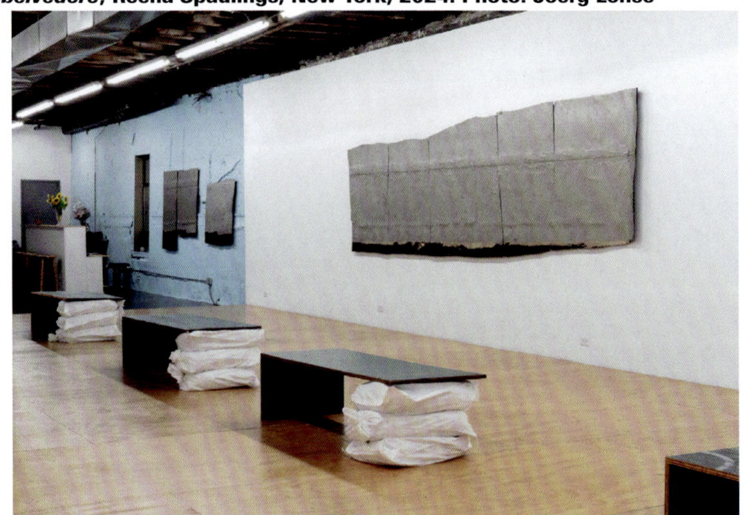

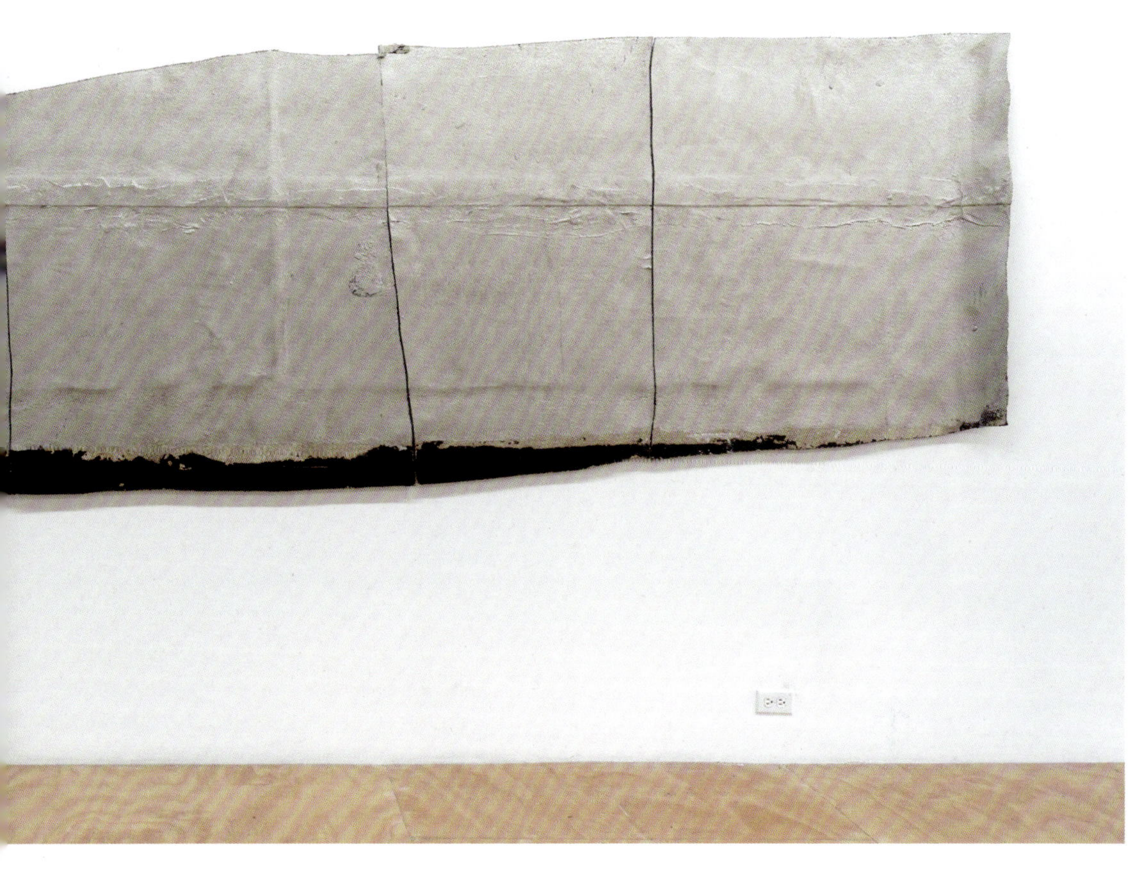

      THE GATHERERS   Ruba Katrib

Fig. 17   Klara Liden, *Untitled (Dunmoore, right)*, 2023.

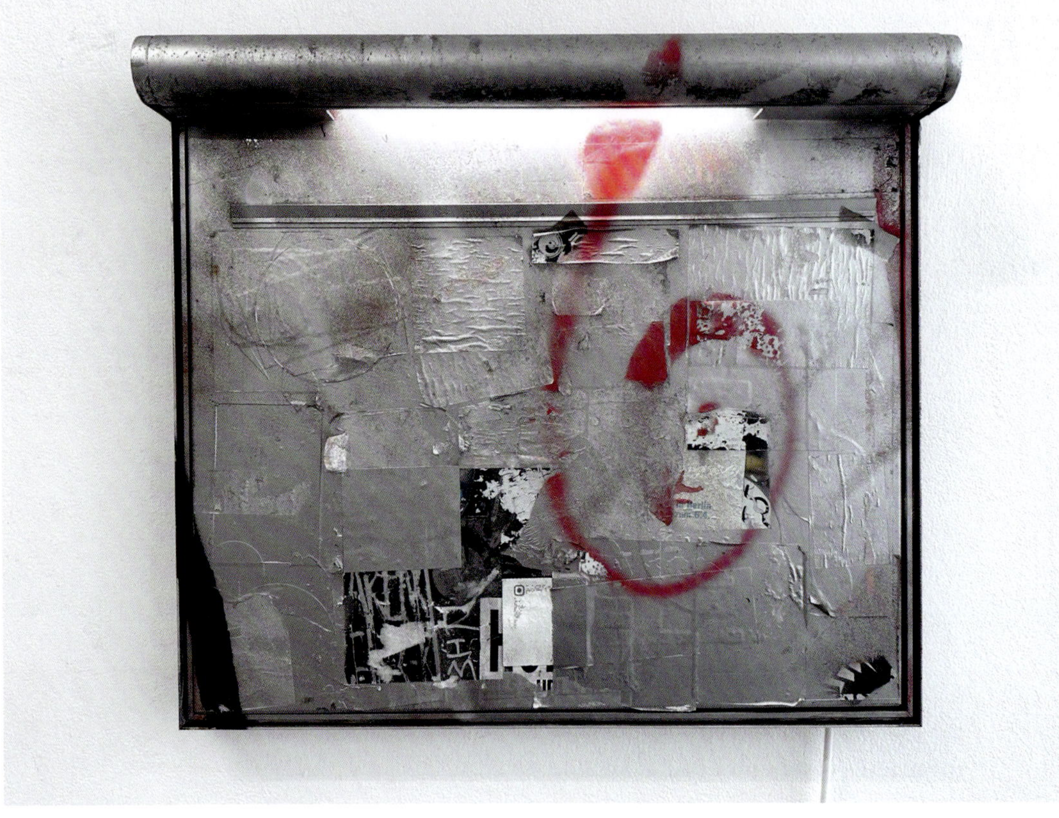

Fig. 18   Nick Relph, sketch for *Lusty Ghost (56)*, 2025.

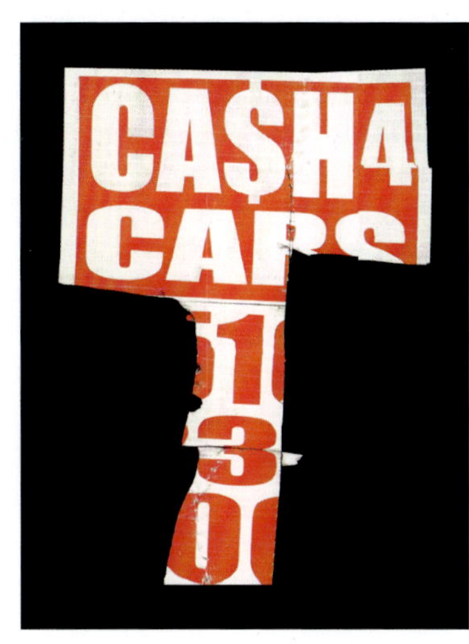

Fig. 19   Klara Liden, *Untitled (Invaliden 2)*, 2024. Photo: Arthur Gray

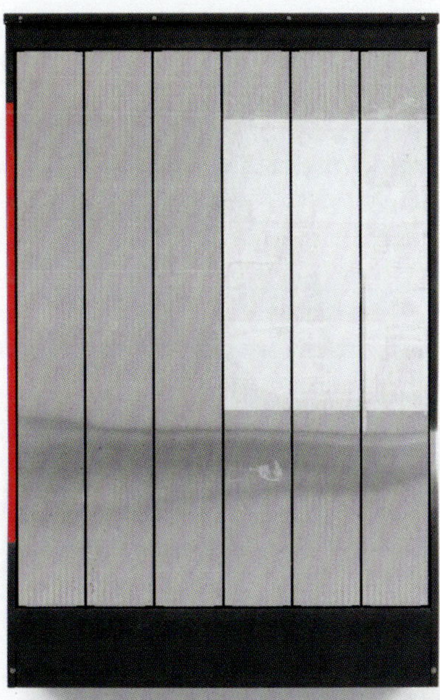

            THE GATHERERS   Ruba Katrib

comprises a mechanical variable-message sign that Liden has spray-painted over. These signs, which are often used on highways, feature options of fixed text that can be cycled through to reflect traffic changes. As these mechanical displays have been increasingly replaced by LED versions, Liden's blank sign is emphatically obsolete (Fig. 19). The artist is interested in a type of object that is so common it is nearly invisible; by removing these objects from their intended contexts, she asks us to consider how they—and the authorized and unauthorized messages many of them display—quietly shape our environments.

The surfaces of Liden's sculptures feature layers of mark-making and erasure, such that textuality, or its absence, is as much a subject of the work as the found object itself. Similar dynamics are at play in Relph's Chaos photographs, which center on text that is integrated into the cityscape. During his walks through the streets of Rome, Relph used a portable scanner to catalogue the various GAS signs he encountered (Figs. 20–21). Indicating the location of gas lines, these signs feature letters composed of small holes punctured in metal surfaces. Relph's prints are to scale, and they capture the modulating textures and colors of the pictured surfaces; the artist pierces each image in accordance with the punctured letters. Not unlike Liden's junction boxes, these signs foreground the sites where the resources that flow throughout a municipality are made visible. Closer to home, Relph scans flyers offering cash for junked cars in New York City (Fig. 18). These circulars litter intersections around the city; they are the kind of thing that is easy to ignore but, once noticed, looms everywhere. Across Relph's collection of scans, one can see that the signs have their own vernacular, with catchy fonts in bright colors and dollar-sign illustrations. Often, they simply provide a phone number and promise cash. These messages are most legible when they are relevant to the passerby, most likely due to some urgency. Gas, cash, junk—they all circulate abstractly throughout the city's spheres.

Urban excess and detritus as art historical subjects are critical to *The Gatherers.* While many of the included artists expand on traditions outlined earlier in this essay, another salient precursor is Robert Smithson's 1967 notion of "ruins in reverse," which commented on the expansion of an anonymous suburbia, referencing forthcoming constructions whose failure and obsolescence were already in view.[24] Working in this vein, Samuel Hindolo processes vestiges of the future that are latent in the present. His collaged paintings create environs that suspend notions of place and time. *Gare de Bruxelles-Nord* (2024) doesn't depict the station that is the subject of the work but rather offers the perspective from its platform (Fig. 22). The twilight scene features a narrow sliver of skyline that could easily belong to any metropolis. The work is painted on paper, creating a rippling and distressed effect that makes the image appear worn or unstable. Warped substrate is utilized in most of Hindolo's works. However, to create *Galgenberg Hill* (2025), he painted directly on canvas. The work bridges disparate elements—discordant staircases, a sculpture of a sphynx, the façade of a neoclassical building—to compose the

Fig. 20   Nick Relph, sketch for *Chaos*, 2025.

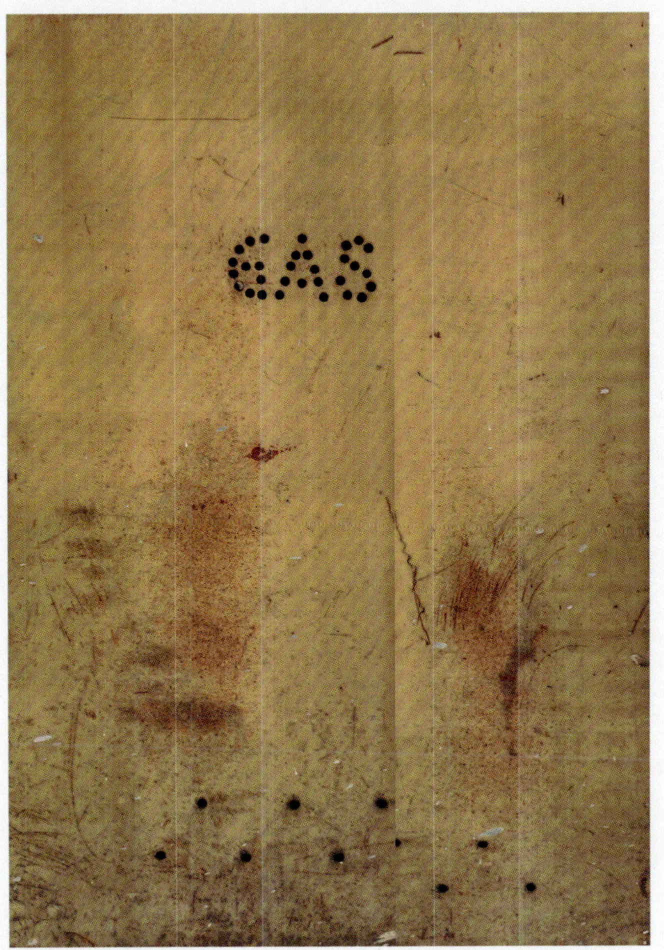

    THE GATHERERS   Ruba Katrib

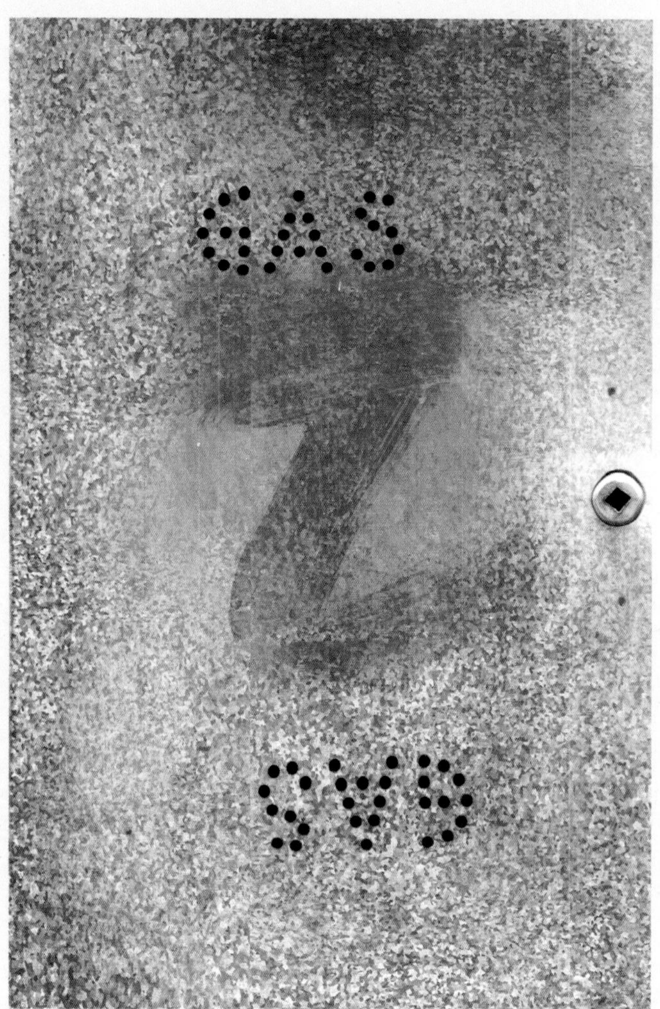

titular site anew. In the sixteenth century, Galgenberg Hill (or Gallows Hill) was the site of public hangings in Brussels; today, it is the location of the notoriously decrepit Palace of Justice. Hindolo's palimpsestic composition returns inscrutable traces of this history to the site, suggesting that future ruins can extend from the distant past. In both works, a sense of absence pervades, conveyed through the superimposition of place markers into otherwise abstracted environments. With their unsteady grounds and spectral imagery, Hindolo's paintings evoke afterimages; after long observation, the viewer might discover a haunting quality of erosion in the pictured surfaces.

The distinctions between mess and waste, or viable goods and trash, are slippery; they are constantly made and unmade. Yet there is some meaning to be found in the spaces between these categories. Arrangements of objects can tell us about how these determinations are made in the eye of the beholder. Geumhyung Jeong's work relies on this process. Working across media—in performance, installation, video, choreography, and sculpture—she considers the dynamics between the body and objects, drawing on a vast collection of fragmentary parts, tools, toys, robotics, and segments from medical models (Fig. 23). In her new work, *Removed Parts: Restored* (2025), the artist removes parts of these collected objects to use them in performances and then restores, or recovers, them by generating new objects. Jeong arranges her collection in grids that emphasize the formal qualities of each object, stripping away any sense of its original context. Though they are here abstracted, these objects are shiny and pristine, summoning the effects of the new commodity. Jeong makes and unmakes her work. Depending on the artist's engagement, the status of each object—or extracted parts of an object—changes, and is brought into new fields of purpose and purposelessness, use and disuse. Like other artists in *The Gatherers*, Jeong works in a way that privileges not the individual object, but the relationships objects enter with other objects, bodies, and contexts. These works evoke the mass, the heap, the endless stream of goods that are found on store shelves and in trash bins alike.

Restaging, remaking, and cataloguing are central strategies for many of the artists in *The Gatherers*. Tolia Astakhishvili's new video work *so many things I'd like to tell you* (2025), made with Dylan Peirce, is an ambivalent example of this activity (Fig. 24). The video is shown on two channels, each framing a scanner bed on which various objects are placed. As each item is scanned, a wand of light illuminates it, generating a sense of movement that recalls an assembly line. Every time the scanner whirs, it offers a familiar yet unsettling sound akin to that of a shutter going off or a printer starting up. In the artists' seemingly endless cycle of things—pages torn from books, a bone, a zipper, a spoon, a feather, photos—there is no obvious association between one article and the next; these images seem to evade subjectivity altogether. These accumulated things—found, used, trashed—have surfaces that indicate broader narratives and durations. This is also a central characteristic of Astakhishvili's large-scale sculptural installations, where architectures and

                                    THE GATHERERS   Ruba Katrib

Fig. 22   Samuel Hindolo, *Gare de Bruxelles-Nord*, 2024.

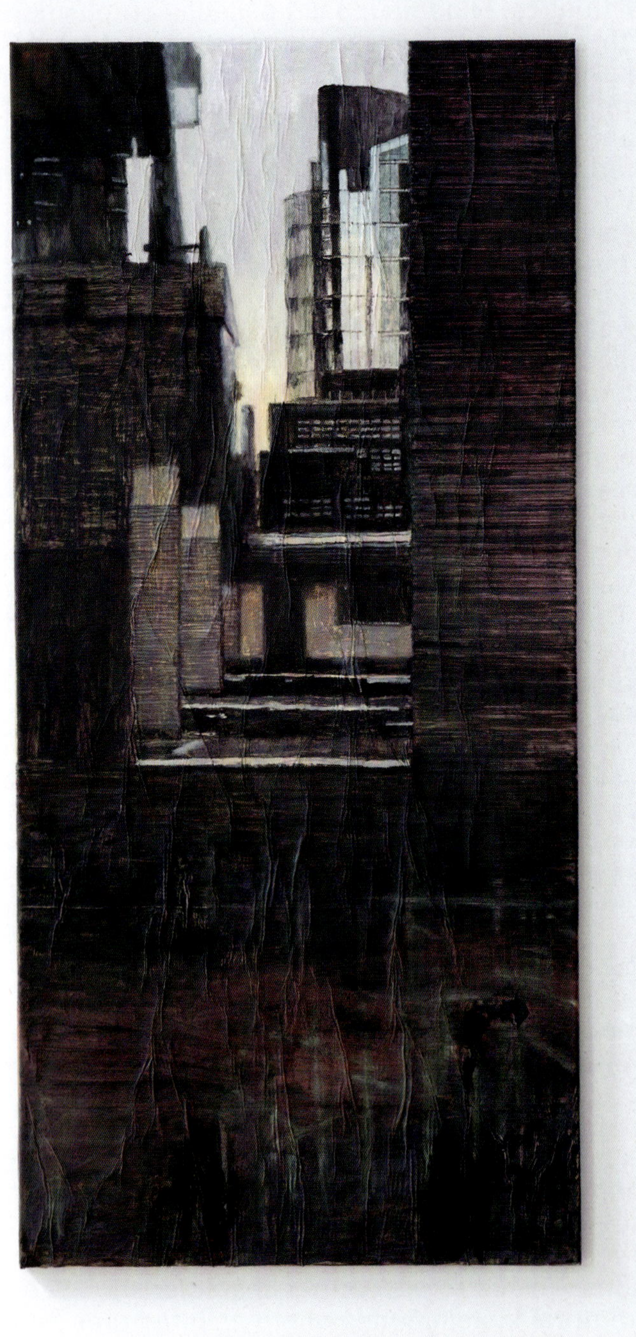

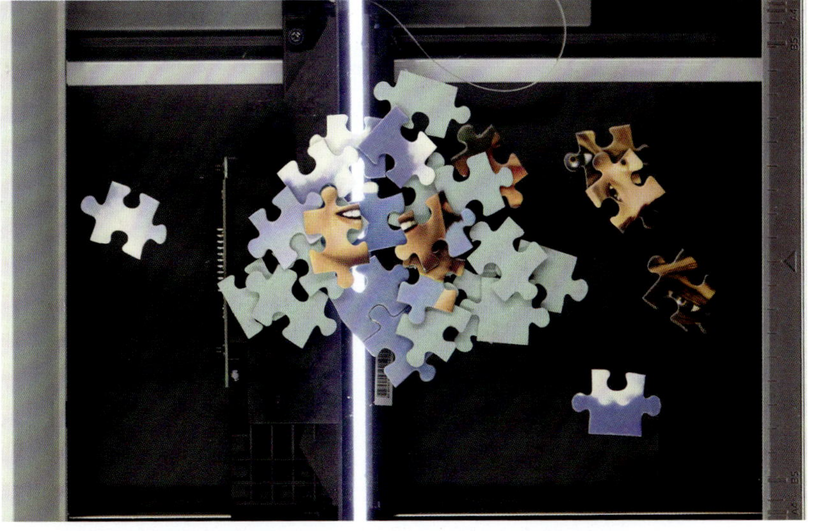

    THE GATHERERS   Ruba Katrib

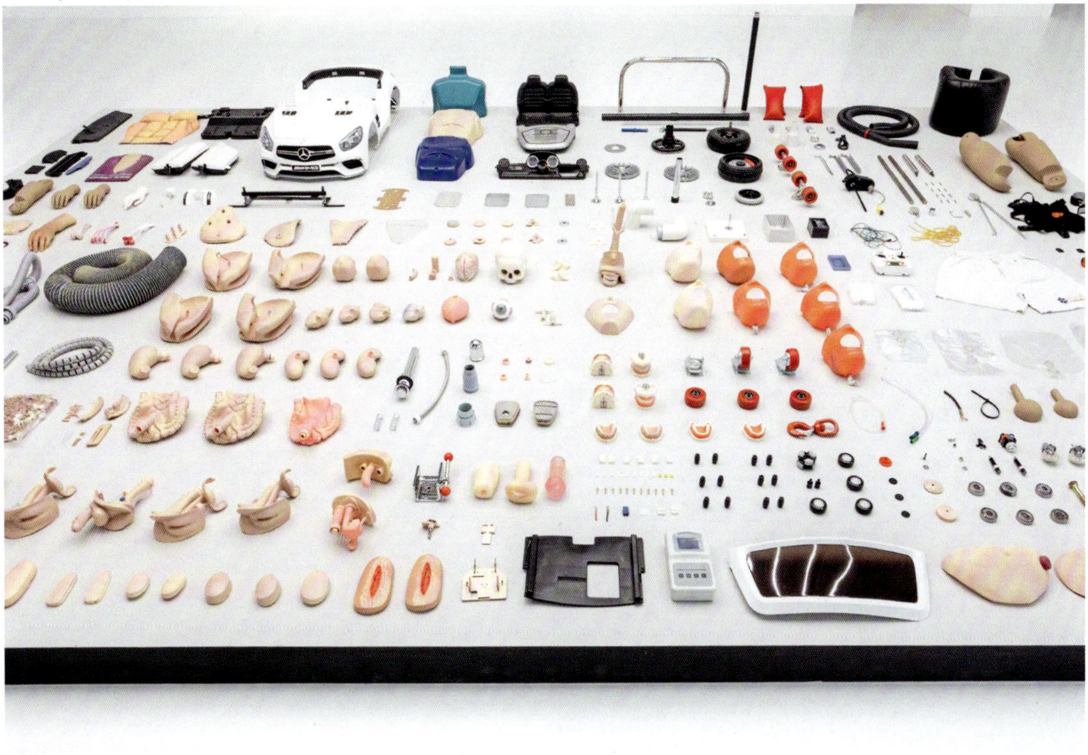

Installation view, Tolia Astakhishvili, *And how I care for*, 2024, in *between mother and father*, Sculpture Center, New York, 2024.

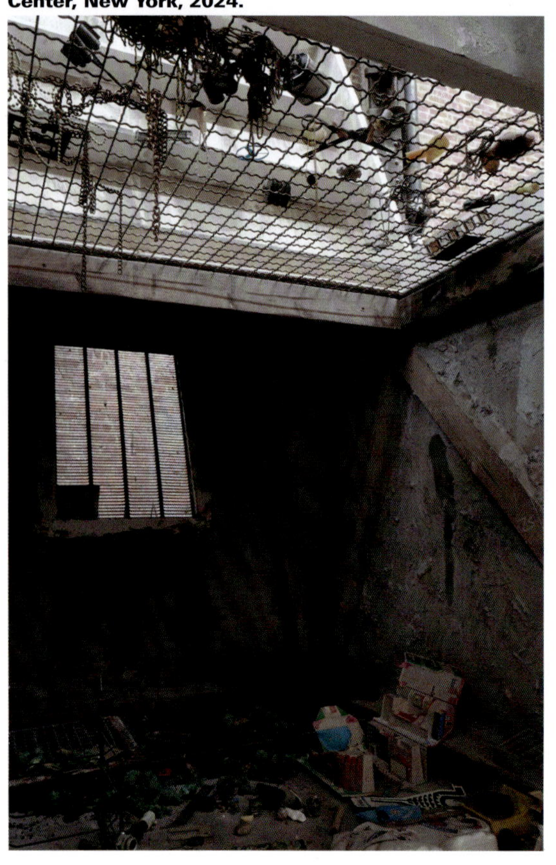

Installation view, Tolia Astakhishivi, *When the others are within us*, 2024, in *Post Scriptum. A museum forgotten by heart*, MACRO Museum, Rome, 2024.

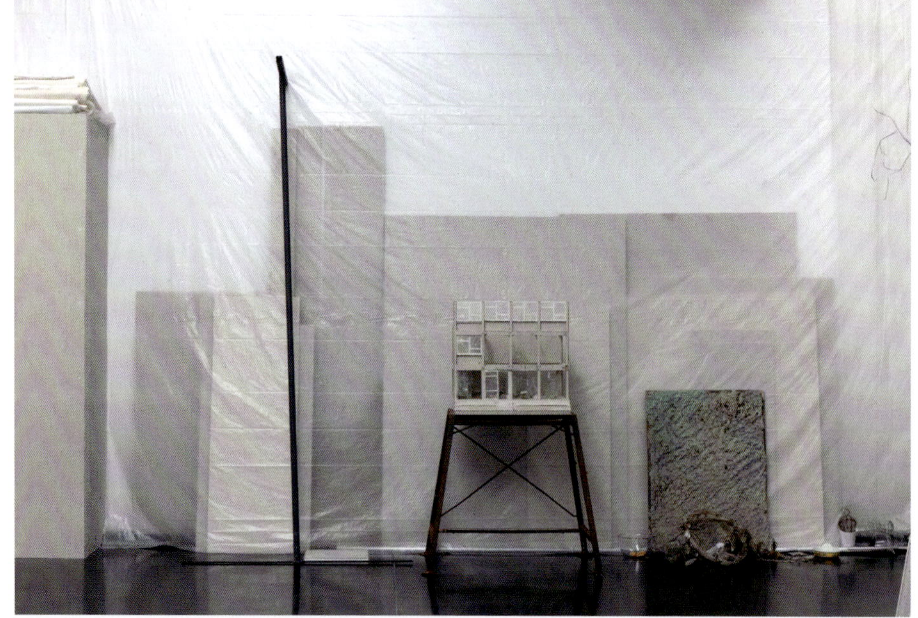

heaps of objects merge in environments that carry ambiguous histories and marks. These spaces offer a totality that exceeds the individual elements that comprise them, conjuring a distant yet familiar sense of place. The objects therein—small trinkets, scribbles, bits and bobs—evoke remnants of a faded past, as if they were caught in a net or remained in a sieve. It seems their endurance isn't arbitrary but is owed to some inherent stubbornness or stickiness. The viewer becomes engaged in a charged act of seeking evidence or logic, their plight recalling David Trotter's writing on how "rummagings release the memory of desire."[25] Sifting through the information at hand, the viewer is confronted with the interrelation of forgetting and the accommodations of memory; here, accumulation invokes absence.

Writing at mid-century, the philosopher Georges Bataille argued that the central problem facing society isn't the scarcity of production (per Marx)—there is plenty on earth to sustain life—but our management of the excess and destruction of both objects and energy. In his 1949 thesis for a "general economy," he contends there is a need to account for the energetic and psychological expenditures that exceed established notions of production and exchange.[26] Art, as a nonproductive activity, is a key aspect of this accounting, requiring, as it does, surplus resources of time and materials. A decade later, the structural anthropologist Claude Lévi-Strauss formulated the concept of *bricolage*, describing practices that make do with "whatever is at hand," all the contingent "leftovers from earlier constructions and destructions."[27] The bricoleur thus traverses the contours of what remains—used or unused, operational or broken—bridging the intrinsic relation between production and waste. In 2012, Claire Bishop identified a shift in this activity, noting that older models of bricolage treated found elements "as raw materials whose histories are incidental," but since the 1990s, bricoleurs are more likely to "maintain the cultural integrity of the reused artifact—to invoke and sustain its history, connotations, and moods."[28] Perhaps, then, we might locate another modulation in the activities of the contemporary bricoleur that acknowledges the scale of leftovers to draw from—the unthinkable, malignant volume of what is at hand.

One such artist is Miho Dohi, who works on an intimate scale, transforming bits of cast-off paper, wood, metal, textiles, and other scraps into surprising constructions (Figs. 25–28). She collects anonymous waste and responds to its material and symbolic dimensions, often manipulating it with paint, cuts, and glue. Working without a destination in mind, she makes one decision at a time, each directing what comes next. The resulting compound arrangements evoke worlds with their own inherent logic. Dohi allows the natural balance of each form to dictate the sculpture's orientation in space, and whether it should rest on a surface or hang on the wall. These works resemble abstracted architectural models, microcosmic proposals of worlds to come from what's been left behind. He Xiangyu also allows the dimensions of his materials to instruct the shape of his sculptures. His works *Opaque Loop* and *Rock Tongue* (both 2024) feature stones collected from a river in China and

　　　　THE GATHERERS　　　　Ruba Katrib

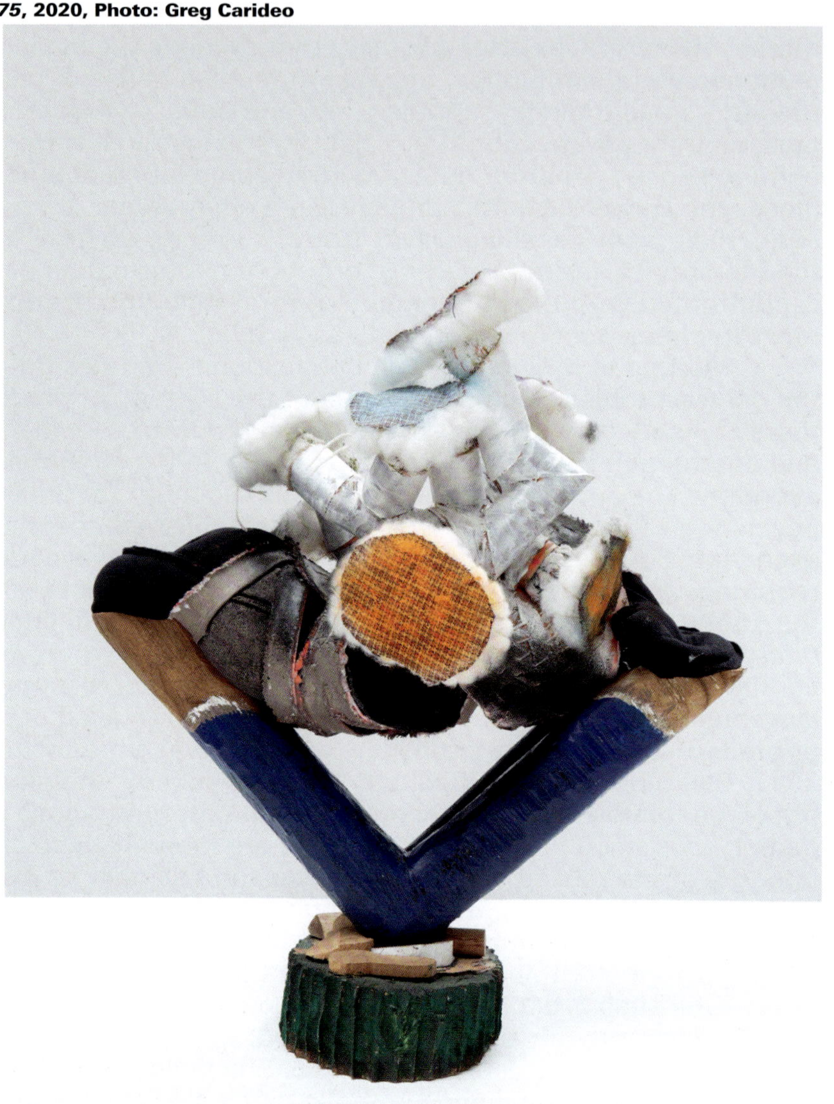

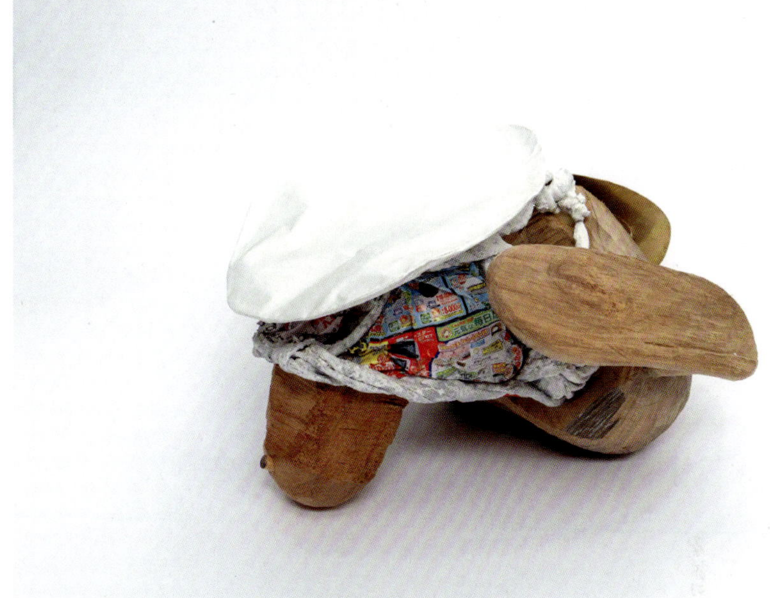

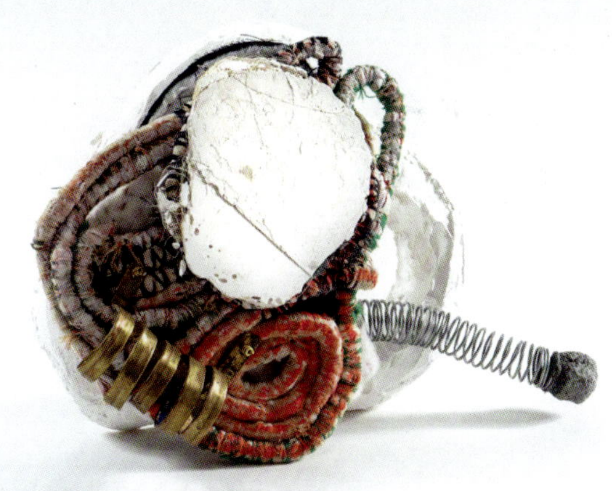

            THE GATHERERS   Ruba Katrib

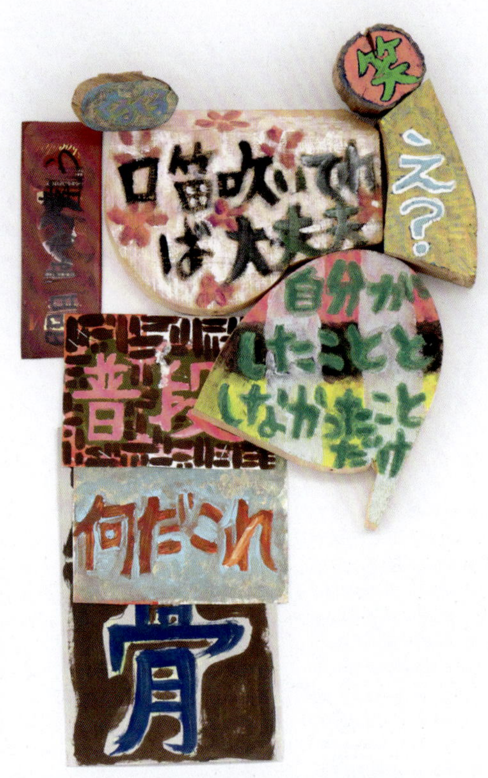
笑
こえ？
口笛吹いてれ
ば大丈夫
自分が
いたことと
しなかったこと
だけ
普段
何だこれ
骨

strung up on metal rods that bend under their weight (Fig. 29–30). Each stone has been differently worn down by the fluctuating pressures of water over centuries, quite literally shaped by time, and so each differently sits on (and depresses) the metal support. These assemblages generate a tension between erosion and accumulation, highlighting the potentiality in processes of flux in the natural world. For his 2024 sculptural installation *Vessel Project: Yellow Houses*, He built up layers of saggar clay to create forms that resemble rectangular buildings (Fig. 31). The features and hard lines of the structures appear worn down, such that the works read as if they were contoured by erosion instead of constructed over time. Visually, the sculptures seem to refute the nature of their production. Exploring the nature and expressive capacity of sediment, He situates his work in the space between being and not being, finished and not finished.

The relentless speed of cycles of production, consumption, and waste, echoed as they are in the temporalities of our news cycles and social media feeds, casts a radical light on slower durations (even as slowness, wellness, mindfulness, and artisanship are themselves rapidly branded and monetized). Andro Eradze's new film *Flowering and Fading* (2024) seems to decelerate as it speculates on the hidden lives of objects (Fig. 32–34). A dreamlike sequence departs from a scene of a person and dog sleeping in a bedroom. The camera moves around the house, animal, and human, exploring the nuanced relationships between the interior and exterior states of each. A gust of wind comes through an open window, tipping over a jar of honey, and as the nectar drips between the jar and the floor, gravity is suspended. Objects—a lamp, a table, chairs—begin to levitate. This supernatural event gives way to a sense of unease. What animates this stuff? The events of Eradze's film recall Marx's assessment of the metaphysical qualities of commodities. When basic materials are transformed into goods, Marx contends, they enter a world of "sensuous" and complex relations and symbols. The commodity of a table, for example, makes wood seem transcendent, as if it could start "dancing of its own accord."[29] The product, in other words, is granted the appearance of an existence that exceeds the facts of its material makeup. Eradze's film alludes to these symbolic distinctions, asking, perhaps, what would happen if we perceived the mystical quality we grant to goods in other aspects of our world. The film's title suggests cycles of becoming and becoming undone, and its sequencing blurs realities, offering changes of perspective. Everything is turned on its head. Breaking the axis of gravity, Eradze suggests the possibility of transformation under even the most intractable laws. *Flowering and Fading*, among other works in the exhibition, portrays an unfettered world that unfolds without, and even despite, the climactic logics of human narrative; it reveals other scales and other durations.

Attending to the forms that shape our narratives, and thus our attention and values, Ursula K. Le Guin's 1986 essay "The Carrier Bag Theory of Fiction," draws on the anthropological theory that the first human innovation was not a

         THE GATHERERS   Ruba Katrib

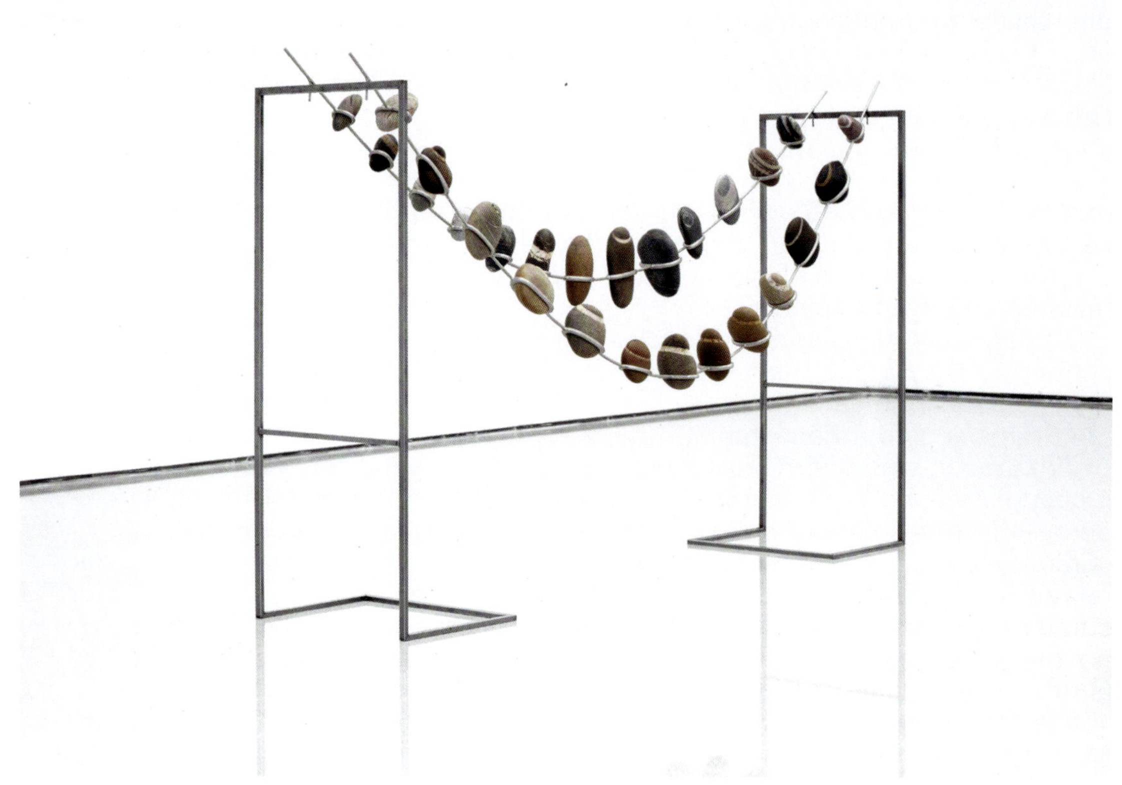

Fig. 29   He Xiangyu, *Rock Tongue*, 2024.

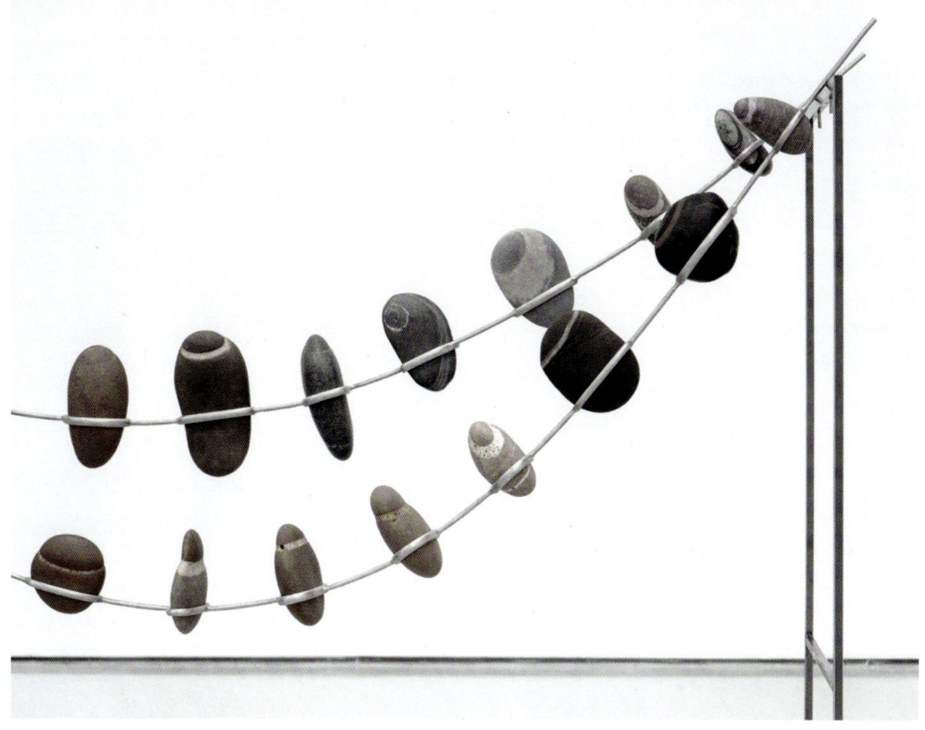

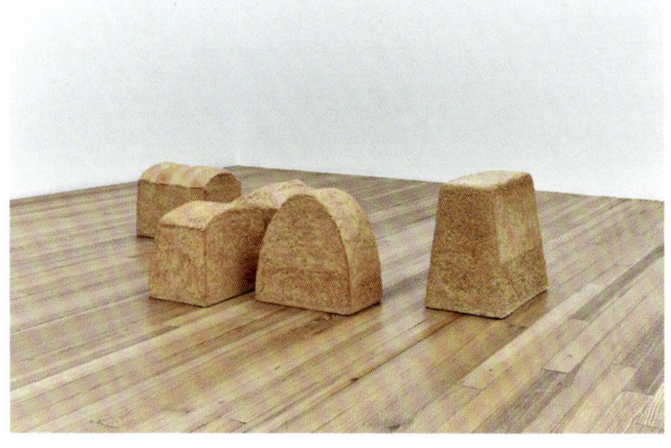

51   THE GATHERERS   Ruba Katrib

Fig. 32   Still, Andro Eradze, *Flowering and Fading*, 2024.
Fig. 33   Still, Andro Eradze, *Flowering and Fading*, 2024.
Fig. 34   Still, Andro Eradze, *Flowering and Fading*, 2024.

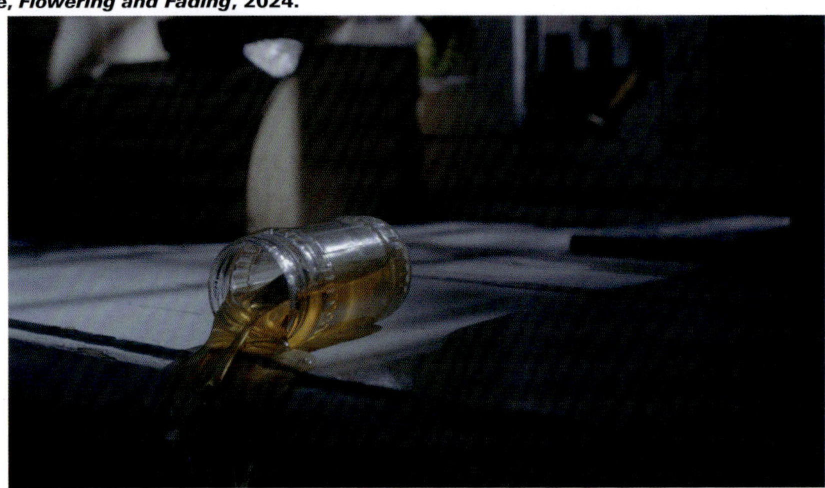

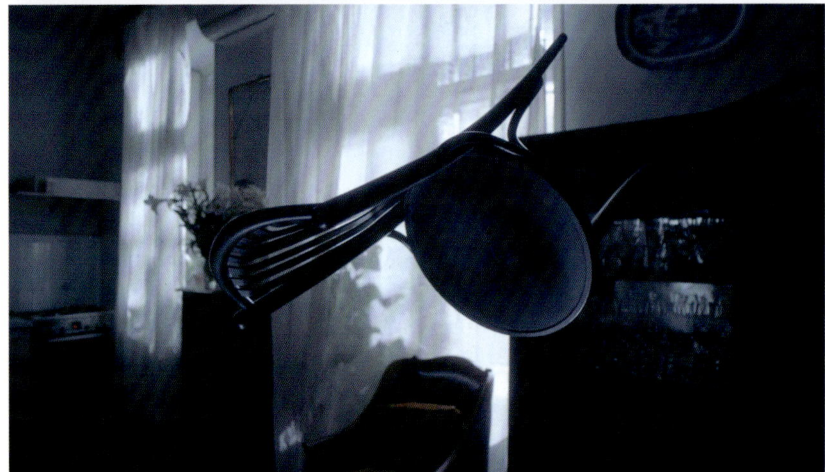

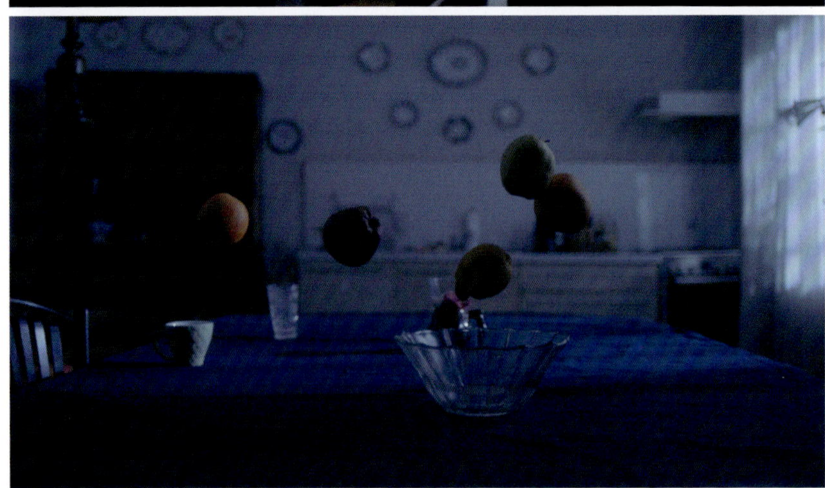

tool or a weapon, but a container, or a sack. While whittled sticks evoke tales of building, hunting, and killing that are fantastically heroic, she observes, bags or slings are critical for the quotidian aspects of life: gathering, storing, and preserving, holding food or children. Le Guin notes that the stories civilization is wont to tell are those of the heroes, not the gatherers, and thus there is less attention paid to the context of gathering. And "it is the story that makes the difference," she writes. The hero, she goes on, doesn't work in the stories of gatherers; "you put him in a bag and he looks like a rabbit, like a potato."[30] Commodities are this way: they lose their luster once acquired, once they are contextualized in the real world, with the waste they will become. In the millennia since the bag was conceived, our relationship to everything we might put in it has changed, has been intoxicated by the promise of fetishistic surfaces and overwhelmed by the magnitude of our scrap heaps. As Le Guin articulates, the stories we tell about what we gather (and leave behind) make a difference. The artists in this exhibition offer vantages onto the unresolvable dialectic between creation and destruction. Their works generate narratives that move not only between discrete objects and heaps, but between the formal and informal systems that manage both our perception and the material flows of those objects. Ultimately, the artists in *The Gatherers* are captivated by the idea that the aftermaths of production exceed the narrative forms of today—they extend into inconceivable eternities.

1   Wendy Brown, foreword to *Capital: Critique of Political Economy, Volume 1*, by Karl Marx, ed. Paul North and Paul Reitter, trans. Paul Reitter (Princeton University Press, 2024), xxix.

2   Franco "Bifo" Berardi, *Quit Everything: Interpreting Depression* (Repeater Books, 2024), 21.

3   Here, I am evoking Berardi's notion of "the slow cancelation of the future." "When I say 'future,'" he writes, "I am not referring to the direction of time. I am thinking, rather, of the psychological perception, which emerged in the cultural situation of progressive modernity, the cultural expectations that were fabricated during the long period of modern civilization, reaching a peak in the years after the Second World War." Franco "Bifo" Berardi, *After the Future*, ed. Gary Genosko and Nicholas Thoburn (AK Press, 2011), 18.

4   Michel Foucault, *The Order of Things: An Archaeology of the Human Sciences* (Vintage Books, 1994), 387.

5   See Stephen Shankland, "The Secret Life of the 500+ Cables That Run the Internet," CNET, August 6, 2023, https://www.cnet.com/home/internet/features/the-secret-life-of-the-500-cables-that-run-the-internet/.

6   Political theorist Fredric Jameson contends that the "effacement of the traces of production" from the commodity frees the consumer from "guilt" and from having to remember the "innumerable others" who produced their objects. He writes, "You don't want to have to think about Third World women every time you pull yourself up to your word processor, or all the other lower-class people with their lower-class lives when you decide to use or consume your other luxury products." In Fredric Jameson, *Postmodernism, or, The Cultural Logic of Late Capitalism* (Duke University Press, 1991), 314–15.

7   The philosopher Georges Bataille discusses these distinctions in Bataille, *Visions of Excess: Selected Writings, 1927–1939*, ed. Allan Stoekl, trans. Allan Stoekl, Carl R. Lovitt, and Donald M. Leslie Jr. (University of Minnesota Press, 1985).

8   David Trotter, *Cooking with Mud* (Oxford University Press, 2000), 16.

9   Norman Bryson, *Looking at the Overlooked: Four Essays on Still Life Painting* (Reaktion Books, 1990).

10   Bryson, 140.

11   William C. Seitz, *The Art of Assemblage* (The Museum of Modern Art, 1961), 84.

12   Eduardo Paolozzi, quoted in *Eduardo Paolozzi: Writings and Interviews*, ed. Robert Spencer (Oxford University Press, 2000), 81.

13   Pierre Restany, "The Nouveau Réalistes Declaration of Intention" in *Le nouveau réalisme*, trans. Martha Nichols (Union Générale d'Éditions, 1978), 281–85.

14   *Junk Dada* was a 2015 survey exhibition of Noah Purifoy's work, curated by Franklin Sirmans at the Los Angeles County Museum of Art.

15   John Cage, "On Robert Rauschenberg, Artist, and His Work," in *Silence: Lectures and Writings by John Cage* (Wesleyan University Press, 1973), 101.

16   John Ruskin, "The Two Boyhoods," in *Modern Painters, Volume V* (Smith, Elder and Co., 1873), 293.

17   Seitz, 88–89.

18   Such as the accidents at the Chernobyl (1986) and Fukushima Daiichi (2011) nuclear power plants.

19   Walter Benjamin, "Theses on the Philosophy of History," in *Illuminations*, trans. Harry Zohn, ed. Hannah Arendt (Schocken Books, 1968), 257–58.

20   Allan Kaprow, quoted in Seitz, 88. Note reads: Allan Kaprow, *Paintings, Environments, and Happenings* (ms. scheduled for publication in the near future), Old Bridge, NJ, 1960.

21   Trotter, 21

22   Michel Serres, *Malfeasance: Appropriation through Pollution?*, trans. Anne-Marie Feenberg-Dibon (Stanford University Press, 2010), 3.

23   Serres, 71.

24   Robert Smithson, "The Monuments of Passaic," *Artforum*, December 1967, 48–51.

25   Trotter, 26.

26   See Georges Bataille, *The Accursed Share, Volume I*, trans. Robert Hurley (Zone Books, 1988).

27   Claude Lévi-Strauss, *Wild Thought: A New Translation of "La Pensée sauvage,"* trans. Jeffrey Mehlman and John Leavitt (The University of Chicago Press, 2021), 21.

28   Claire Bishop, "Digital Divide: Contemporary Art and New Media," *Artforum*, September 2012, 434–41.

29   Marx, *Capital*, 47.

30   Ursula K. Le Guin, "The Carrier Bag Theory of Fiction," in *Dancing at the Edge of the World: Thoughts on Words, Women, Places* (Grove Press, 1989), 168–69.

Karimah Ashadu

(British-born Nigerian, b. 1985)

Fig. 1   Installation view, *Plateau*, 2021, Secession, Vienna, 2021. Photo: Pascal Petignat

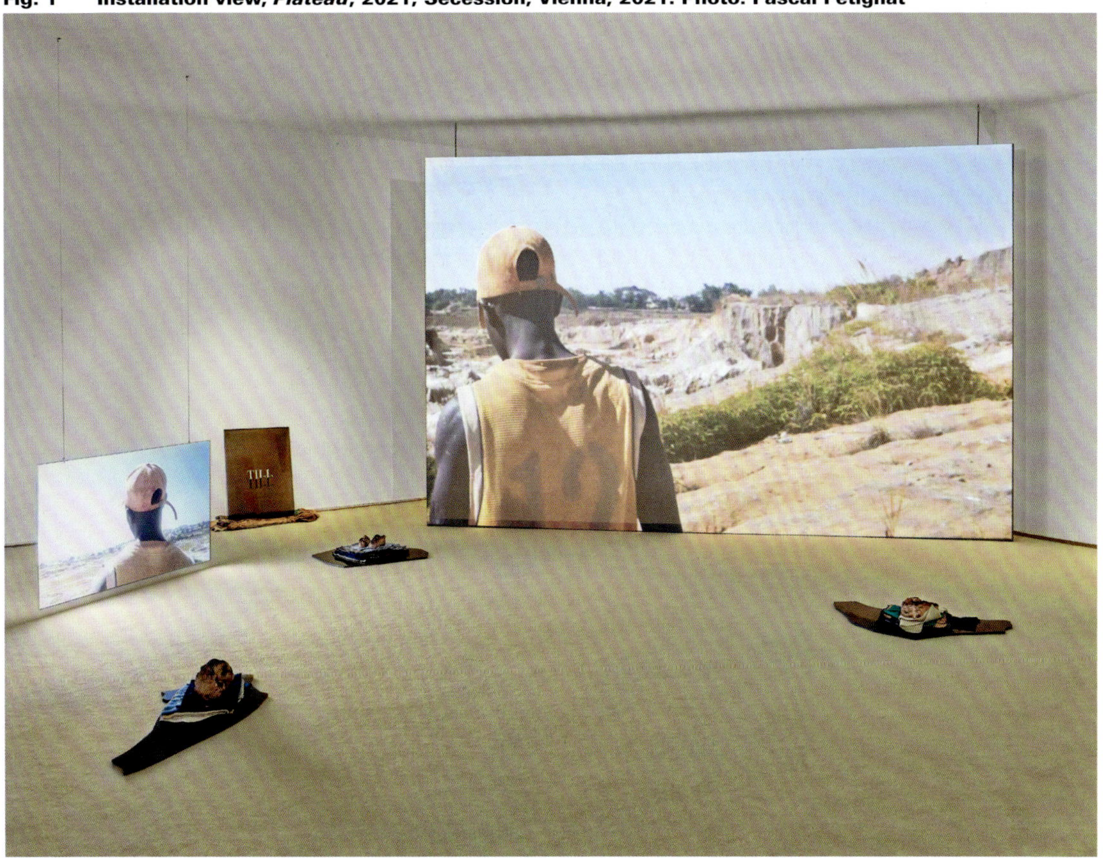

Entering the outskirts of Hamburg by train in 2019, British-born Nigerian artist and filmmaker Karimah Ashadu was struck by the industrial landscape of warehouses, shipping containers, and piles of discarded refrigerators. This scene on the edge of her home city piqued her interest. Over time, Ashadu's work has taught her to recognize the signs of economic activity unfolding in overlooked corners of cities. The industrial street she saw from the train, Billstrasse, would become the setting for her film *Brown Goods* (2020) (Figs. 2–3). Its main character, Emeka, works there alongside fellow Nigerian migrants, finding ways to capitalize on discarded goods—purchasing used tires, cars, and home appliances to resell to buyers in Africa.

As *Brown Goods* explores, this informal trade is a livelihood forged in response to global inequality and colonial legacies. Ashadu composes the desolate warehouse district at dawn with remarkable care, evoking the grandeur of Hudson River School paintings: an expansive sky, distant puffs of smoke from industrial stacks, and soft, dim light. Her camera lingers over piles of secondhand bikes and used tires as Emeka recounts his perilous journey from Nigeria to Libya, Italy, and finally Germany, where he was granted humanitarian status.

With resigned frustration, Emeka describes the trajectory of his status: in Lagos, he was a college-educated man with a good job, and now, as a migrant, he hauls refrigerators on his back and packs cargo containers. His anger is palpable, but Ashadu's refined, measured compositions are grounding. The camera's slow, restrained shots convey not only the physicality of Emeka's work but also the emotional weight it carries. He stares directly into the camera with intense, unwavering eyes; his resentment is both personal and collective.

The manual labor performed on Billstrasse is part of a vast system of informal trade that is as complex as the machinations of the New York Stock Exchange trading floor. Ashadu's film highlights this hierarchical network, where the glut of one market meets the dearth of another. Her exploration underscores the social and economic dynamics of postcolonial exchange: resources and labor flow from former colonies to sustain manufacturing in the

Global North, only to return as detritus in a cycle marked by marginalization and power imbalance. These tensions are emphasized by the film's soundtrack, wherein the rhythmic hum of machinery is met with the sharp clang of scrap metal colliding with cargo containers.

Ashadu's work can be understood through concepts like *kanju*—as Dayo Olopade in her book *The Bright Continent* (2014) termed "the specific creativity born from African difficulty."[1] In *Brown Goods* and her other films, Ashadu examines the entrepreneurial spirit and resilience of individuals building livelihoods against the odds. Having grown up in Lagos, she is intimately familiar with the informal sector—untaxed and unregulated economic activity—which in Nigeria accounts for an estimated 90 percent of employment and 58 percent of GDP.[2] As a megacity, Lagos is home to millions of street vendors, scrap-metal workers, and secondhand-goods traders who rely on

1   Dayo Olopade, *The Bright Continent: Breaking Rules and Making Change in Modern Africa* (Houghton, Mifflin, Harcourt, 2014), 20.
2   "Nigeria's Informal Economy Size," World Economics, accessed January 1, 2025, bit.ly /3XrDsMc.

Fig. 2   Still, *Brown Goods*, 2020.
Fig. 3   Still, *Brown Goods*, 2020.

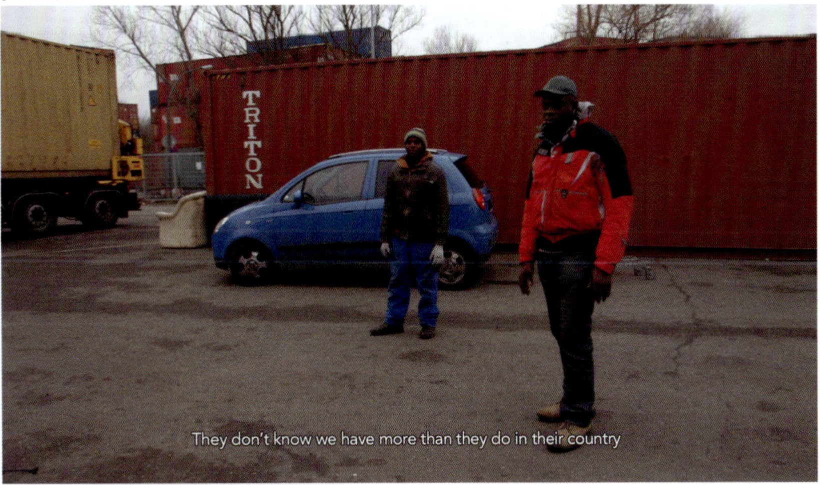

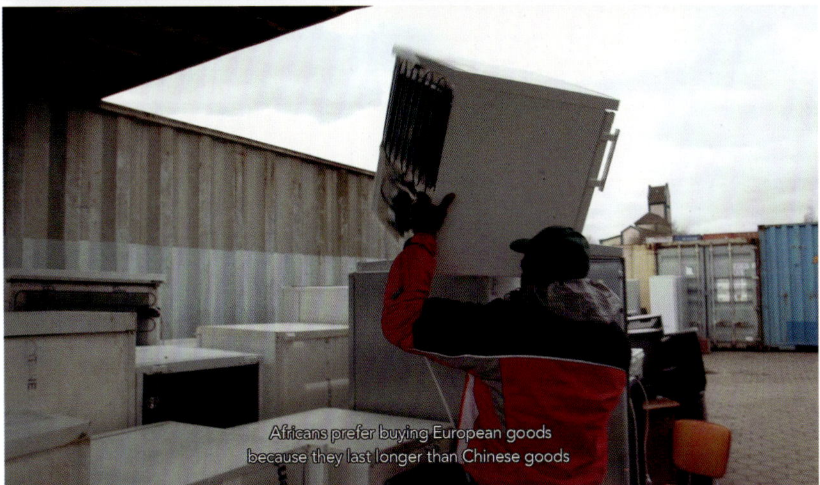

informal labor for survival. Ashadu's films shed light on these vibrant yet precarious economic networks, which are often disregarded by mainstream society despite being the backbone of many local communities. Her work pushes the understanding that this labor constitutes a defiant practice of independence in a postcolonial context.

In the film *Plateau* (2021), Ashadu follows a group of undocumented miners reworking the exhausted tin fields of Nigeria's Jos Plateau, a region ravaged by colonial extraction (Figs. 1 & 4). Navigating dangerous caves without modern equipment, these men risk mudslides and tunnel collapses. Ashadu's camera moves through the landscape, often from the perspective of the workers as they look around at the craggy terrain. Her focus is the relentlessness of their labor: axes swing into the earth and shovels are freighted with wet silt. In one harrowing scene,

Fig. 4   Still, *Plateau*, 2021.

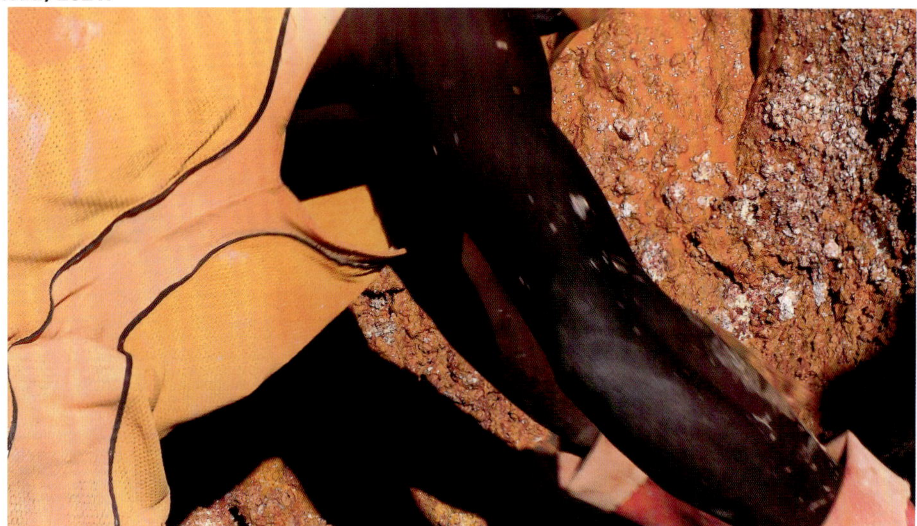

          Karimah Ashadu

a man is lowered into a deep tunnel; an aboveground view of his initial descent shifts to his perspective from below. In subtitled voiceover, the workers express both their frustration at the depletion of the formerly resource-rich land and their determination to persist, driven by the hope of a lucky find and a modest payout. As they attempt to regain control of land long exploited by colonial powers, they seek to restore what those powers stripped away.

Machine Boys (2024) considers another informal industry in Lagos: motorcycle taxis, or *okada* (Figs. 5–6). This service is common throughout Western Africa, despite being outlawed in many cities due to frequent accidents. Ashadu documents a group of young men who make their living as illegal *okada* drivers. Their bravado is on full display as they rev their engines, spin dramatically in clouds of dirt, and drift low to the ground. In voiceover,

Fig. 5   **Still, *Machine Boys*, 2024.**

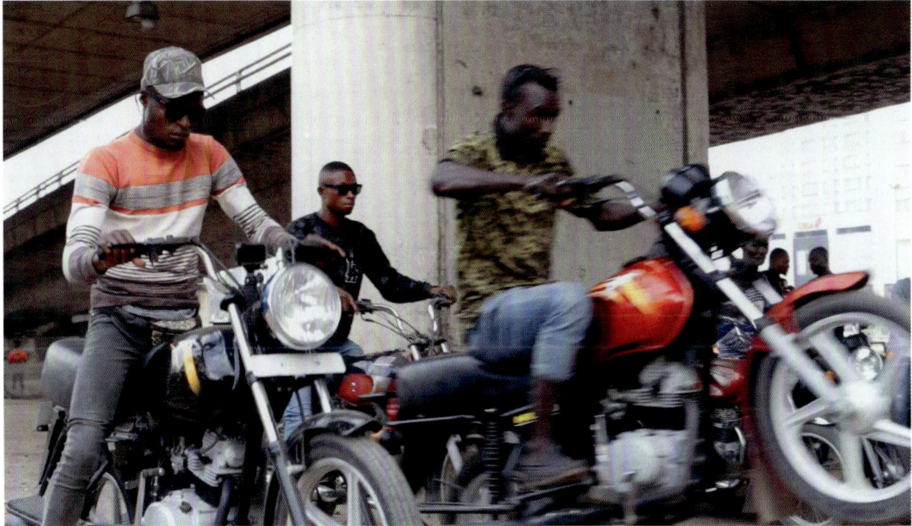

the drivers speak candidly about the challenges they face:
the criminalization of their work, the constant need to
bribe officials, and the sacrifices they make to support
their families. Many express a deep desire to pursue
other careers but lament the lack of opportunities in their
struggling economy, which leaves *okada* as the only viable
option. The film juxtaposes the performative masculinity
and vulnerability of these men in the context of their
precarious, dangerous occupations.

Ashadu's body of work centers on how people
subsist in postcolonial nations, focusing on the remarkable
resourcefulness she sees in those who survive—and
even thrive—within complex economic systems. Her
films suggest that to survive isn't merely to endure harsh
conditions but to adapt, innovate, and find ways to prosper
despite adversity. Nigeria, a nation shaped by proud
tribes and a young democracy formed within the arbitrary
borders of British colonial rule, is both scarred by its imperial past and defined by its resilience. In Ashadu's films, the
legacy of colonial exploitation is ever-present, not as the
central theme, but as the backdrop against which stories of
survival, strength, and ingenuity unfold.

Fig. 6   Installation view, *Machine Boys*, 2024, in *Stranieri Ovunque – Foreigners Everywhere*, La Biennale di Venezia, 2024. Photo: Lorenzo Palmieri

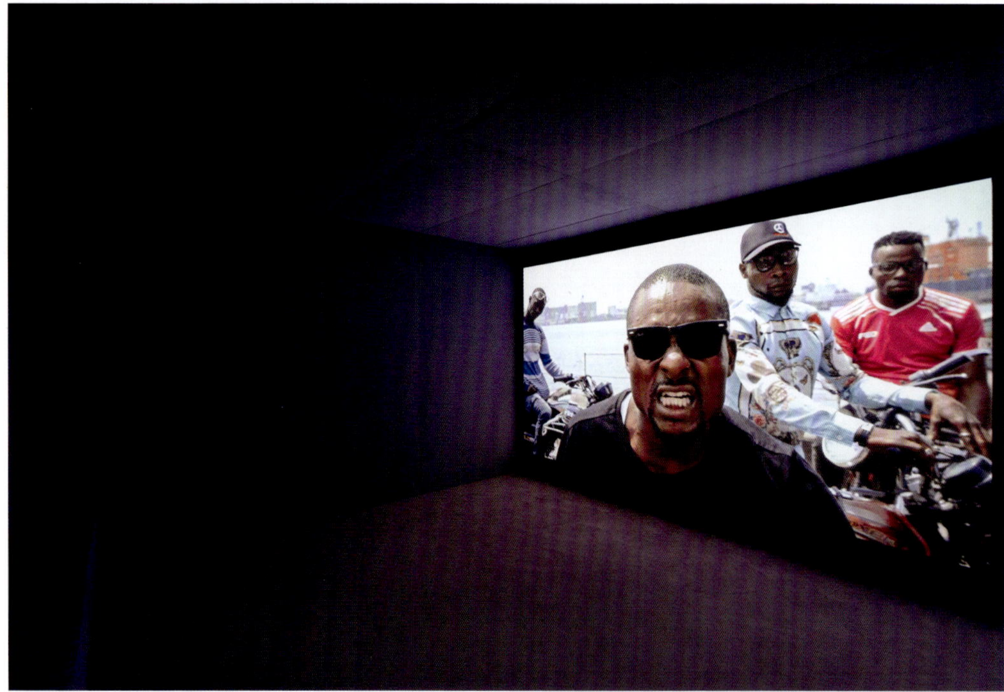

          Karimah Ashadu

Tolia Astakhishvili

(Georgian, b. 1974)

Fig. 1   Still, Astakhishivili with Dylan Peirce, *so many things I'd like to tell you*, 2025.

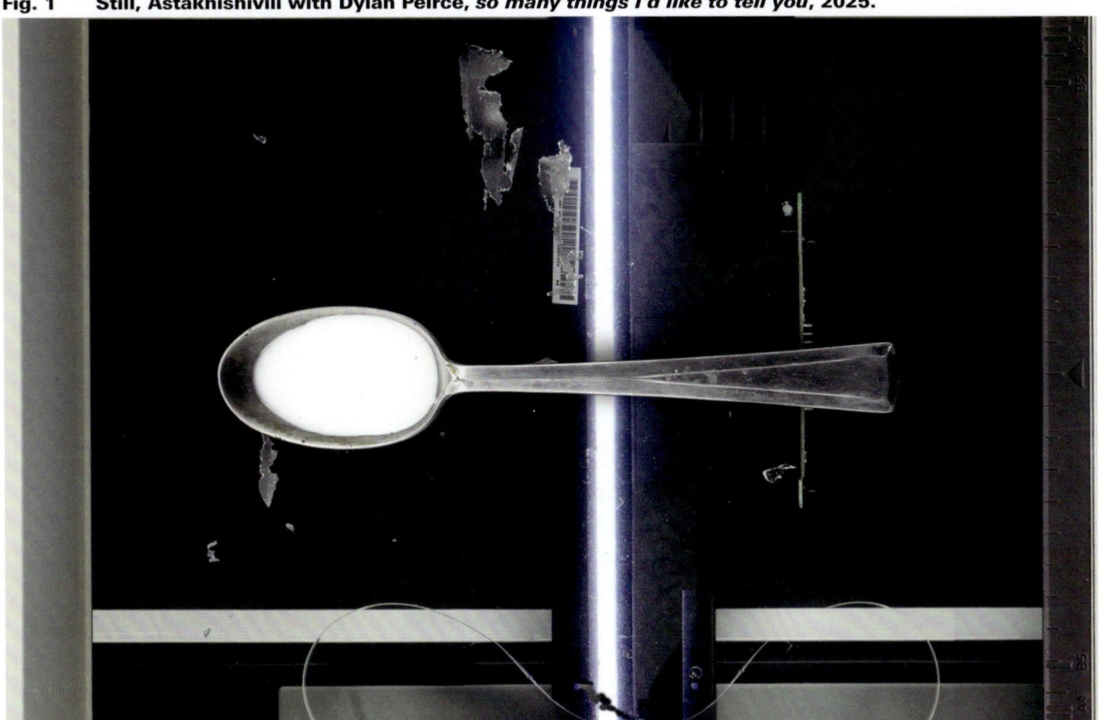

Installation view, *The Holding Environment*, Bonner Kunstverein, Bonn, 2021.

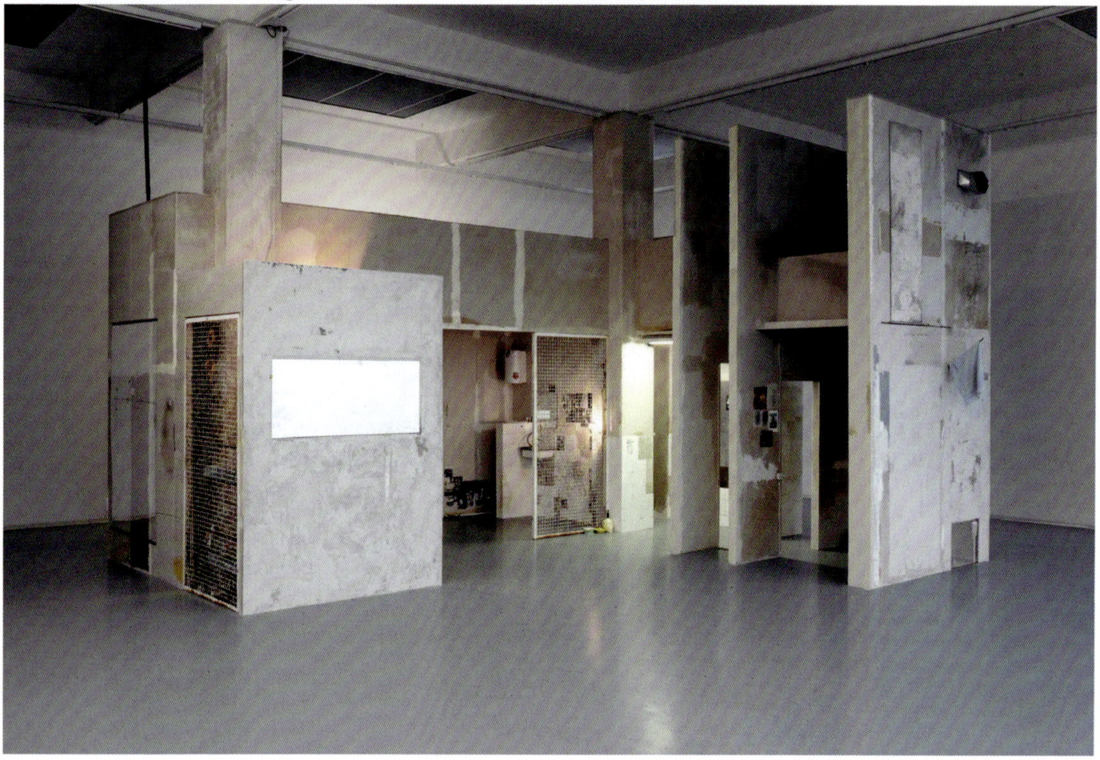

Detail, *The Holding Environment*, Bonner Kunstverein, Bonn, 2021.

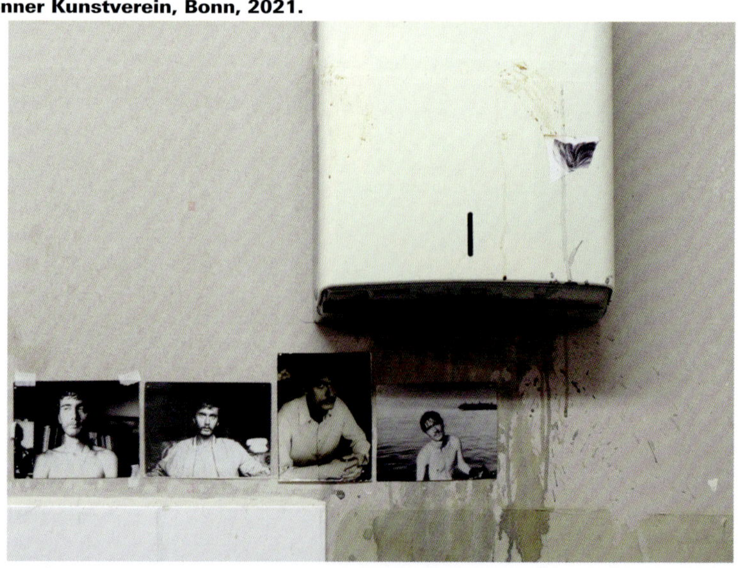

ARCHITECTURAL AFTERLIVES
Kirsty Bell

Tolia Astakhishvili's sculptural work appears to grow from within the spaces it inhabits. The artist inserts surrogate architectures into exhibition spaces; built from drywall or found construction materials, these structures feature strange spatial ambiguities and are seemingly unfinished. Narrow passageways lead nowhere, niches are crammed with domestic detritus, and whole rooms are inaccessible, glimpsed only through chinks in the wall. Elements that are usually concealed—pipes, circuitry, cabling, ventilation systems, and dirt—are visible, while patches of damp or mold appear in high-up corners. The exhibition space is transformed into an alternative interior whose function remains ambiguous. It could be makeshift living quarters or an abandoned construction project. Tarnished and dented, the structures suggest the rub of an unseen dweller's small-scale daily encounters, comings and goings, decisions and mistakes. They do not appear static; rather, they seem like evolving organisms that constantly adapt for existence and its ever-changing requirements.

"I'm not interested in nostalgia," says Astakhishvili. "It is the need to have a home, across all classes of society, that I return to."[1] Growing up in Tbilisi, Georgia, she was surrounded by a patchwork urban landscape that reflected decades of unregulated architectural modification and improvisation. As a teenager, she witnessed close-up the failure and collapse of the oppressive Soviet Union. What followed was not a fresh start, however. The post-Soviet society of the early 1990s remained burdened with ideological baggage, economic precarity, intermittent periods of violent unrest, and political coercion—conditions and forces that persist to this day. Although Astakhishvili left Tbilisi in the late 1990s to study in Germany and the U.K. and has lived in Berlin since 2001, the fractured and ad hoc environment of her home city continues to be an underlying influence.

The artist draws on childhood memories of the built environment she grew up in, but the vernacular she employs has a broad familiarity. The furnishings, building materials, surfaces, and sounds that comprise her installations recall the liminal realms of domestic interiors: basements, cupboards, attics; concealed spaces where

1   Tolia Astakhishvili, quoted in Chris McCormack, "Profile: Tolia Astakhishvili," *Art Monthly*, June 2023, 15.

Fig. 2   Detail, *space reflected owner I*, Bonner Kunstverein, Bonn, 2023.

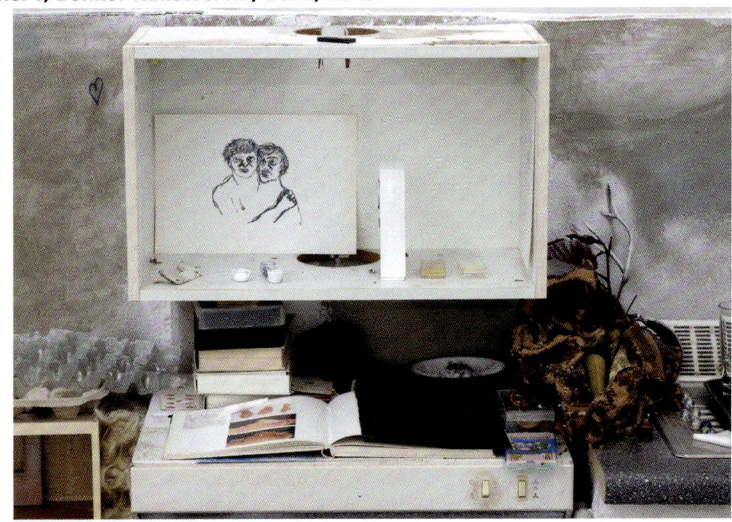

Fig. 3   Installation view, *space reflected owner I*, Bonner Kunstverein, Bonn, 2023.

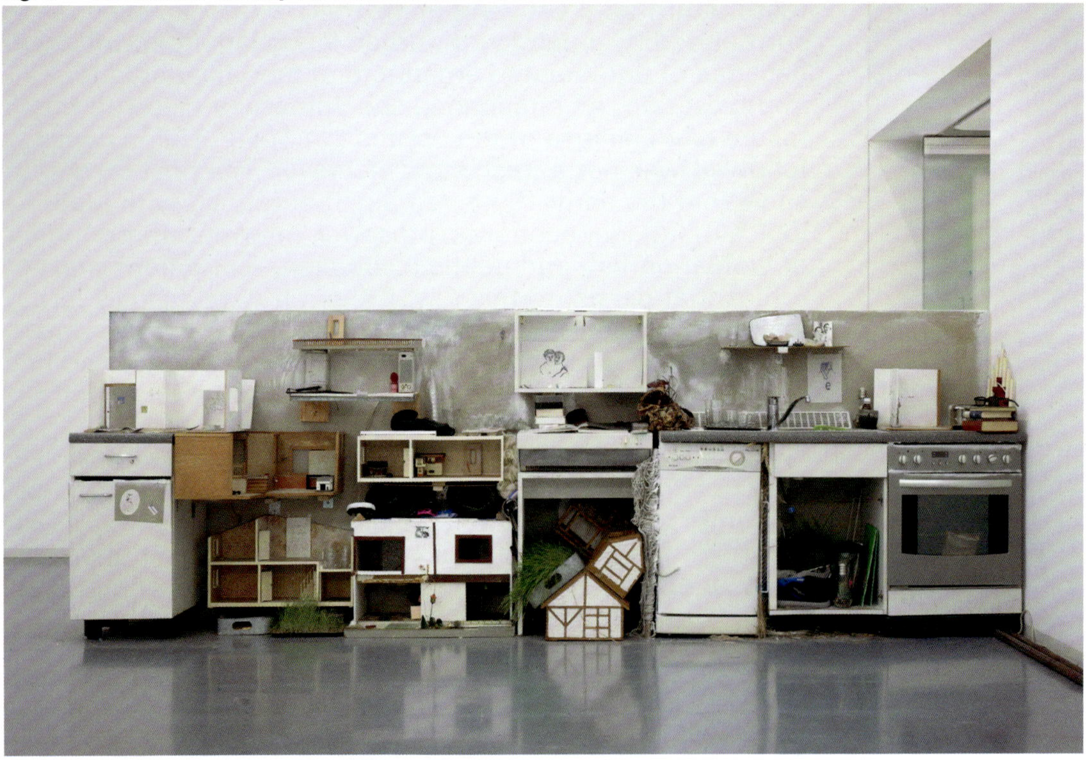

light slips through gaps in the floorboards and boilers or air vents rumble. Her structures seem to tap into the psychic energy of the buildings she works within and to emphasize the uncanny aspects of inhabitation. Recontextualized, the permanent architecture appears to change; patches of damage or clumsy repairs assert themselves, and new spatial alignments create a profound sense of disorientation. The rooms conjured by her work seem to belong as much to the mind as to the material world.

The narratives that emerge in Astakhishvili's work are not linear; they unfold spatially and often entail shifts of scale. Plasterboard configurations and dropped ceilings may alter the dimensions of the exhibition space, and windows are covered over. Zooming in, we find the kind of clutter that lingers in the kitchen drawer or on shelves in the garage; obsolete artifacts not thrown away but kept out of sight to gather dust, becoming sticky or brittle with neglect. Astakhishvili's exhibition at Bonner Kunstverein in 2023 featured a derelict kitchen, its cupboards and appliances stuffed with assorted crockery and cutlery but also with a strange collection of dollhouses and architectural models (Figs. 2–4). Elsewhere, ironing boards and suitcases were jammed into the interstitial spaces of another construction. Domestic inhabitation was indicated, but no protagonist was revealed. At MoMA PS1, a floor-bound debris chute is a repository for accumulations of various hardware fixtures, tangled jewelry chains, and little plastic

Fig. 4   Installation view, *space reflected owner I*, Bonner Kunstverein, Bonn, 2023.

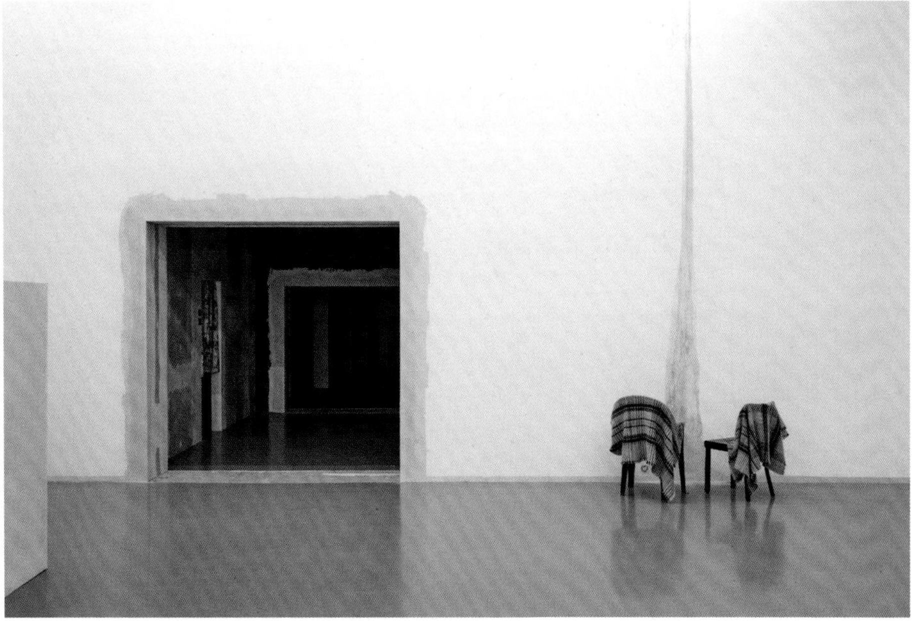

                    ARCHITECTURAL AFTERLIVES   Kirsty Bell

toys. Astakhishvili's work reorders and repurposes such items, extracting them from regular use and suggesting an afterlife that exists somehow out of time. In fact, time itself becomes elastic in her installations, which require the viewer to slow down in order to navigate spatial disorientations and take in obscure details.

Scattered among these mise-en-scènes are drawings on scraps of paper and delicately painted canvases. Picturing intertwined bodies or involutions of landscapes and limbs, these images are infused with eroticism and hints of violence. The drawings' compulsive figurations suggest a state of instability, both corporeal and existential. Meanwhile, fragments of enigmatic text scribbled directly on the walls suggest evidence of previous visitors, if not dwellers.

Detail, *The First Finger (Chapter II)*, Haus am Waldsee, Berlin, 2023. Photo: Eric Tschernow

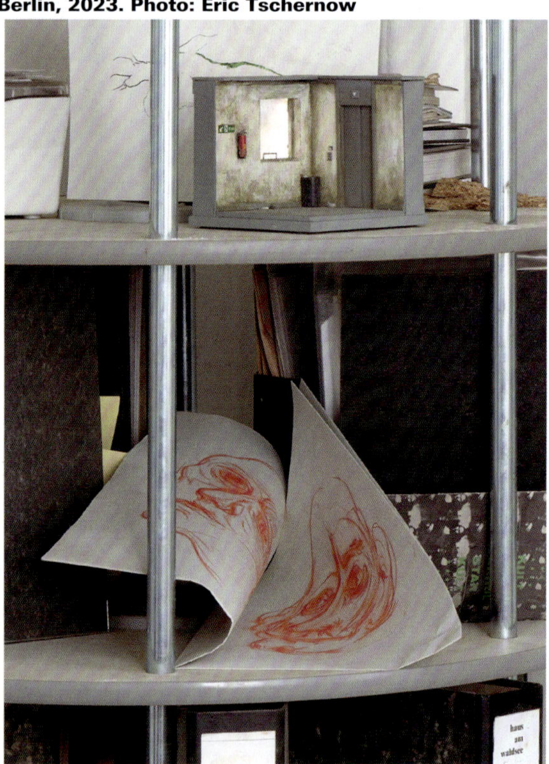

          Tolia Astakhishvili

These drawings and paintings are unmistakably Astakhishvili's own, but her installations are otherwise characterized by authorial slippage. What is existing architecture and what is intervention? Is that ambient sound or composition? Whom do these things belong to? Are they valuable or simply trash? And who is it that makes such appraisals? Astakhishvili further smudges the boundaries of authorship when she integrates works by other artists. In this exhibition are collages made by her father, Zurab Astakhishvili, and works on paper by her mother, Maka Sanadze. The new video *so many things I'd like to tell you* (2025) **(Fig. 1)** was made with her longtime collaborator, the artist Dylan Peirce. Its protagonist is a flatbed scanner that examines an endless stream of common objects and enigmatic images. The scanner's forensic gaze meets our own as we try to make sense of a random flow of items: an analog, materialist version of the everyday image feed we constantly consume.

Astakhishvili's sculptural installations summon an alternative spatial, material, and cognitive arena that nudges the present and common sense aside. In place of floor plans, measurements, and waking hours are ambiguous corners, forgotten rooms, and misremembered passageways. Immersed in these spaces, we understand their constructed nature while giving in to the parallel reality they evoke. Despite the familiarity of the rooms and objects, the work remains mysterious. It never fully resolves or clicks into focus. Every structure exists simultaneously as a model, a memory, and a real place. Buildings, like bodies, are shown to be porous, affected by changes in atmosphere, by time passing, by faulty plumbing and circuitry. In revealing the vulnerability of buildings and bodies, and their ultimate interdependence, Astakhishvili's practice questions the certainties of both.

 ARCHITECTURAL AFTERLIVES   Kirsty Bell

Miho Dohi

(Japanese, b. 1979)

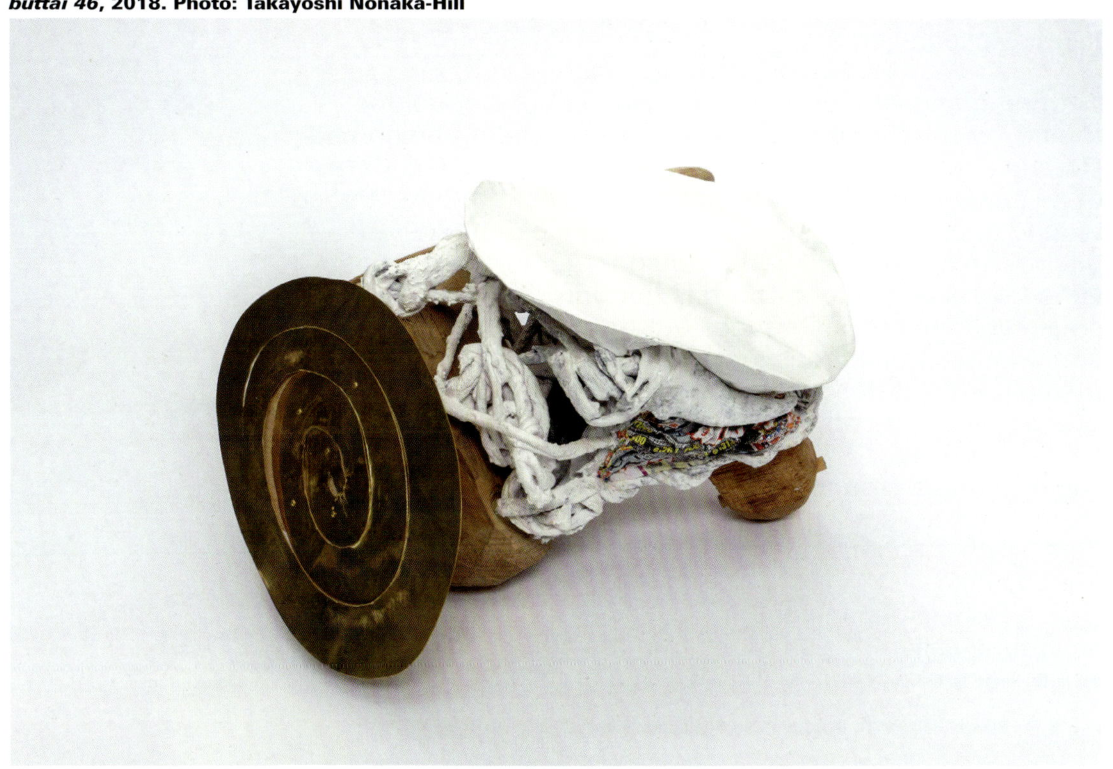

HOUSE SPIRITS
Laura McLean-Ferris

"At first glance it looks like a flat star-shaped spool for thread," wrote Franz Kafka of the curious being he named Odradek, who is the subject of the short story "The Cares of a Family Man." "And indeed it does seem to have thread wound upon it; to be sure, they are only old, broken-off bits of thread, knotted and tangled together, of the most varied sorts and colors. But it is not only a spool, for a small wooden crossbar sticks out of the middle of the star, and another small rod is joined to that at a right angle. By means of this latter rod on one side and one of the points of the star on the other, the whole thing can stand upright as if on two legs."[1] This circuitous description, in which we seem to move around a strange, somewhat unknowable thing—part assemblage, part life-form—uncannily resonates with the experience of looking at the sculptures of Miho Dohi.

Dohi, a Japanese artist based in Kanagawa, makes sculptural assemblages of an intimate and handleable scale, each one roughly the size of a small animal such

1   Franz Kafka, "The Cares of a Family Man," in *The Complete Stories by Franz Kafka*, ed. Nahum N. Glatzer (Schocken Books, 1971), 469.

Fig. 1   *buttai 71*, 2019. Photo: Élise Fourché

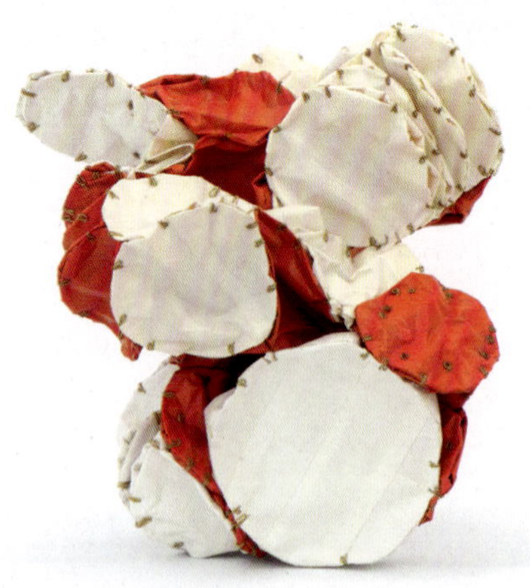

as a kitten or a rabbit. They are mostly constructed from common materials such as wood, cloth, copper, and paint, and household staples such as thread, duct tape, and wire. They can seem to be unassuming composites of the familiar stuff of the everyday: odds and ends from a shelf in a garage or the back of a kitchen drawer. One sculpture, *buttai 71* (2019), is formed mostly from red and white pieces of duct tape (Fig. 1). Yet in Dohi's hands, these folded fragments, which are tessellated and joined together, create a mysterious new form that seems to have popped open into three dimensions like a traveling circus marquee.

Dohi's sculptures are asymmetrical and singular, and they are difficult to comprehend from one vantage point, having a multitude of different features and faces that only come into focus as one moves around them. Surfaces, details, and daubs of color are sometimes concealed, screened, or cloaked by corners or hoods. *Buttai 94* (2023), for example, is built around six solid wooden cylinders that have been painted yellow and joined together in a curving horizontal row like a set of panpipes (Fig. 2). Extending off this central structure are several pieces of copper and brass that have been twisted, pleated, looped, and bent to form squares, hooks, plates, and other forms. Many of these metal sections have been partially painted in blue and green hues, the additions highlighting the shape's interiors or decorating their exteriors like precious stones. Viewed from one side, the sculpture appears to open itself up like a wide jaw, but from another it looks closed like a fist accessorized with baroque metal rings. From certain angles a goofy smile appears in the sculpture's midst, and from others, some googly eyes. Sometimes its coherence

Fig. 2   *buttai 94*, 2023. Photo: Ken Kato

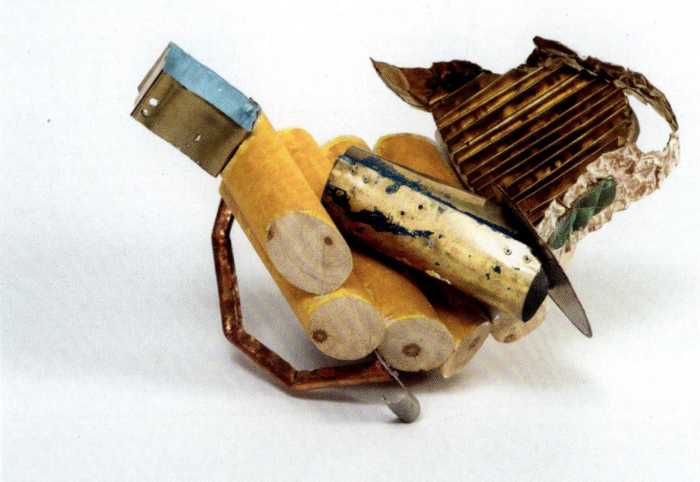

seems to collapse, leaving a simple pile of stuff for a moment, before it reassembles itself, finding new form. For an assemblage of hard, solid matter, it is surprisingly fluid, a shape-shifter made of wood and metal.

Since 2008, Dohi has titled each of her sculptures *buttai* (物体). The word, which means "object," brings together two kanji characters: 物 / *but-* (meaning "thing"), and 体 / *-tai* (meaning "body"). This synthesis connotes a liveliness that is important to the artist. As she has said, "All of my works are 'objects' and 'bodies'.... A 'thing' that also has an element of 'body' which involves movement."[2] Indeed, certain elements of Dohi's sculptures—colors, shapes, or textures—seem to rush forward in the way they might in a painted composition. In a sculptural form, this creates a sense of motion.

But like Kafka's Odradek, who is made of household bits of wood and string yet moves "nimbly" and laughs in a lungless voice like "the rustling of fallen leaves," Dohi's *buttai* are in possession of something like a voice, or a soul: not just in motion but fully and curiously animated.[3] By what, exactly? To look at several *buttai* in succession is to see charged objects in full possession of the different energies that lie latent in their unassuming materials. And it's the long duration of the artist's attention, her continued study and testing of objects, that allows for this

2   Miho Dohi, quoted in "Miho Dohi," Gordon Robichaux, accessed January 16, 2025, https://gordon robichaux.com/exhibitions /miho-dohi.
3   Kafka, "The Cares of a Family Man,"470.

buttai 111, 2024. Photo: Takayoshi Nonaka-Hill
buttai 66, 2019. Photo: Greg Carideo

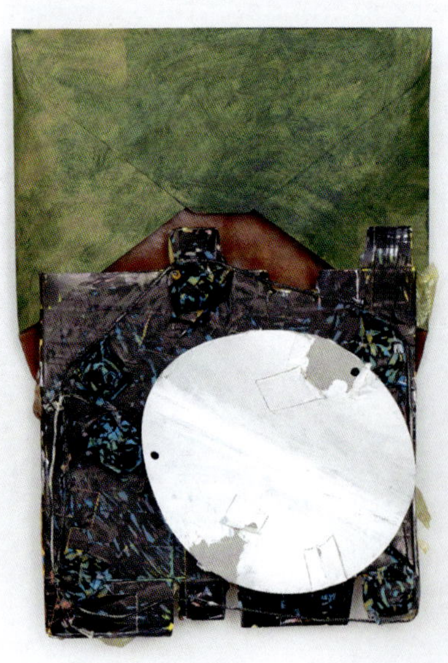

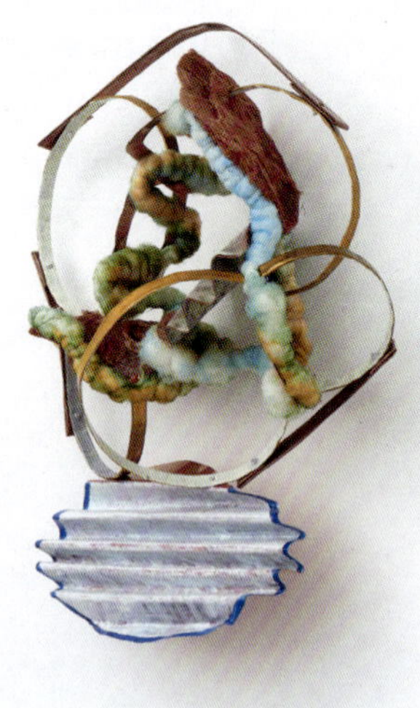

          Miho Dohi

transformation, for the bringing of a new form into being from "beyond [the] imagination."[4] Like a new species, each *buttai* appears to have been dictated by its own interior logic. The artist describes her process as a kind of decreation, a creative undoing. "Once an object has completely collapsed," Dohi has said, "something that hadn't existed in me becomes something that is there now."[5]

It's also significant that Dohi's sculptures sometimes seem dragged from places where things are stashed so they can be forgotten about, corners where objects might dull from lack of attention. At first glance, *buttai 91* (2022) looks like a small model of an animal on a display stand (Fig. 3). A mangled little rocking horse is what comes to mind, made of white bones and gray mothballs and raised on a copper pedestal attached to a clamshell-like box. Each element echoes something recognizable—a toddler's toy, an old jewelry case, insulation, wiring, a broken machine part—the type of object that might collect dust in an attic. In Dohi's work these half-seen, half-recognizable forms come together in new hybrid creatures, as though memories and bits of matter could coalesce into a new substance. Things aren't used up when we have stopped using them, or when they lie out of sight. Quite to the contrary, they mostly outlast us.

4   Dohi, "Miho Dohi."
5   Miho Dohi, quoted in "Miho Dohi," Fondation d'entreprise Pernod Ricard, accessed January 16, 2025, https://www.fondation-pernod-ricard.com/en/exhibition/miho-dohi.

Fig. 3   *buttai 91*, 2022. Photo: Ken Kato

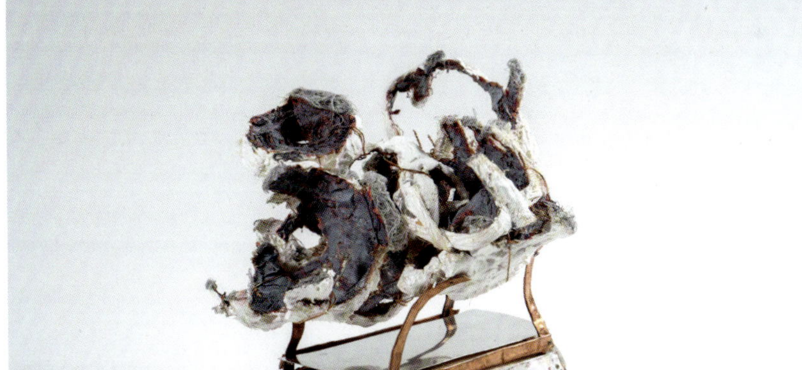

     HOUSE SPIRITS   Laura McLean-Ferris

Andro Eradze

(Georgian, b. 1993)

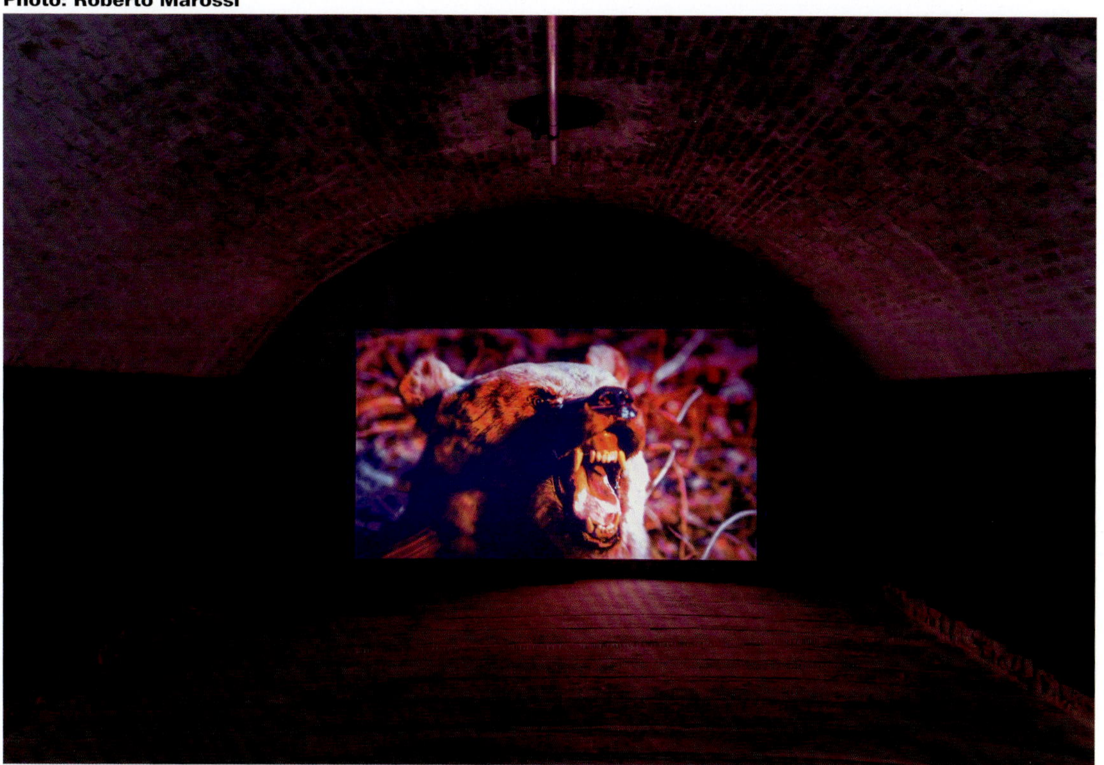

Fig. 1   Installation view, *Raised in the Dust*, 2022, in *The Milk of Dreams*, La Biennale di Venezia, 2022.
Photo: Roberto Marossi

SHIFTING THE STILLNESS INTO TURBULENCE
Filipa Ramos

Surrealism, influenced by theories about consciousness and the mind, was interested in people's dreams. Imagining and depicting the plausible and outlandish oneiric worlds that populated our sleeping lives, artists affiliated with or attracted to the Surrealist movement shaped the ways in which dreams were narrated, imagined, and depicted. Through their speculative exercises, these artists gave birth to even more dreams. Proposing an ensemble of figures, resources, and states of mind, their work triggered a new organization of the unconscious that also defied conventions of time.

Once given an important stage in people's lives, dreams—in their absurd, unruly, meandering plots and lack of pragmatism—troubled the linear order of things that modernity had naturalized. These disruptions not only concerned the construction of the rational mind of the modern (civilized) individual; they also challenged the logics of the assemblage and productivity lines at the base of industrialization and the supposed distribution of efficiency, progress, and success to society at large. The invention of industrial time—with its operative vectors and divisions between production and recovery, prescription and performance, planning and contingency—likewise informed the structuring of cinematic time, in its assigned linearity and sequential arrangement.[1] Fittingly, certain filmmakers associated with Surrealism (namely Maya Deren and Luis Buñuel, as well as more contemporary artists such as Joan Jonas) brought together the representation of dreams with the rethinking and re-worlding of domestic spaces. By associating the container that is the house with the vast universe of dreams, they questioned a bastion of society's organization; they proposed that other ways of living, feeling, and dreaming were possible. As such, they contributed to a reconceptualization of domesticity, recasting the haven of the reproduction of stability as a site where the otherwise could be summoned and actualized.

Dialoguing with this history, Andro Eradze's film *Flowering and Fading* (2024) locates the house as a symbolic and concrete site of dream expression (Figs. 2–3 & 6–7). This departs from several of his earlier works, which

1   On this subject, see Mary Ann Doane, *The Emergence of Cinematic Time: Modernity, Contingency, the Archive* (Harvard University Press, 2002).

Fig. 2   Still, *Flowering and Fading*, 2024.
Fig. 3   Still, *Flowering and Fading*, 2024.

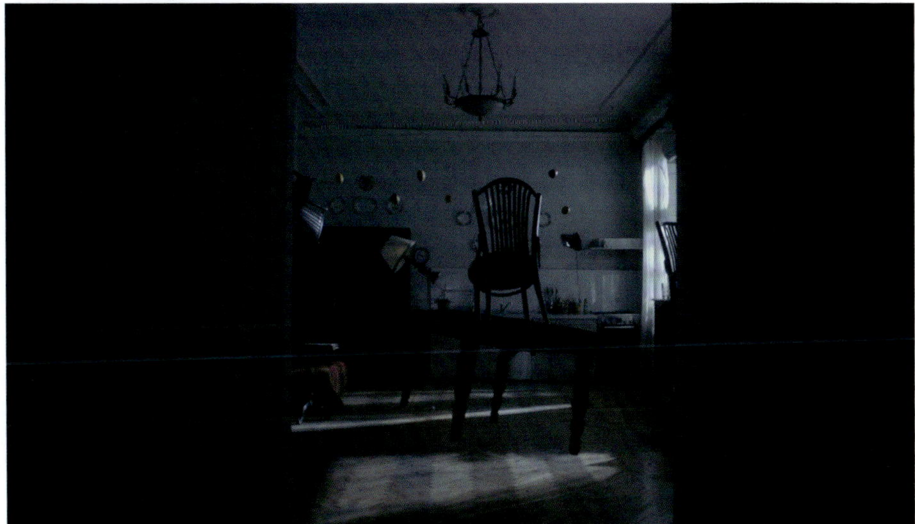

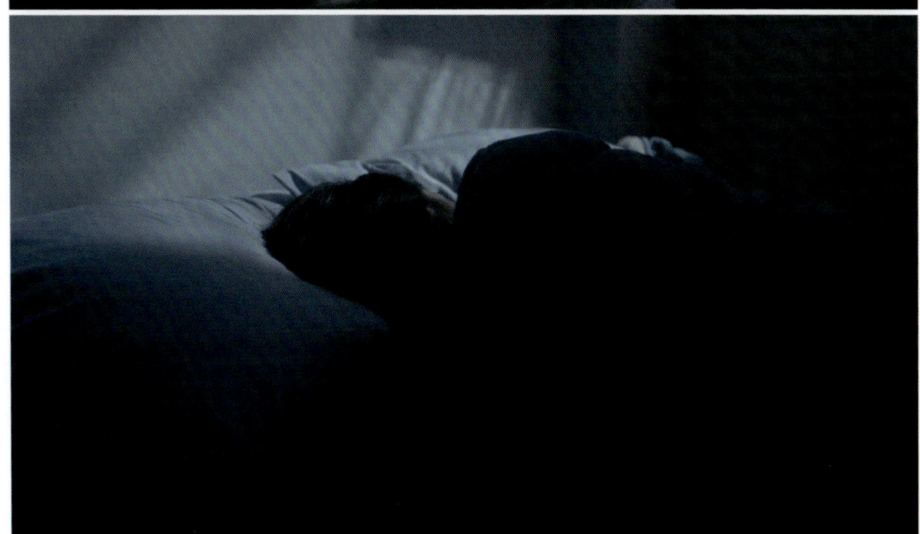

81

take viewers to forests and liminal spaces where tensions among the feral, the natural, and the human are permanent. Such is the case with *Nightvision, Limited Access* (2021), a film that follows a pack of stray dogs roaming the empty streets of Tbilisi, Georgia, at night, their presence challenging the definition of the urban in a space of total human control and ownership **(Fig. 4)**. A subsequent film, *Raised in the Dust* (2022), alternates images of fireworks and taxidermy animals that have been placed in a forest at night **(Figs. 1 & 5)**. The triangulation among human celebration, at once joyful and violent; the stereotyped positions of animals preserved as trophies or museum props; and the somber forest further accentuate the zones of friction where distinctions and values of civilization and wilderness collapse.

In *Flowering and Fading*, Eradze further pursues his interest in portraying that which happens at night. The film was shot in the historic home of Simon Virsaladze (1909–1989), a renowned Georgian stage and costume designer. For decades, Virsaladze set the atmosphere of Georgian and Soviet ballets, films, and operas, and his collection of

Fig. 4   *Nightvision, Limited Access*, 2021, in *Between Dog and Wolf*, screening at Fondation Vincent van Gogh, Arles, 2023. Photo: Grégoire d'Ablon

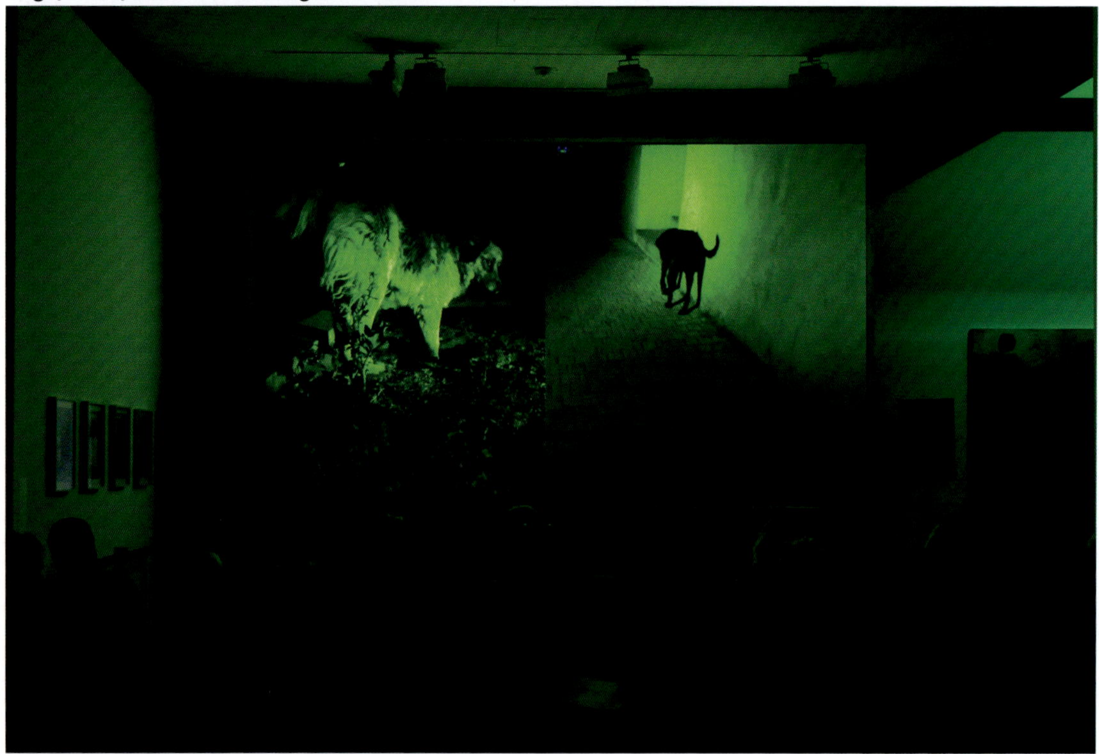

     Andro Eradze

objects gathered during his world travels is still preserved in the house. Eradze's camera moves around the abode at night. Alongside a wind that traverses it, coming from the outside, the camera is the only presence that breaks an otherwise serene situation, in which a woman and a dog sleep, "shifting the stillness into turbulence."[2] While they sleep, something happens around them, an activity that is outside the usual functioning of the house and seems alien to those who inhabit it. The unusual, quasi-magical events that occur put the film in conversation with Deren's *Meshes of the Afternoon* (1943) and Buñuel's *The Discreet Charm of the Bourgeoisie* (1972), which conceive of the house as the incubator of irrational, oneiric human activity. Yet here, the surprising episodes captured by the camera seem to come not from the unconscious minds of the house's inhabitants but from the house itself.

In the ebb and flow of the night, attuned to the rhythms of breezes and gusts, matter and spirit are recombined, and the house is the one who dreams. Unlike cinematic tropes in which a house is possessed and animated by disruptive entities that slam doors or turn

2   "Shifting the stillness into turbulence" is a phrase Eradze used to describe the wind's effect on the atmosphere of the house. Email exchange with the author, December 2024.

Fig. 5   Still, *Raised in the Dust*, 2022.

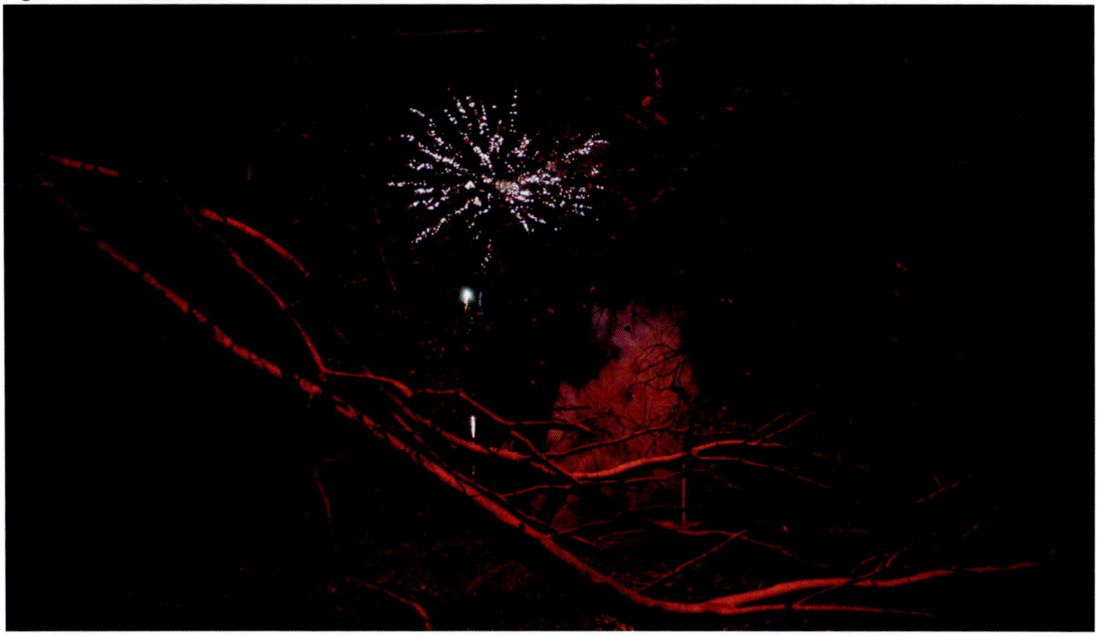

SHIFTING THE STILLNESS
INTO TURBULENCE

Filipa Ramos

lights on and off, here the home's inner life is peaceful and smooth. Ignoring the laws of gravity, objects such as a table, a chair, a lamp, and fruit—classical constituents of *vanitas* paintings—float in space, slowly and softly suspended in midair. A tiny mouse is also caught in this moment of beautiful strangeness. A creature of the threshold, neither wild nor domestic, the mouse reveals the porosity between the human and nonhuman realms while floating atop a chair, seemingly indifferent to the unusual levitation of the furniture. While everything floats, gentle underwater noises can be heard, enhancing a sense of otherworldliness.

A honey jar, felled, slowly spills its thick liquid, a liberatory vision that feels both wrong and magical. The beauty of the golden amber liquid seeping out is timeless. The scene is imbued with still life pictorial traditions, which it also updates. Could this house be dreaming of a new order, a different arrangement of things that attends to the poetry and potency of minor events? And what about the dog? Is he dreaming *with* the house, asserting his own domestication—his belonging to the domus—a bond that broke his own species's pact with wilderness? Or, aligned in his animality with the mouse, is he also aware of the house's dream, accepting its fluidity with that sagacious acquiescence that only animals have? Or maybe these are unnecessary distinctions and classifications that see divisions between humans, other animals, and things where there should be none. Maybe together they dream, and in their dreams they follow the poem and *"understand flowering and fading at once."*[3]

3   Like those of other works by Eradze, the title of the film *Flowering and Fading* is inspired by a poem. In this case, it references the fourth elegy from Rainer Maria Rilke's *Duino Elegies* (1923):

O trees of life, when is your winter?
Our nature's not the same. We don't have the instinct
of migrant birds. Late and out of season,
we suddenly throw ourselves to the wind
and fall into indifferent ponds. We
understand flowering and fading at once.
And somewhere lions still roam: so magnificent
they can't understand weakness.

Translation by A. Poulin Jr. in *Duino Elegies and The Sonnets to Orpheus* (Houghton Mifflin, 1977), 27.

    Andro Eradze

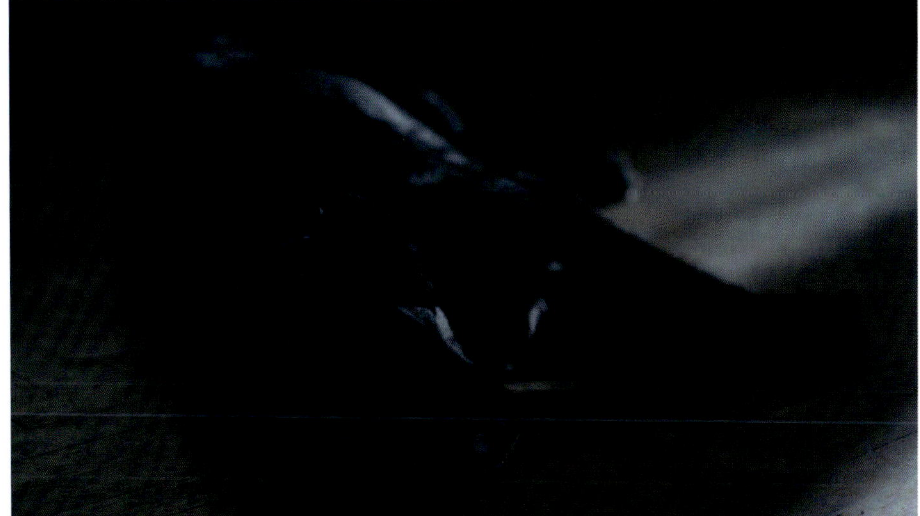

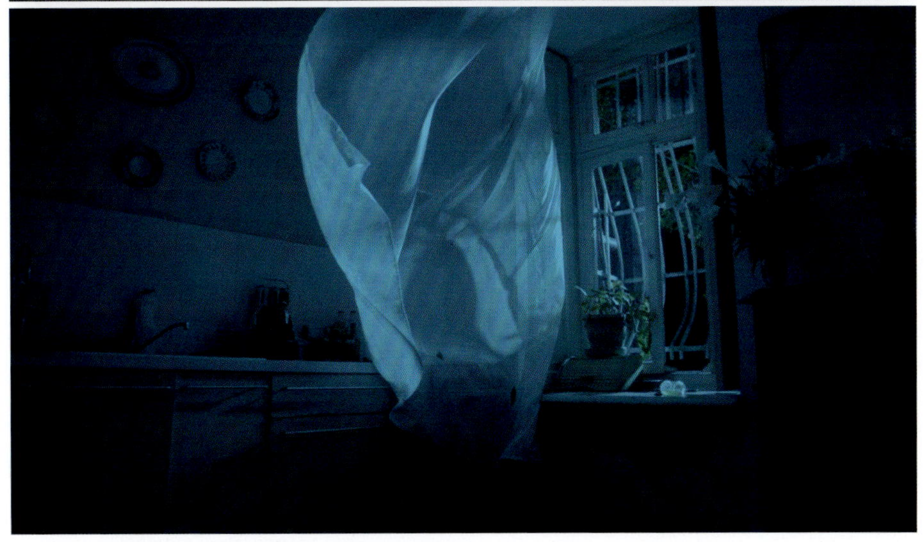

SHIFTING THE STILLNESS
INTO TURBULENCE

Filipa Ramos

He
Xiangyu

(Chinese, b. 1986)

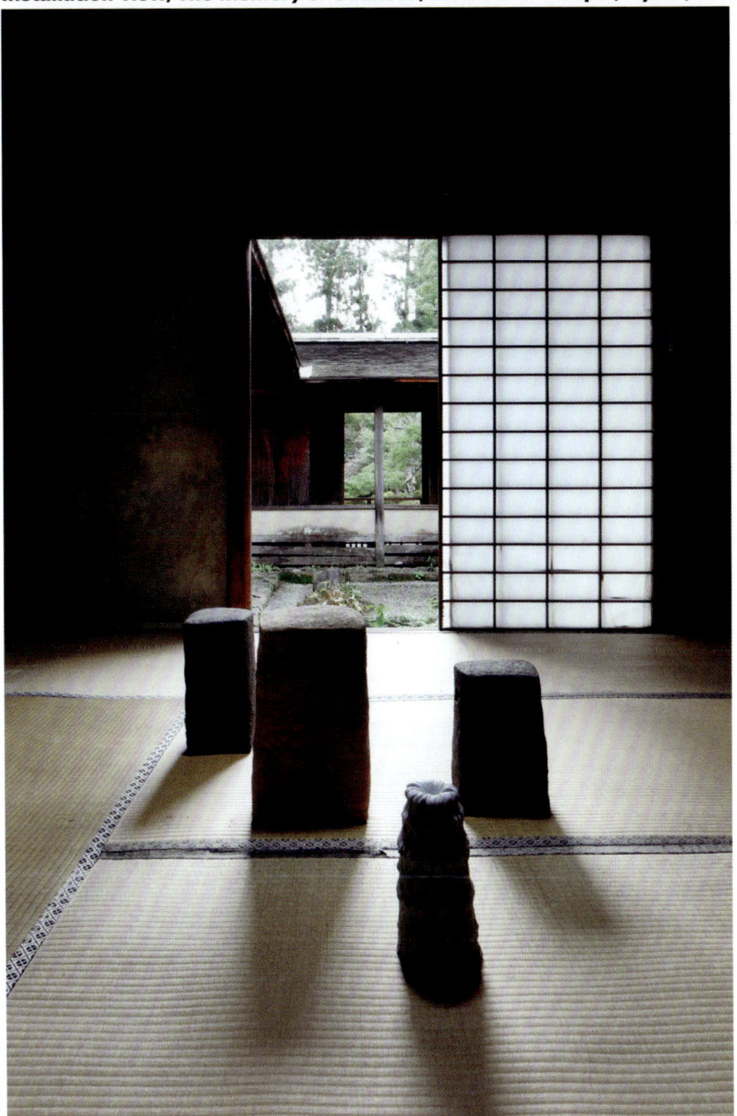

OBSERVATION AS MATERIAL
Fabian Schöneich

He Xiangyu's *House of Nations* is a 2021 short film that
intimately portrays the life of a young Chinese exchange
student residing in Berlin during the initial COVID-19 lockdowns (Figs. 1–2). The protagonist moves through his daily
routines—cycling through the city, socializing with fellow
students, and finding solitude in moments like bathing in
lakes—against the backdrop of global isolation. A quiet,
poetic observation of a young person's journey, the work
also serves as a sharp critique of society, exploring globalization just as much as it delves into the protagonist's
personal experiences. Indeed, the student's fear of an
uncertain future and his struggle with loneliness reflect the
concerns and conditions of many migrant communities.
In a world that has become increasingly interconnected,
He focuses on minor histories and in-between moments,
weaving a nuanced narrative of childhood, tradition, and
ideology. Yet he does not lose sight of what truly matters:
humor, friendship, and community take center stage
in his work.

Born and educated in China, He lived briefly in the
United States before moving to Berlin, then back to Beijing,
and in early 2025 to Milan. His life and work are thus
shaped by diverse political ideologies, cultures, and social
systems. This background is crucial to keep in mind when
engaging with He's films, paintings, drawings, sculptures,
and installations. He often adds a witty touch to his
otherwise earnest contemplation of social and societal
realities, isolating and suspending small physical actions.
For example, the sculpture *Asian Boy* (2019–20) features
a prepubescent boy opening an absent can of soda (Fig. 3),
and the multimedia series *Palate Project* (2012–ongoing)
centers on the mundane sensory experience of touching
one's tongue to the roof of one's mouth while learning a
foreign language. These works highlight the subtle, often
overlooked aspects of daily life.

In recent years, He has created a remarkable
number of sculptures that, incorporating various artisanal
traditions such as metalworking and ceramics, distill
trenchant political commentary into formal gestures.
There is *Asian Boy* again, a work that seems so innocent
yet critiques China's one-child policy. And then there is

88

Fig. 1   Still, *House of Nations*, 2021.
Fig. 2   Still, *House of Nations*, 2021.

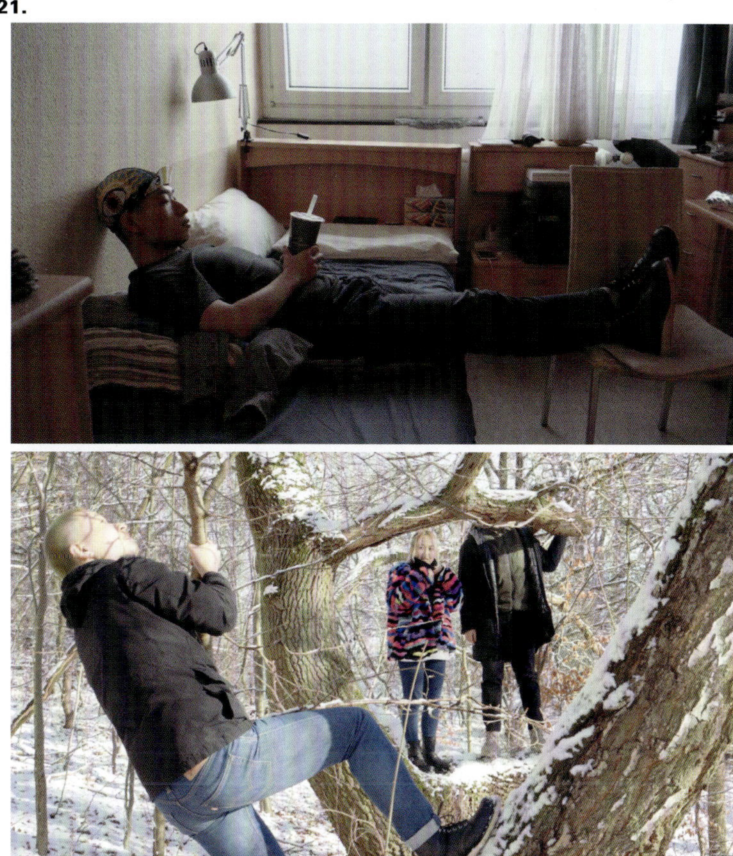

Fig. 3   Installation view, *Asian Boy*, 2019–20, in *Afterimage*, MAXXI L'Aquila, 2022.
Photo: Andrea Rossetti

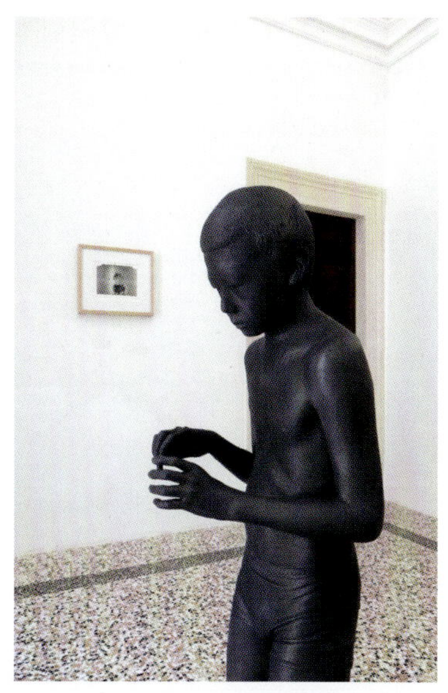

Practical Opacity (2020), an assembly of found school chairs covered with careless, almost violent, scribbles, scratches, stickers, and graffiti, always shown with an exacting arrangement of miniature copies (Fig. 4). The viewer must decide which set of chairs is "real." The work calls to mind the sculptures of Robert Gober, who, like no other, has made his own upbringing the subject of his work. The challenge of precisely re-creating objects and bodies, building on the past while decidedly not repeating it, connects the artists. Both consciously choose to see something in a way that it has not been seen before.

Fig. 4 *Practical Opacity*, 2020.

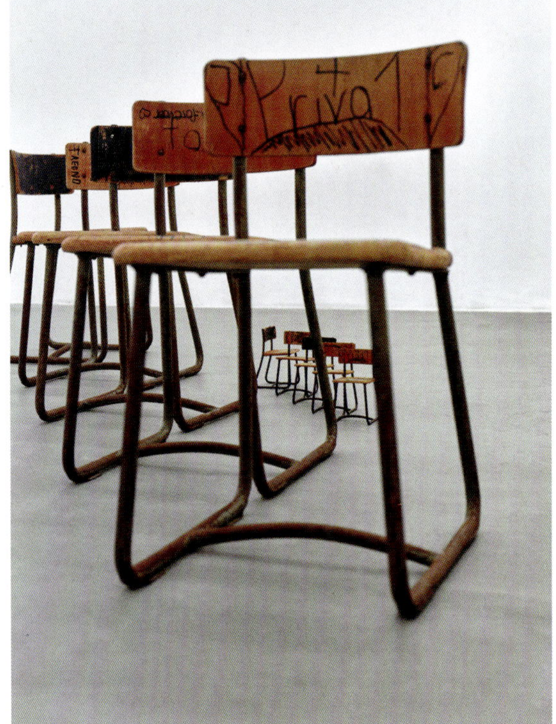

 He Xiangyu

     The installations *Rock Tongue* and *Opaque Loop* **(Fig. 5)** (both 2024) reflect on the very idea of uniformity. Each is made from steel and found river stones. Stone has many resonant valences: a natural resource, it is among the oldest conceivable sculptural materials and evokes early tools. In China, as in many countries, stones are popular and significant collector's items, often valued for their imperfections and distinguishing features. He collects stones that are small to medium-size, with minimal inclusions or fractures; their coloring is relatively unchanging, and each is marked by a white circle that stands out from the rest of the surface. These rings are formed by calcium carbonate deposition and subsequent wavy mineral segregation. The stones are not sought-after collectibles, but rather are universal objects found anywhere.

Fig. 5   ***Opaque Loop*, 2024.**

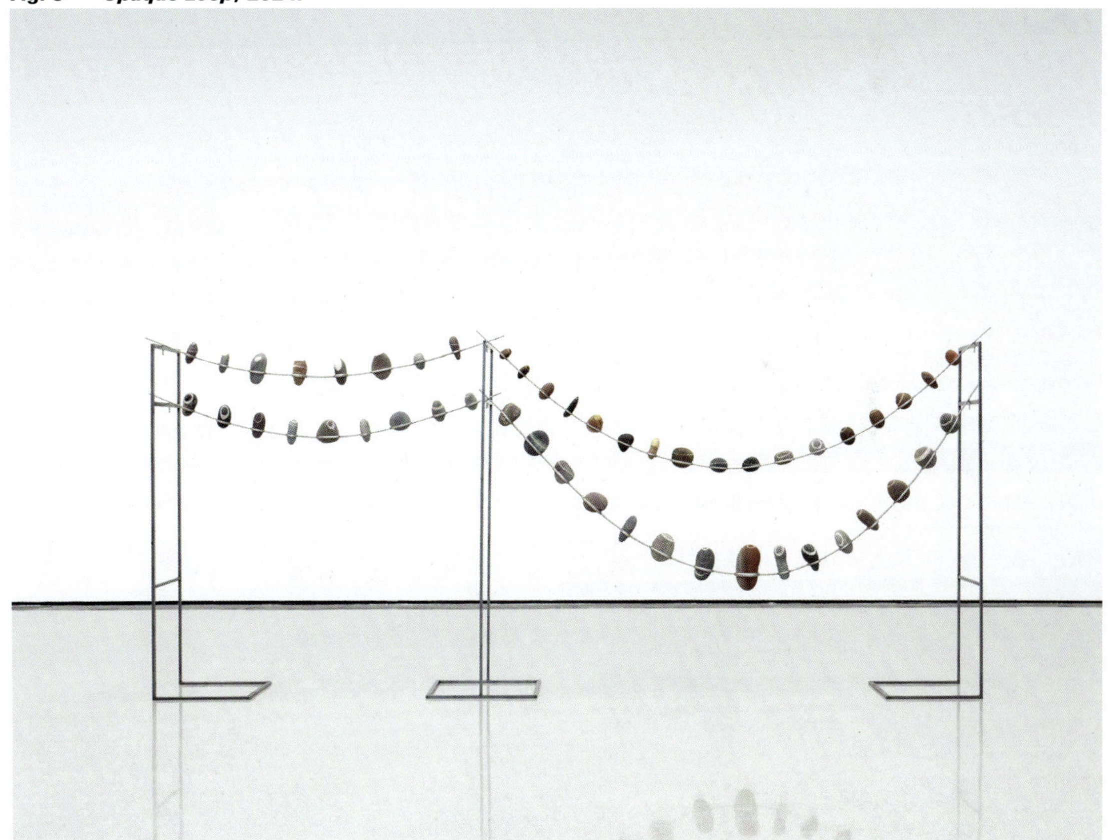

    OBSERVATION AS MATERIAL   Fabian Schöneich

Installation view, *The Essence of Early Morning*, 2024, in *The Memory of Stillness*, Manshu-in Temple, Kyoto, 2024. Photo: Takeru Koroda

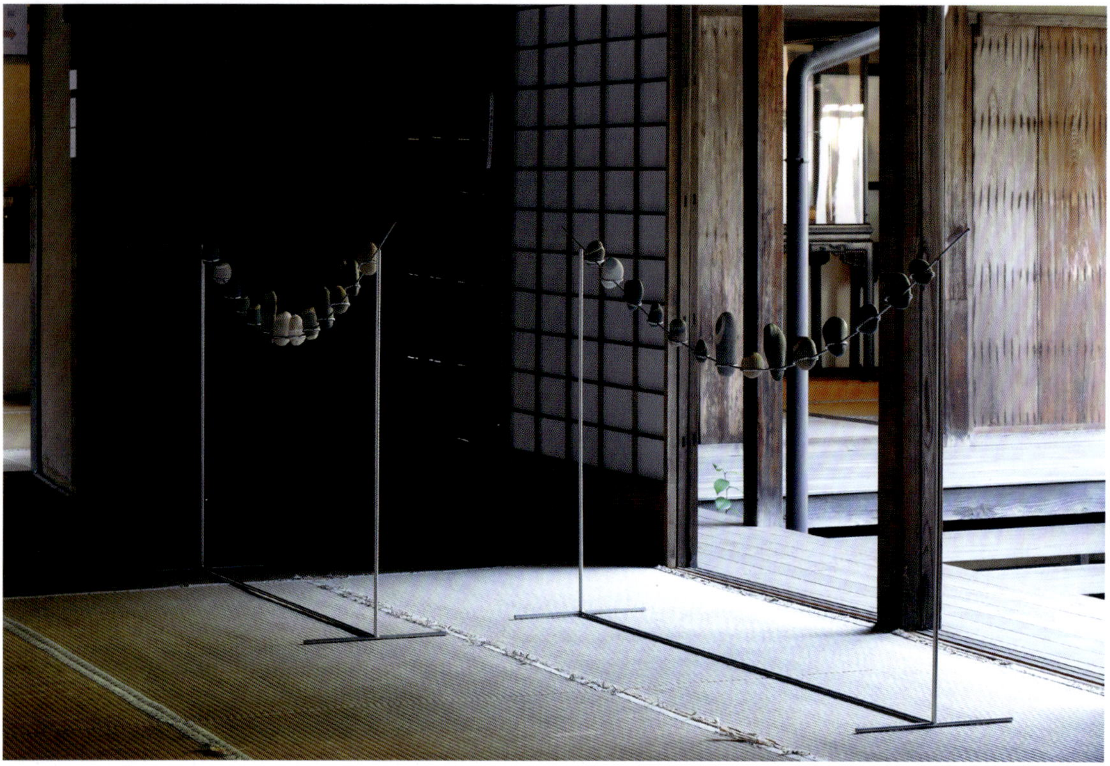

Installation view, *The Essence of Early Morning*, 2024, in *The Memory of Stillness*, Manshu-in Temple, Kyoto, 2024. Photo: Takeru Koroda

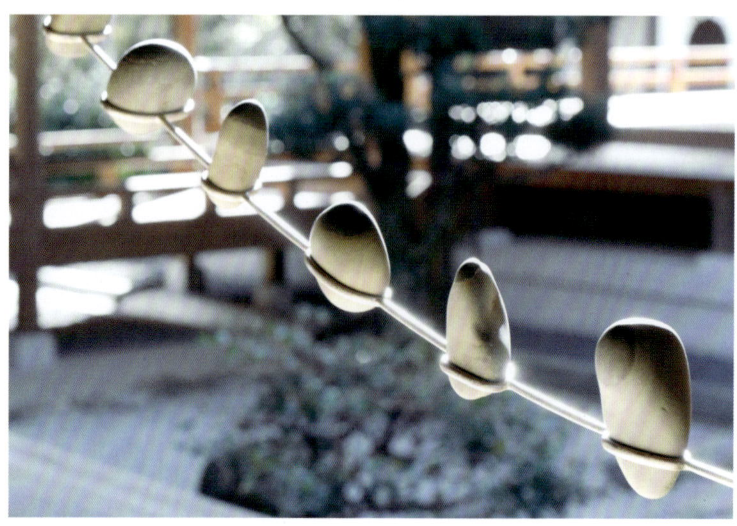

The artist builds custom steel structures that feature rods balancing between larger supports; the rods are designed with small, equidistant circles in which He places the ringed stones upright. Each installation contains between 20 and 50 stones, whose weight causes the steel framework to sag. History has shown us that in social or political systems where uniformity is prized and subjects are confined within rigid parameters, the structures created to uphold those restrictions inevitably bend until they collapse. The rings that gently hold each stone can also be seen as restrictive clamps that are ultimately powerless to prevent the system's collapse. The work does not destroy itself like Jean Tinguely's *Homage to New York* (1960)—at least, not yet—but it teeters on the brink. It plays with tension while evoking a certain harmony—a lethal combination.

He's upbringing in China, and his later reflection on this experience from an outsider's perspective, informs much of the artist's work. Being the "one" child generates a lot of attention and a great deal of pressure. He found that when he left his immediate family structure to enter the daily routine of school, his worldview changed. Suddenly, he was one of many "ones" that a teacher was supposed to educate and shape into uniform servants of a system. How does one deal with that experience as a person, as an artist? He's more recent work explores his detachment from the world of his childhood, and his decision to lead a self-determined life as free from systems as possible. The work also reflects an awareness that to live in a "free" society is, alas, to participate in yet another system.

     OBSERVATION AS MATERIAL   Fabian Schöneich

Vessel Project: Yellow Houses (2024) features ceramic architectures created by the artist in Jingdezhen, a region renowned for ceramics production (Fig. 6). He uses the coil-building technique and then carefully fires his structures for over a week, ensuring greater durability and stability. Notably, these buildings lack the elements that make architecture livable and inhabitable: windows and doors (light and access) and other identifiable features of human-made structures. What are these houses? Empty shells or uninhabitable relics, they gesture to a future world that is unlivable. As attractive as their ocher appearance may be, their insides are hollow and presumably dark—ominously so.

Fig. 6   Installation view, *Vessel Project: Yellow Houses*, 2024, in *The Radiance of Liberty*, Andrew Kreps Gallery, New York, 2024. Photo: Kunning Huang

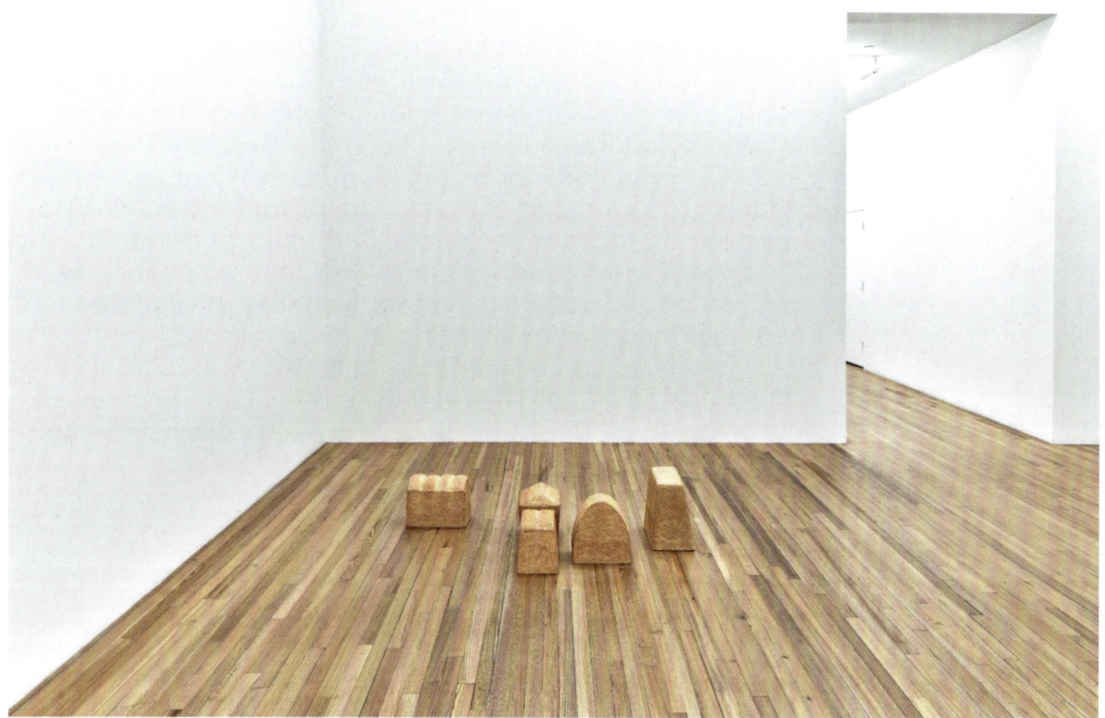

          He Xiangyu

Time is an element that connects many of He's works—not in terms of the duration of the artist's efforts (although many of his projects involve extensive production processes; he frequently collaborates with specialized craftspeople). Here, time is understood as a material—something that was, is, and will be present. Will our structures collapse? Will our houses become untenable? He moves through the world as artists have always done, living within systems while observing them from the outside. His work—a series of proposals generated from collected allegories, materials, techniques, and experiences—is at once aesthetically pleasing and uncannily distancing.

     OBSERVATION AS MATERIAL   Fabian Schöneich

Samuel Hindolo

(American, b. 1990)

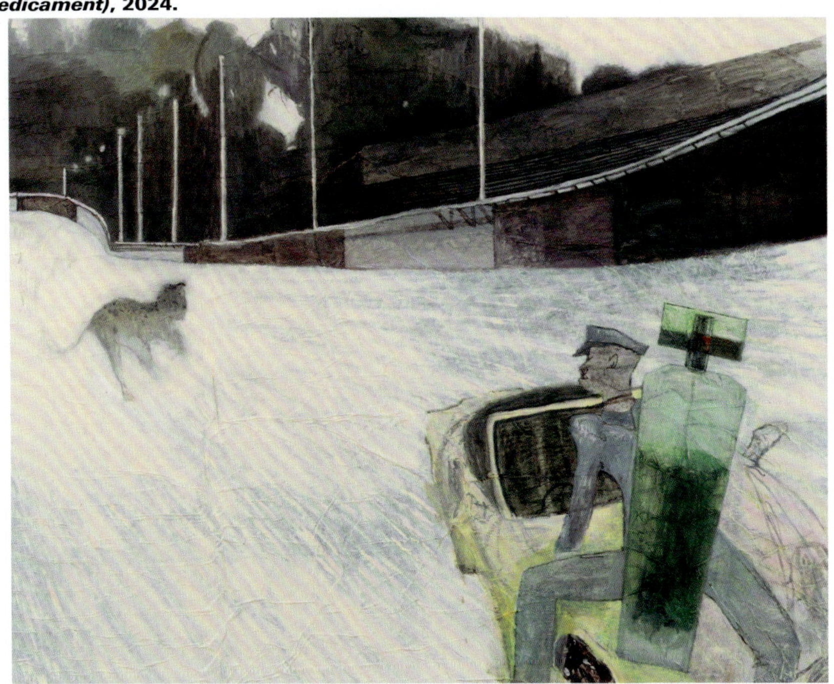

Saïda (Two Scenes, One Predicament), 2024.

FIGURES
Anette Freudenberger

Samuel Hindolo's paintings explore the way images transform and even empty out over the course of their history as they are utilized in different contexts, sometimes linking these progressions to the global circulation of goods. The artist focuses on the immediacy of his materials and on the spatial and conceptual organization of his imagery, generating multi-perspective compositions where narratives intersect. Across his work, he allows room for discrepancies and ruptures of logic.

Consider the collage painting *Saïda (Leap)* (2024); Hindolo's work usually features elusive figures in urban environments, but here, the artist arranges three leopards and their prey, a limp human body, alongside collaged floating perfume bottles and islands of text in an obscure location extending toward a vast, featureless horizon (Fig. 1). One perfume is NNN by the brand Napoleon, and the other is named after poet, philosopher, and politician Leopold Sédar Senghor, who theorized the anticolonial concept of Négritude in the 1930s and served as the first Senegalese president (1960–80) after the country's liberation from

Fig. 1   *Saïda (Leap)*, 2024.

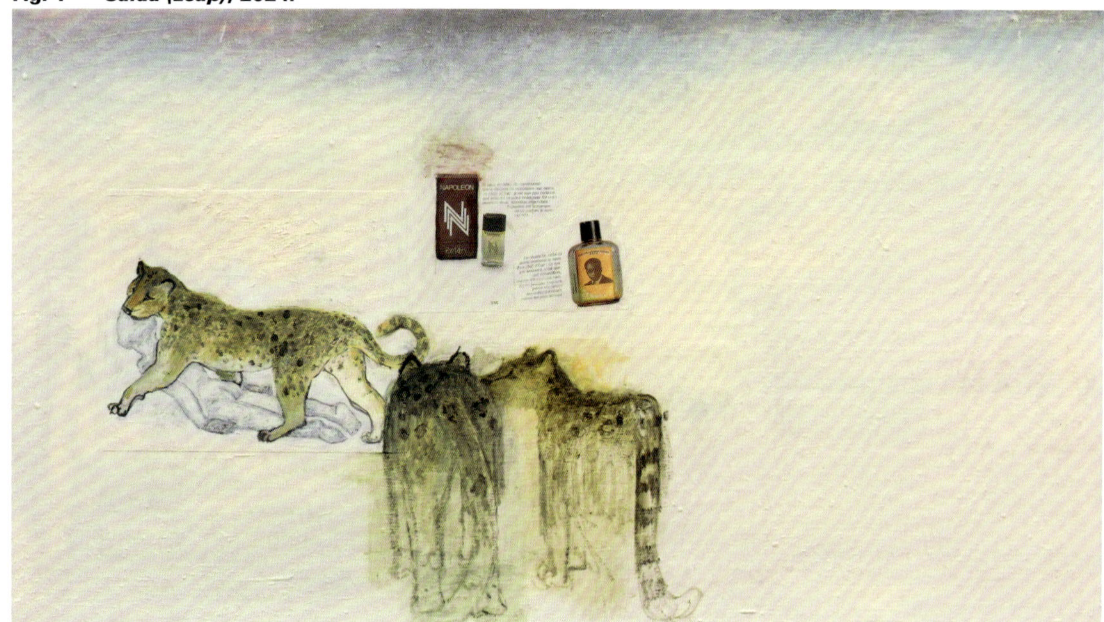

France. The texts offer no clues about the political figures referenced, but instead address the viewer—or, rather, the collector—with suggestions for collecting according to such categories as perfumes named after heads of state. Hindolo hints at the context of the statesmen in the painting, yet declines further comment.

Napoléon Bonaparte's systematic art theft during his invasion of Egypt at the end of the eighteenth century is largely responsible for the Western construction of the exotic, which continues to inspire marketing strategies in the fragrance industry today. In such campaigns, encounters between wildcat and perfume are a widespread trope. Hindolo revisits the leopard motif over a series of works. He draws reference from the 1913 Belgian silent film *Saïda a enlevé Manneken Pis* (Saïda Makes Off With the Manneken Pis), a parody by Alfred Machin that follows a leopard as she escapes from a fairground and tears a Belgian landmark (the odd bronze of a little pissing boy) from its pedestal and claims power. As she chases a crowd of clumsy police officers deployed to apprehend her through various locations, including a velodrome, Saïda goes from hunted to hunter, even triggering cannon fire in the direction of her pursuers. Hindolo's appropriations demonstrate an interest not only in cultural histories, but in cinematic processes. He transfers information from different shots and perspectives in the film and arranges them sequentially.

The artist's confrontation of feline and statesman calls to mind the numerous variations and caricatures of Jean-Léon Gérôme's iconic painting *Bonaparte Before the Sphinx* (1886), which pictures the military general, during the Battle of the Pyramids in 1798, standing face-to-face with the statue—a moment that never actually took place. Photographs of the monument served as a model for Gérôme's painting, but no horseman was ever present in them; Napoléon's lifetime predates the invention of photography. Yet nearly every film about him, including Ridley Scott's historically inaccurate 2023 biopic, includes this scene.

The inscrutable sphinx has occupied Hindolo for some time. In an untitled 2023 painting, he reconceives the Belgian painter Fernand Khnopff's *Caress of the Sphinx* (1896), a symbolist depiction of the mythical, androgynous creature (that channels the artist's incestuous desire for his sister) (Fig. 2). Hindolo's equally ambiguous and somewhat macabre scene unfolds before the Palace of Justice in Brussels—a monumental, dilapidated building, erected under King Leopold II, that has been awaiting renovation for forty years—outside of which sits another statue of a sphinx.

Hindolo intentionally locates many of his works in a Belgian context, confronting us with the colonialist background of Europe's cultural production. Traces of colonial history and its consequences are evident everywhere, particularly in Brussels, home to the headquarters of many European institutions and, for some time, to Hindolo. The title of his 2024 exhibition *Eurostar* connected the New

Fig. 2   *untitled*, **2023.**

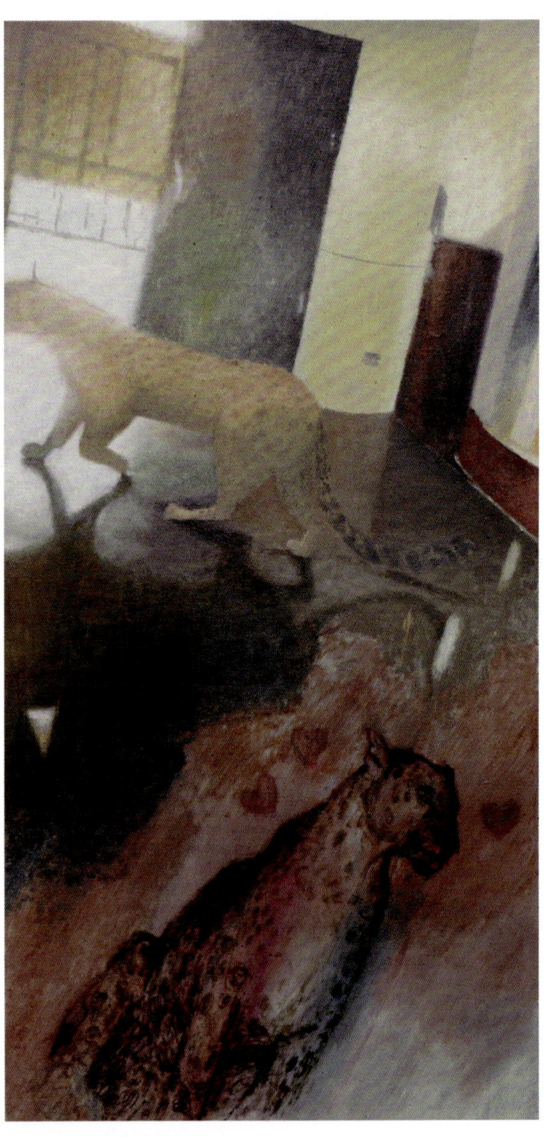

            Samuel Hindolo

York venues 15 Orient and Buchholz Gallery, while the eponymous train links major cities like Paris and London. Brussels's biggest train station, Gare du Midi, is the hub of a (Western) European transport network that bears witness to an idea of a political and economic union that has long since cracked. However, Hindolo's *Gare de Bruxelles-Nord* (2024) depicts a regional train station whose urban surroundings are reminiscent of New York **(Fig. 3)**. If one were to take the train as a metaphor for moving images, this scene would be a still that radiates tranquility, capturing the transition between night and day. Whether the twilight glimmering between the gloomy skyscrapers is full of expectation or melancholy remains an open question, as does any notion of what is buried beneath the overpainted and collaged layers of the image. Another version of the painting, *Gare de Bruxelles-Nord (Twin)*, features an image of Prince in its bottom right-hand corner **(Fig. 4)**.

Yet the true Euro star is actress and supermodel Donyale Luna, the first Black model to appear on the cover of *Harper's Bazaar*. In 1965, the magazine featured an illustration of her, which was enough to scare off

Fig. 3   **Installation view, *Gare de Bruxelles-Nord*, 2024, in *Eurostar*, 15 Orient, New York, 2024.**
Fig. 4   ***Gare de Bruxelles-Nord (Twin)*, 2024.**

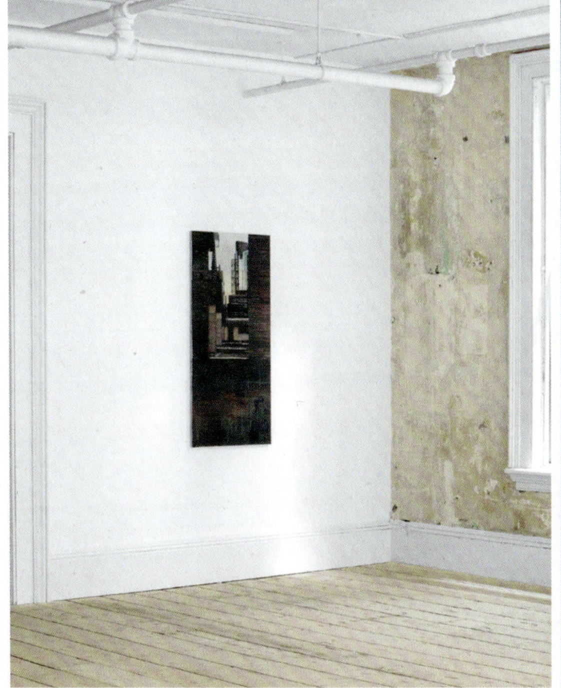

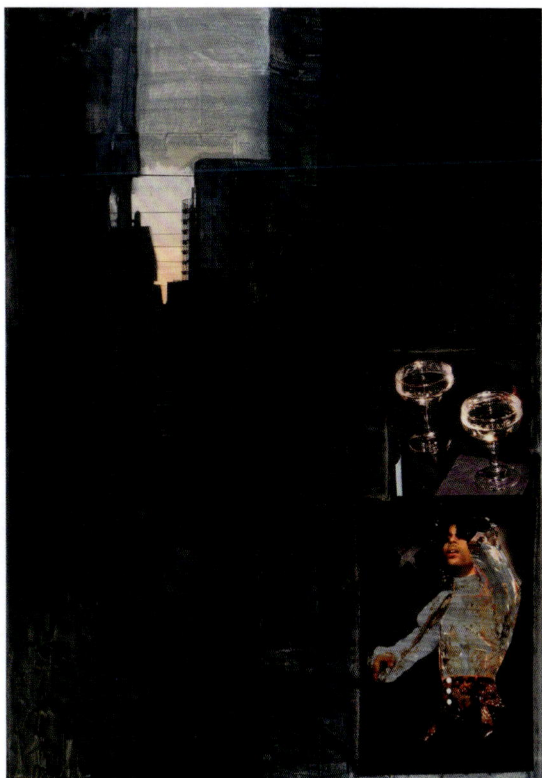

subscribers and sponsors. But Luna was not deterred; she twisted and turned the projections cast upon her as she pleased to create her own fluid identity. She claimed to be from the moon, or Egypt, or Mexico, and went on to build a career in Europe. Hindolo's paintings demonstrate how he originally encountered Luna: as a set piece of a mediatized world, a photographic or cinematic detail. *Vitrine I* (2024) portrays only her upper body, which was probably all that was visible in the source image (Fig. 5). The artist positions her at the bottom edge of the picture and, to compensate for her missing bottom half, renders mannequin legs in another area of the same work—as if onto a subsequent frame (in yet another filmic strategy).

Hindolo seizes the opportunity to point out the differences and reciprocal registers between the medium of painting and those of photography or film. Media-reflexive moments like this show up again and again in his works. He transforms fragile narratives and materials into a visual form that correlates fragments of historical events with subjective experiences, delivering it all with complexity, ambivalence, and opacity.

Fig. 5 *Vitrine I*, 2024.

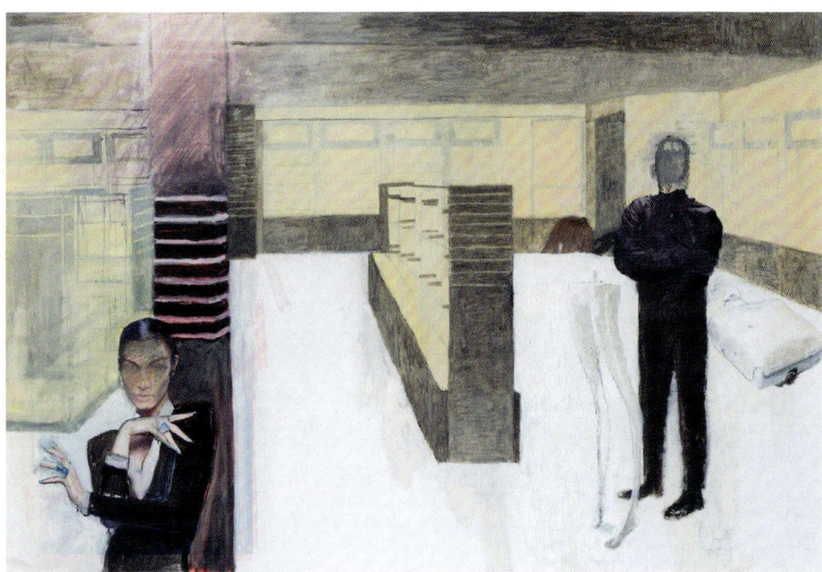

     Samuel Hindolo

Geumhyung Jeong

(Korean, b. 1980)

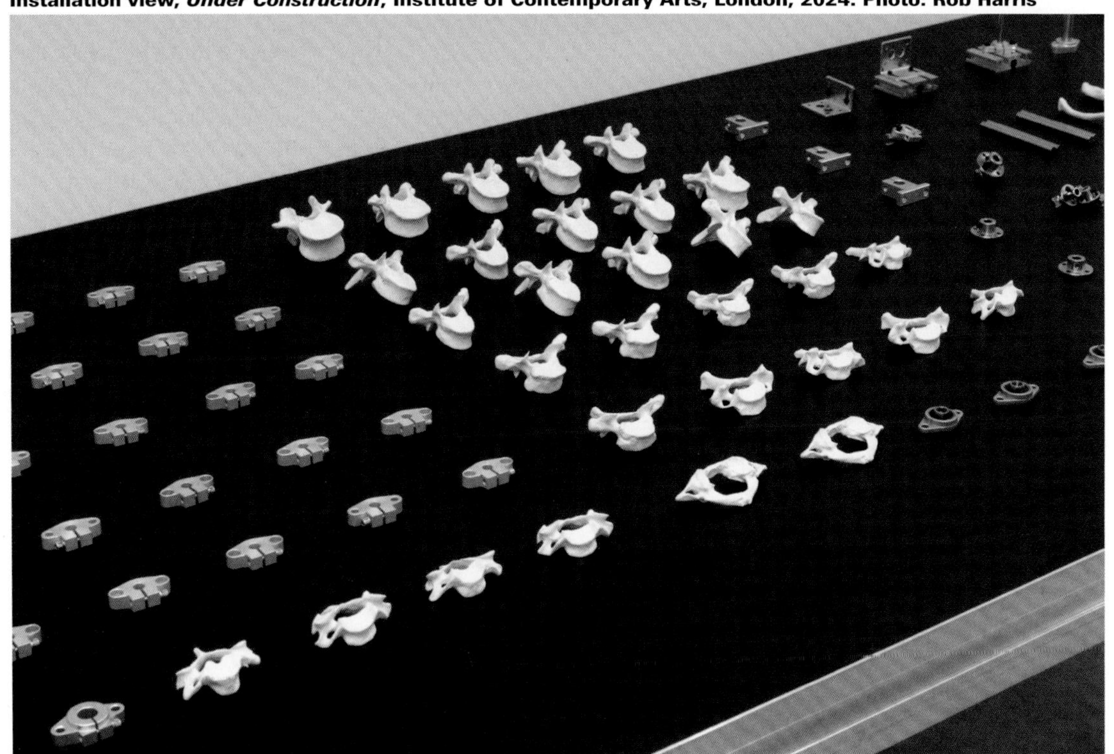

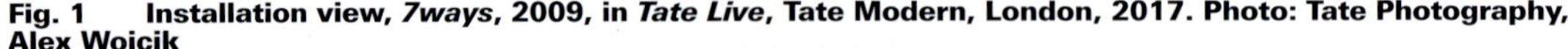

Fig. 1   Installation view, *7ways*, 2009, in *Tate Live*, Tate Modern, London, 2017. Photo: Tate Photography, Alex Wojcik

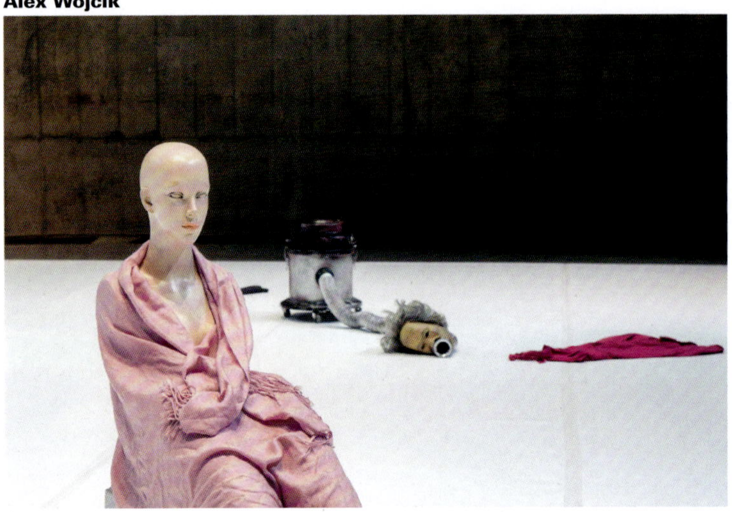

Fig. 2   *Oil Pressure Vibrator*, 2008, premier appearance, Seoul Marginal Theatre Festival, 2008. Photo: Gajin Kim

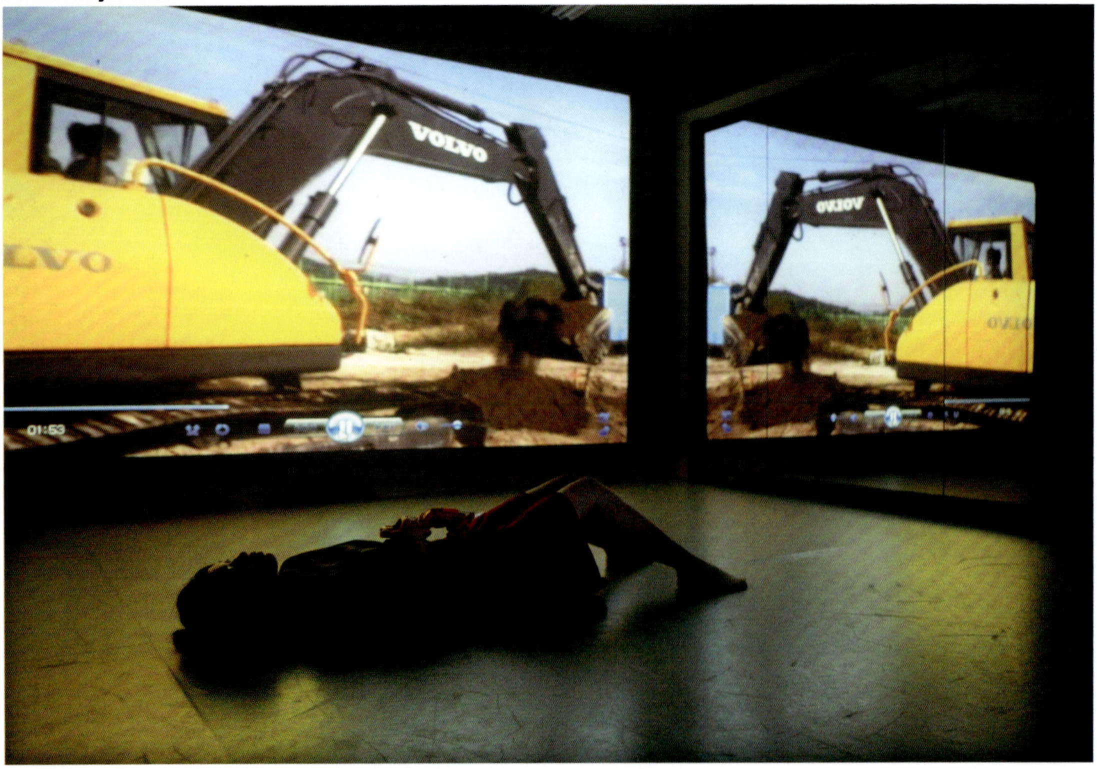

PERFORMING OBJECTS
Jeppe Ugelvig

In the early 1980s, anthropologist Frank Proschan coined the term "performing objects" to refer to "material images of humans, animals, or spirits that are created, displayed, or manipulated in narrative or dramatic performance."[1] His exploration of puppets, masks, and ritual objects coincided with the emergence of Europe's *théâtre d'objets*, a genre of works for the stage performed entirely by everyday objects. Both acknowledge that all sorts of things (can) perform—that is, if they are given the right stage and a sense of kinetic vitality, that ever-delightful illusion of life. Yet in these contexts, objects only ever indicate a certain dimension of performance because their animated capacities inevitably point back to their instructor, the human puppeteer or mechanical designer, on whom they are dependent for their choreography.

Geumhyung Jeong's work is less an aesthetic engagement with the puppet than an attempt to centralize the affective intensities of its tinkering controller. The artist's practice, spilling across performance and sculptural installation, lays bare the erotics of puppeteering by suggesting that humanoid objects might be collaborative performers with agency and desires of their own. Prosthetics, toys, robots, mannequins, rescue and crash dummies—the artist collects all types of commercial objects that aim to reproduce the human body, however crudely. She methodically breaks them apart, rewires them, and puts them together anew, creating makeshift constructions that, like skeletal cyborgs, miraculously move (if in an uncertain fashion). They are the fine art version of the "Mutant Toys" of *Toy Story* (1995), and they share with them an identity: hybrid products of joyfully macabre free play.

Jeong, who is trained in acting, first developed this methodology with the stagework *7ways* (2009), wherein she generated makeshift supernatural puppet forms by attaching simple masks and mannequin parts to her own limbs (Fig. 1). She offered audiences a series of dramatic vignettes that, rather than directing attention away from the visible puppeteer, boldly centered her. The stories were unnerving and perverse, alluding to each puppet's sexual appetites and its evident erotic exchange with its master.

1 Frank Proschan, *Puppets, Masks, and Performing Objects from Semiotic Perspectives* (Mouton, 1983).

Separate motorized agents—a wig that journeyed across the stage—broke with the unity of puppet and puppeteer, leaving the viewer in illusionistic suspense.

The erotic motif of *7ways* is apt, for the exchange between human and nonhuman, like any choreographed duet, is contingent on a collaborative corporeality between two actors who must negotiate each other kinetically. This dynamic can be abstracted ad infinitum. Jeong's 2008 lecture performance *Oil Pressure Vibrator*, for example, centered on the artist's quest for sexual liberation, which was ultimately found in an encounter with a hydraulic excavator **(Fig. 2)**. Video projections of such machines surrounded the artist as she lay onstage, gently caressing herself with a miniature version of the device. Rather than explore theories of the uncanny, Jeong considers the way human desires are projected onto innocent objects and, moreover, the way desire is scalable *via* machines.

All of Jeong's subsequent work attests to the simple fact that encounters with objects are often imbued with latent eroticism. Desire overflows in our navigation of the physical environment, and we use objects to help us channel, sublimate, or displace affects to better control them in our social interactions. This may involve

Fig. 3   Installation view, *Condition Check*, artist's studio, Seoul, 2023. Photo: Kanghyuk Lee

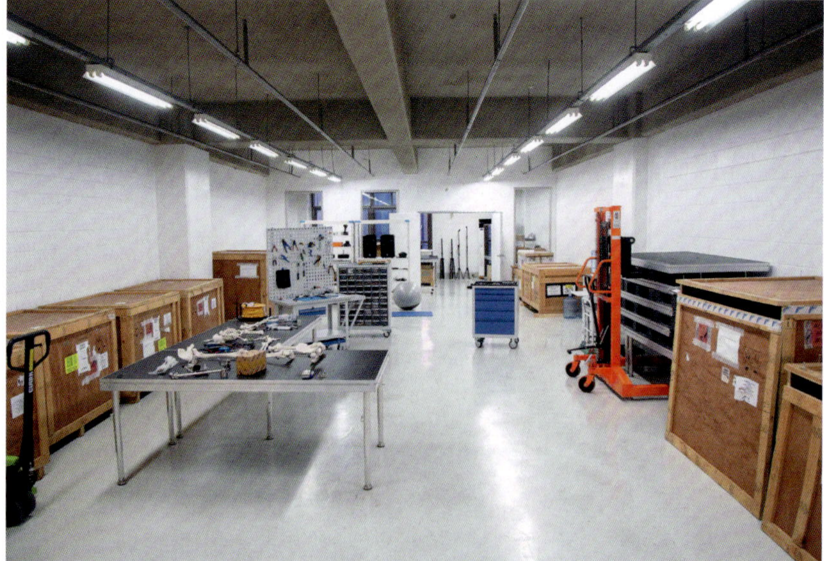

                Geumhyung Jeong

routines of fetishistic care (consider the exhibition and performance *Condition Check* [2023], which document the artist methodically caring for her sprawling collection of animatronic objects) **(Fig. 3)** or fantasies that eschew the human body completely (see *Toy Prototype* [2021] **(Fig. 4)**, a series of sculptures and a video installation in which mutant robots with partial human visages clumsily make out in some posthuman sex factory). In Jeong's work, makeshift robotics are not props so much as characters and actors that, rather than obey the artist, seem to impose themselves *on* her. While these works can be funny, they are never absurd, for they exhibit the artist's earnest love for and dependency on her object-subjects. They document Jeong getting to know her puppets as she makes, maintains, interacts with, and repairs them.

The vitality of the performing object is only realized in the moment of its kinesis. Thus, the stage, as robotics theorists Elizabeth Ann Jochum and Todd Murphey argue, is "a narrowly defined domain in which automated figures can excel."[2] Nam June Paik was early to explore this in the field of contemporary art with *Robot K-456* (1964), a 20-channel remote-controlled robot produced in collaboration with Japanese engineers. While the automaton did

2   Elizabeth Ann Jochum and Todd Murphey, "Programming Play Puppets, Robots, and Engineering," in *The Routledge Companion to Puppetry and Material Performance*, ed. Dassia N. Posner, et al. (Routledge, 2014), 313.

Fig. 4   Installation view, *Toy Prototype*, 2021, in *The Milk of Dreams*, La Biennale di Venezia, 2022. Photo: AVZ - Andrea Avezzù

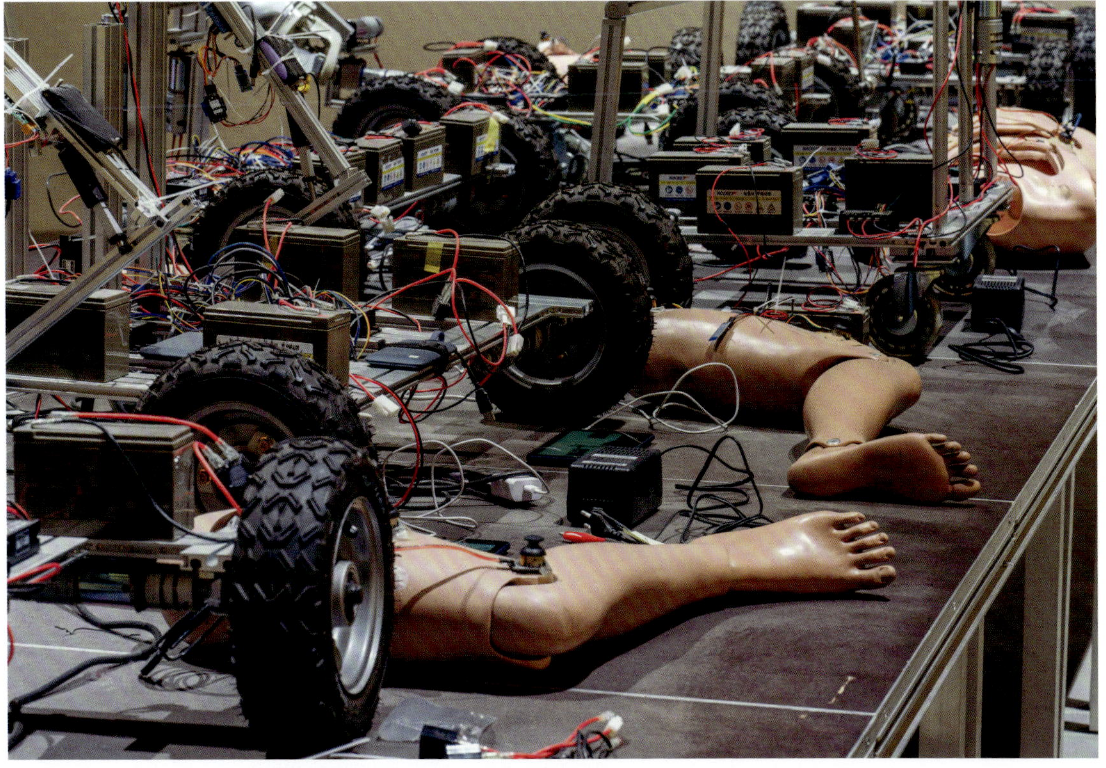

     PERFORMING OBJECTS   Jeppe Ugelvig

accompany its maker in performances around the world, its most vivid performance was no doubt the one outside the Whitney Museum of American Art in New York, where it was fatally struck by a car while crossing the road. With this intentional "catastrophe," the artist made two salient points: machines can be theatrically humanized to solicit human empathy, and the rationality of modern technology is a convenient fiction.[3]

Jeong's work is similarly fascinated by the dramatic lives of objects in the moment of their performative mediation. And yet it exhibits a deconstructive impulse, as the context of the stage is constantly reformatted or rescaled (consider her video *Test Run* [2021], where tables are made into an impromptu racecourse for her works in progress). At times, she mimics the movement of her animatronics with her own fleshy body, which serves as a kind of translator. These studies in movement show that ecstatic, jarring, nervous, and looming qualities can be conveyed by mechanically rendered choreographies. They aren't as dependent on the human body as we'd like to think. In the performance *Find, Select, Copy and Paste* (2020), the artist returned to her own (naked) body as a kinetic entity, displaying its ability to replicate the movements of her absent machines (Fig. 5).

3   "Robot K-456," Nam June Paik Art Center, accessed February 2025, https://njpart.ggcf.kr/collections/251.

Fig. 5   *Find, Select, Copy and Paste*, 2020. Photo: Haewook Park

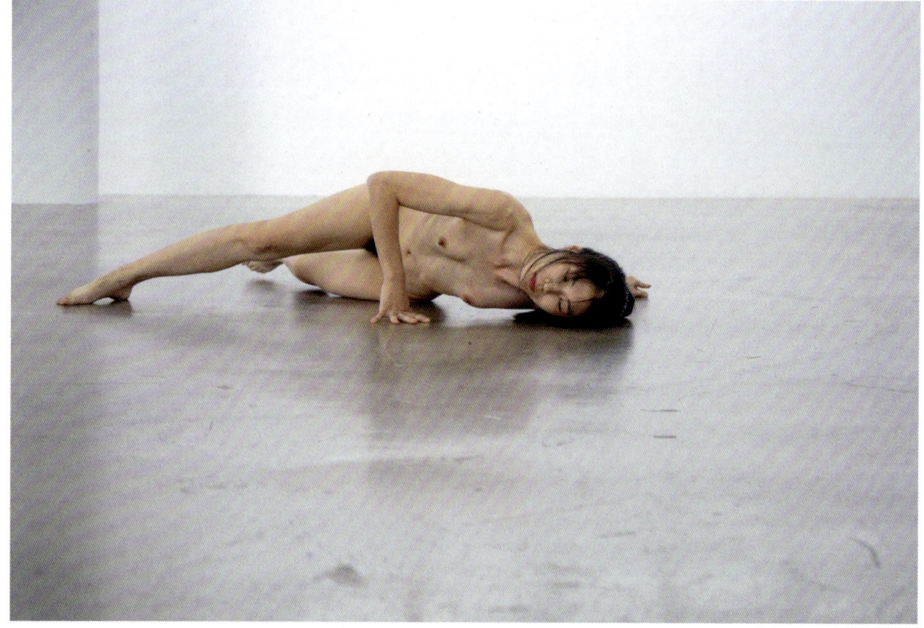

    Geumhyung Jeong

Anything can perform when it moves; but is stillness, then, not also a type of performance? It is here that
Freud's uncanny returns—not as a horror of the uncertain
aliveness of objects but as a nervous sadness pertaining to
the most ordinary *un-aliveness* of objects. In 2017, Jeong
evoked this in her first static exhibition, *Private Collection:
Unperformed Objects* at Delfina Foundation in London,
which culminated a decade of collecting and making props
for performances. The exhibition presented her humanoid
animatronics in an "unperformed" and thus effectively
lifeless state, mere prosthetics to be categorized and
stored. In such a context, Jeong's objects become what
anthropologist Sara K. Schneider calls "vital mummies,"[4]
body archives that, like fashion display mannequins,
are destined to exist in a strange ontological purgatory.
Somehow, these hardworking, precarious machines trigger
a sense of unlikely compassion in the viewer. In this way,
Jeong's investigation of the object as performer is touched
by a sense of tragedy regarding the very question of what
constitutes "life" in a world of moving things. The victims
of these affects are not objects, of course, but human
spectators, confronted with a desire for objects to be
helped, dignified, and even happy—for them to move with
us, sensually.

4   Sara K. Schneider, *Vital
Mummies: Performance
Design for the Show-Window
Mannequin* (Yale University
Press, 1995).

          PERFORMING OBJECTS   Jeppe Ugelvig

Klara Liden

(Swedish, b. 1979)

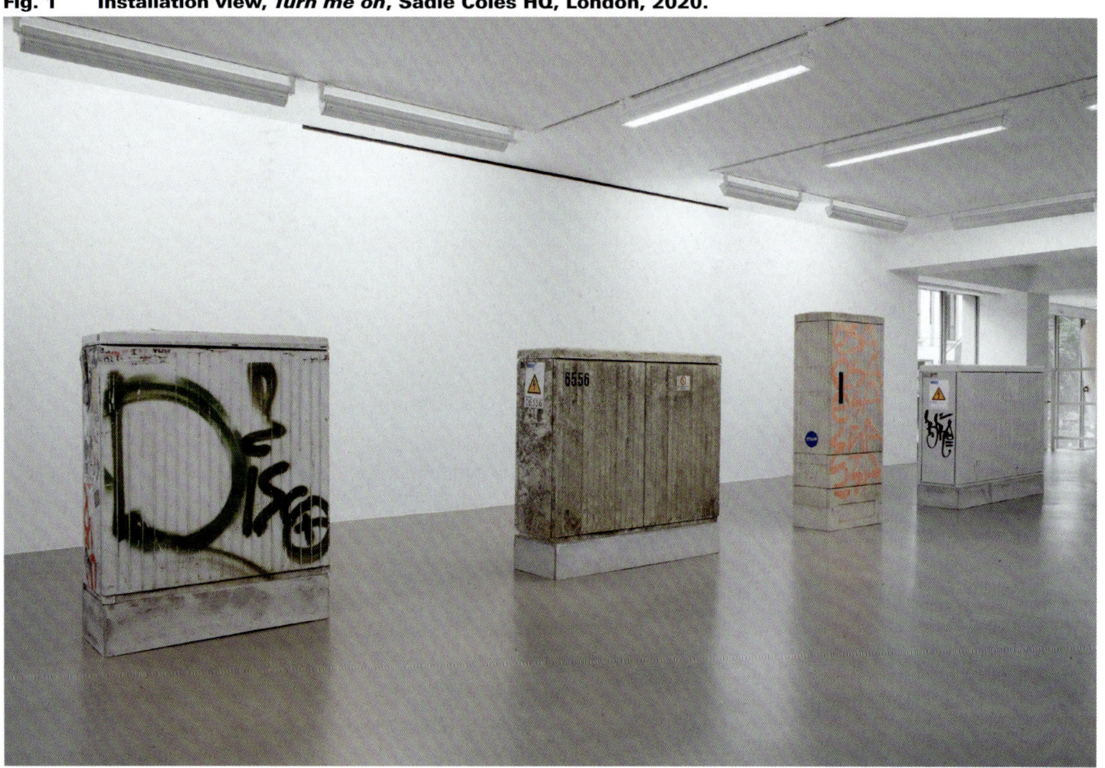

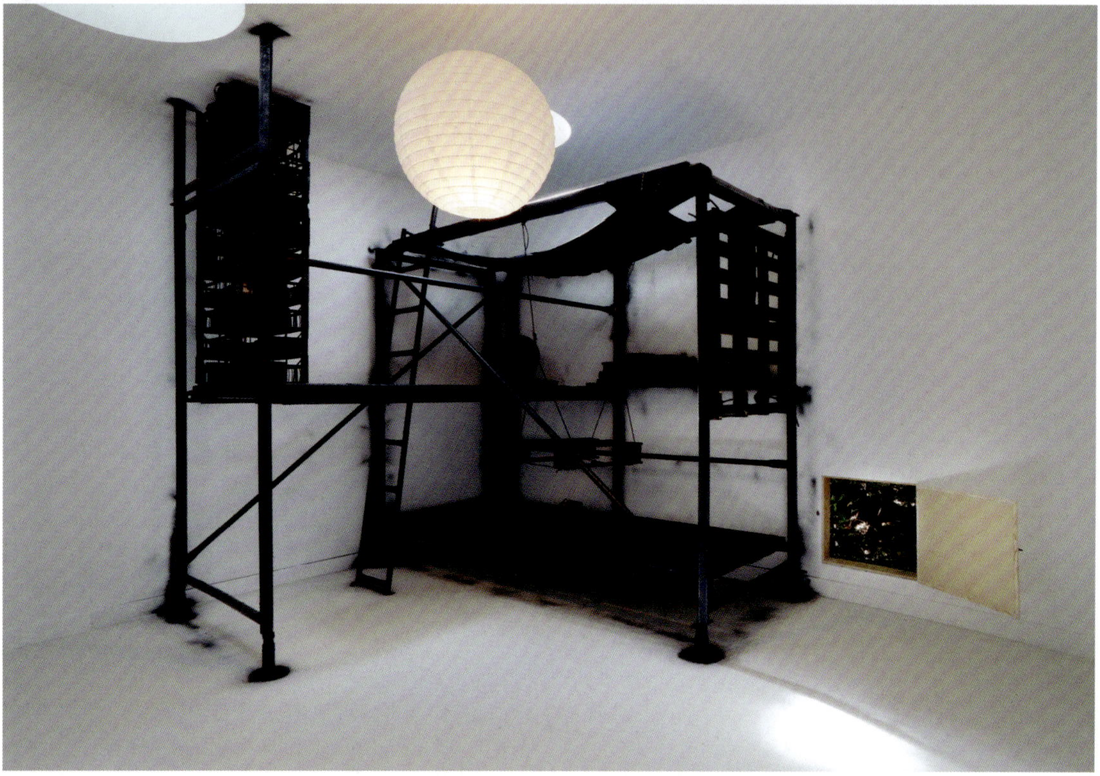

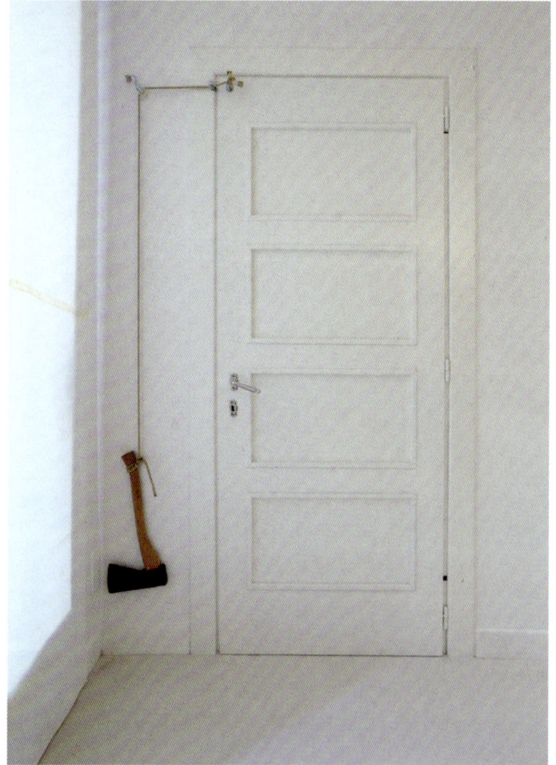

Fig. 3   Installation view, *Teenage Room*, Danish and Nordic Pavilion, La Biennale di Venezia, 2009.

LO-FI AND DIY
Estelle Hoy

Goodbye, yellow brick road.
—Elton John

Gleaning recyclables is a dirty, single-minded pursuit. In it,
Klara Liden never lacks jouissance. She takes the garbage
untouchables of our pungent envionment—the posters,
jagged cans, bunk beds, cardboard, scratched-up petrol
bottles, scaffolding, tar, and sheetrock, the residue of our
consumer-driven society—to the titillating edge of what it
means to waste away. What survives, what perishes? Good
grief, what's her obsession with the guttural dregs of our
nauseating, overmedicated, divisive urban environment?!
Liden's method, like a teen tantrum, is to meticulously
deconstruct a shifting social context around a word
and elaborate on its variations: in this instance, the two
definitions of *refuse*. In this way, she reveals obscured or
suppressed divergencies and correspondences in institutional circulations of meaning across time.
     It's the Venice Biennale, 2009, and the Danish
and Nordic Pavilion nominates Liden to take over part
of the architecture with, well, whatever takes her fancy.
Teenage Room (2009) (Figs. 2–3) unveils a bleak installation:
a blackened bunk bed and charcoaled crates piled to
the ceiling in a miserable, precarious scaffold; the sonic
embarrassment of Linkin Park snuffed out on a boom box
drenched in bargain-bin paint. For the record, she likes
bargains. But the unmoored, sparse, pathetic architectural
installation doesn't nod to the melancholic, withdrawn fury
that is adolescence (I would know) so much as it reflects
social thresholds. Stay with me here. Liden lives in Berlin,
and *Teenage Room* could easily be a corner in a WG (a
share house…shudder) decked out with IKEA furniture and
a stained mattress from hard trash Tuesday, a home to
artists pursuing their "Promised Land." Positioning herself
at the intersection between individual and neoliberal
society, Liden wades into the faux assurances of artistic
sustainability under the neon sign of capital. (And the faux
sustainability of a share house, but that's another story.)
Liden's garbage-ass lifestyle installation reminds us that
the market economy is rudely unstable and the artist is
an involuntary participant in it—an unwilling gamete. The

upshot is that the passing of time can be artificial, suspect, and ultimately corrupt. See, you can position an artwork as "I," and it can have nothing to do with the "self," which is exactly the case with Liden.

What was and always will be a defining feature of Liden's work is her precise and understated attention to our divisive environment. Why tend to our natural world when we can replicate it with polystyrene or metal and wage war with it instead! In 2024, greenwashing New York's Reena Spaulings Fine Art, tongue-in-cheek, Liden presents *Verdebelvedere*, installing pre-prefab gallery benches (verdant planks of worn wood mimetic of our natural world, propped up by white rubbish bags) and vertical TVs, hijacking that natural *verde* (green) belvedere surreptitiously promised in the title—I'm pretty sure there's a covert anagram or three in there; Liden's stealthy like that (Fig. 4). The artist moonwalks into a DIY Trojan horse and then into the exhibition space, interrupting an environmental narrative by pilfering material from the world and using what she's scavenged to create her own ecosystem. This is also a kind of politics. When refuse materials are made visible, highlighting our calamitous relationship with nature, it becomes clear that decisions we make can turn around and decide on us, too: when we take from the life

Fig. 4   Installation view, *Verdebelvedere*, Reena Spaulings, New York, 2024. Photo: Joerg Lohse

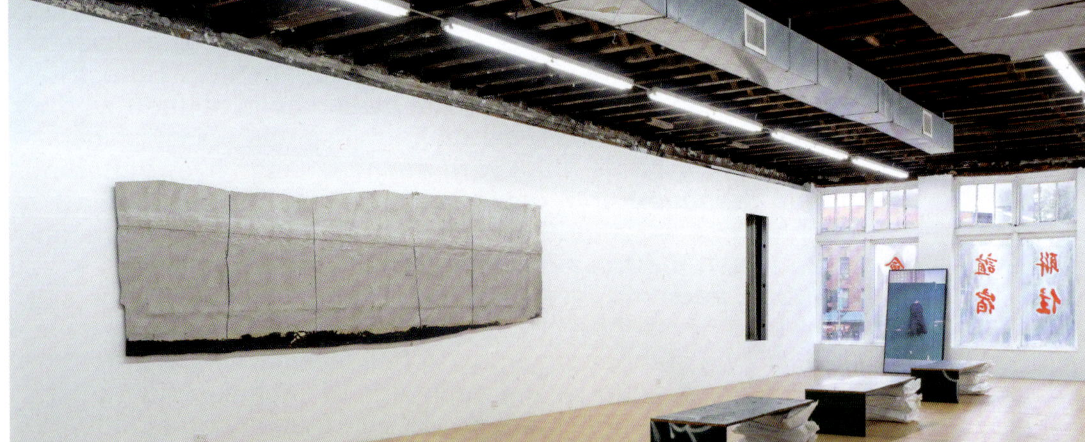

          Klara Liden

force of nature, nature takes the life force right back out of us. Which is all to say that everything is reversible, including our insufferable appropriation of our native conditions. Everybody walks out on nature.

Maybe all Liden really wants is for humans to assume a sense of civic responsibility and refuse to succumb to shortcuts and short circuits. To make her junction box works, the artist culls found concrete electrical boxes, each a meeting spot for conduit wires and shared community energy (Figs. 1 & 5). One sculpture, *Kahba* (2020), boasts rebellious graffiti in will-o'-the-wisp neon orange, green, and pink spray paint (Fig. 5). Dust circles on top of the fuse box mark once-present bottles, since recycled for eight cents in the Pfand system many use to supplement pitiful state welfare checks, which could never cover the rising cost of living under the hellish spruce

Fig. 5   ***Kahba*, 2020.**

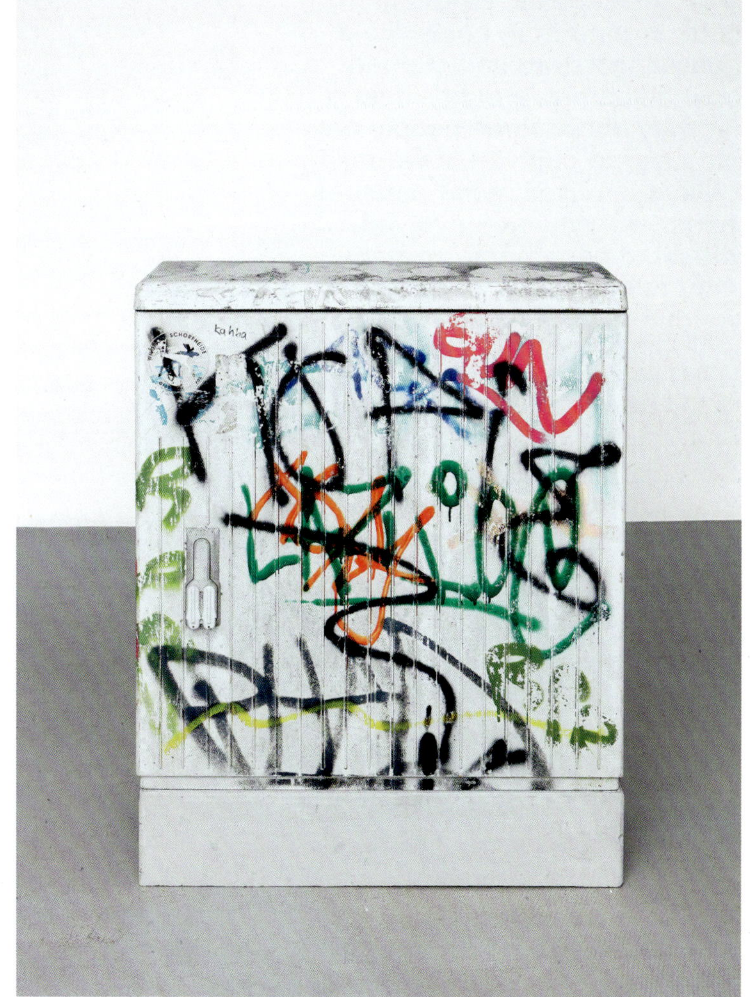

          LO-FI AND DIY   Estelle Hoy

of gentrification. *Kahba* is the charged-up Arabic slang term for "bitch," which is likewise what Liden becomes if anyone dares divide the neighborhood up according to race or any other caustic, circuit-breaking category. The artist's gleaned junction boxes are poorly tended, undoubtedly harvested from a neighborhood underserviced by local council. (La-di-da Prenzlauer Berg residents have gloriously white connection boxes…and connections, just generally.) Directing artistic currents—albeit discreetly—she sends no mixed signals: Liden has a short fuse.

One shortcut any well-adjusted person might take is a hop, skip, and jump past any metro line in Stockholm. Tiptoeing over cigarette stubs, empty cans, liquids, and all the degradation of shared space and its discontents, Liden conceives *Paralyzed* (2003) **(Fig. 6)**. It's just one of many videos she's shot over her career and is fittingly considered one of her finest. Performing *Ett*, *två*, *tre* convulsions and awkward dance movements on the subway, writhing on the piss-covered floor, she curls around train poles like a stripper. Totally nonplussed passengers are half-clipped from the frame. They've seen it all before, and besides, they know that we know that they know some people are scum, and as such, there's no need to cultivate a warm, nonhierarchical community. What survives, what perishes? Rather, who survives, who perishes? Why get involved? Liden advocates for some refusal of hegemonic strategies based on geographic repulsion, public space, and communal denial. But one has to wonder whether such garbage things and nauseating refutations of paralyzing individuality are all that's being indicted when Liden is underground and undercover? She hides deep in the hood of her jacket, totally silent, dancing a hoedown like a reverse cowgirl, hell-bent on anonymity; we're asked to engage through disengagement.

     Klara Liden

Shared space permeates Liden's oeuvre, and it's no coincidence that so many of her videos, sculptures, performances, and installations are unmoored from any stable geographic or architectural foundation. We citizens constitute ourselves according to the movements and drives of subjectivity in the public arena. We negotiate conventional borders and political junctures that dictate our collective and individual rights to engage or withdraw from shared realities. Humans are innovative in reckoning with the shapes and failures of defiance, and no binary is indicated in Liden's restrained artistic interventions; each material element and conceptual embodiment bears the unquantifiable potential of cotransformation. Stepping off pristine golden roads onto the raw sediment of her structural intercessions, she quietly mutters the words of Hannah Arendt: "The only indispensable material factor in the generation of power is the living together of people. Only where men live so close together that the potentialities of action are always present can power remain with them."[1]

1   Hannah Arendt, *The Human Condition* (The University of Chicago Press, 1958), 201.

Fig. 6   Still, *Paralyzed*, 2003.

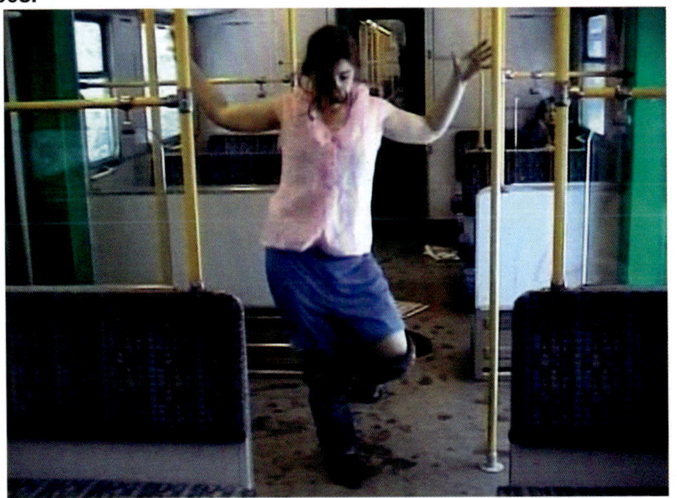

     LO-FI AND DIY   Estelle Hoy

Jean Katambayi Mukendi

(Congolese, b. 1974)

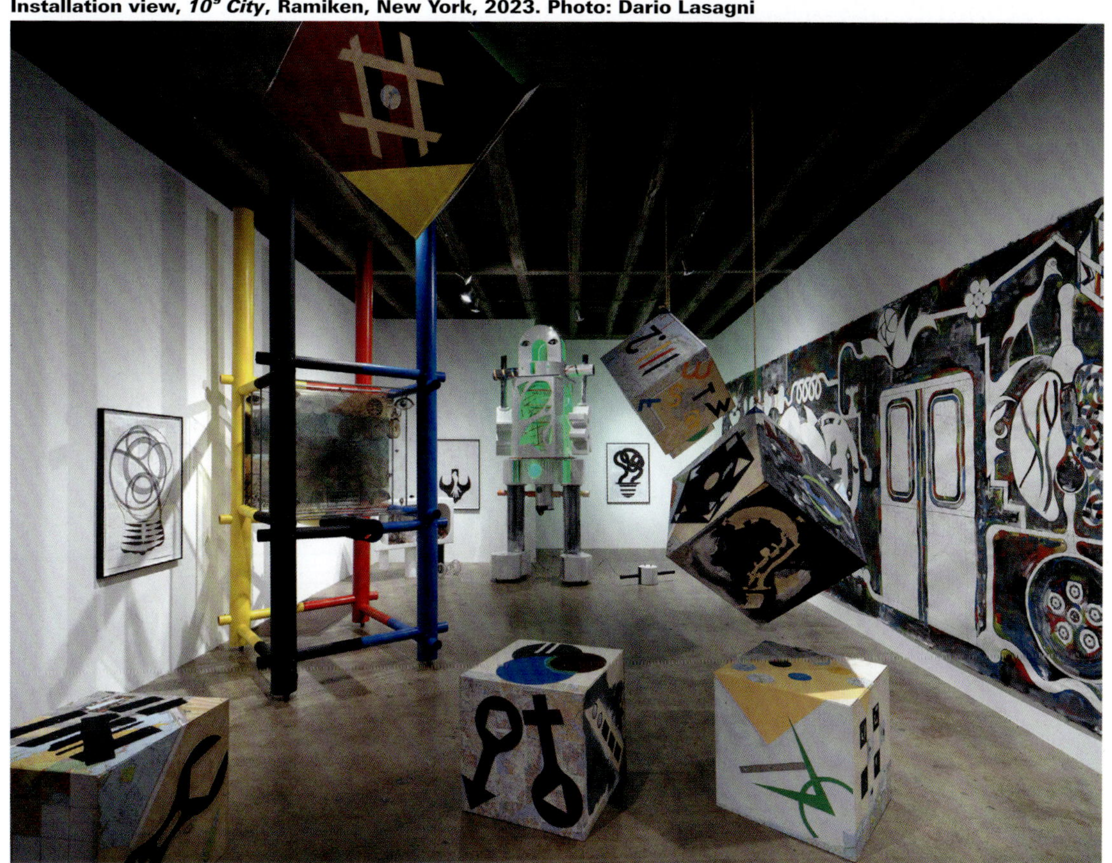

Installation view, *10^9 City*, Ramiken, New York, 2023. Photo: Dario Lasagni

OPEN-CIRCUIT DREAMING
Sheldon Gooch

In 2020, Apple announced its ten-year plan to achieve carbon neutrality across the entirety of its business.[1] Since then, the company has committed to using 100 percent recycled raw materials in several of its products: rare earth elements in its magnets, tin soldering and gold plating in its circuit boards, and cobalt in its batteries.[2] While the implications behind the question of *why* the company made this significant decision may be clear, the inquiry into *where* and *how* these resources are available in the first place may prove just as harrowing. For Congolese artist Jean Katambayi Mukendi, the answer is apparent.

Born and raised in Lubumbashi, Mukendi is intimately familiar with the plight of artisanal mining. The catchall term is used to describe an act of mining the earth with few to no resources. In the Democratic Republic of the Congo, men, women, and young children scratch at the earth, pulling toxic metals such as cobalt and lithium from its cracked surface. The demand for these materials, which are needed to power rechargeable batteries in smartphones and electric vehicles, has forced the country into a central position in trade disputes between China and the United States. And although the latter economies generate billions of dollars in their extraction of the region's resources, the miners are left impoverished, their land ravaged and water contaminated. Created in this context, Mukendi's assemblages and works on paper underscore the gross imbalances of value and power assigned to these social and material relationships. Playful at times, the work incisively prompts inquiry into these ascriptions and proffers a world in which imperial peripheries benefit from the exchange of resources for which they are so often exploited.

Mukendi is trained as an electrical engineer, and electric currents are a primary motif in his drawing practice. His series *Afrolampes* (2016–ongoing) is a morphological study of what appears to be the most quixotic set of light-bulbs (Fig. 1). Each enigmatic ink-drawn form is set against a diagrammatic grid; the energy that might power these bulbs is pictured flowing within rigid parameters. At the crux of compositional coherence, the lightbulbs give way to totemic emblems and absurd cartographies. Their contours come undone, transforming into exotic flora and fauna,

1   "Apple Commits to Be 100 Percent Carbon Neutral for Its Supply Chain and Products by 2030," Apple Newsroom, July 21, 2020, https://www.apple.com/newsroom/2020/07/apple-commits-to-be-100-percent-carbon-neutral-for-its-supply-chain-and-products-by-2030/.
2   "Apple Will Use 100 Percent Recycled Cobalt in Batteries by 2025," Apple Newsroom, April 13, 2023, https://www.apple.com/newsroom/2023/04/apple-will-use-100-percent-recycled-cobalt-in-batteries-by-2025/.

retrofuturistic architectural renderings, and speculative technologies—constituent parts, one might say, of a progressive African imaginary. In *Covid 28 Afrolampe XXIV Métastase Mai 2020 14h00* (2020), a dense procession of thin lines encircles a thicket of tangled marks whose effect is that of a black hole; the composition seems to beckon viewers toward this central form's singularity (Fig. 2). Here, Mukendi evokes a tension expressed in chaos theory, in which the energy present in a chaotic system remains constant if it is subjected to unwavering pressures—an apt metaphor for this era in which global superpowers steadily foment disaster in lower-income countries for profit.

If *Afrolampes* proposes structural reconfiguration as a liberatory model—an idea the artist links to Congo's fraught economic position—then *Doors* (2023), Mukendi's largest work on paper to date, abstractly envisions flows of

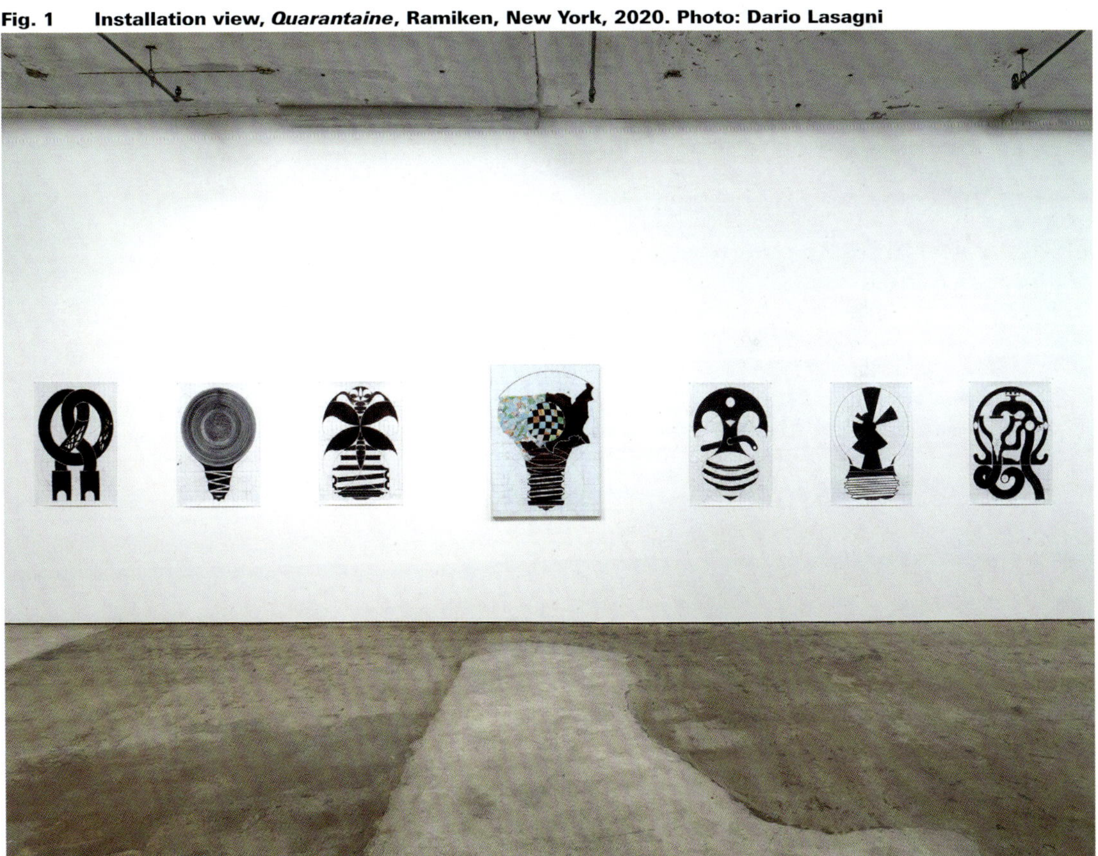
Fig. 1   Installation view, *Quarantaine*, Ramiken, New York, 2020. Photo: Dario Lasagni

123

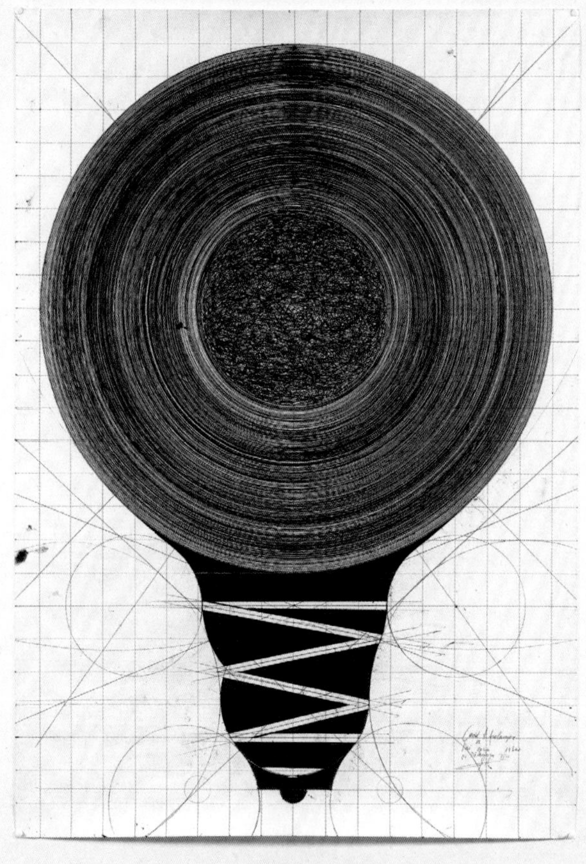

energy unencumbered by hegemonic imposition (pp. 22–23). During an artist residency at Ramiken in New York City, Mukendi was struck by the city's seemingly futuristic operations, marked by a mechanized precision in relation to time and productivity. According to Mukendi, time in the city felt "official and political," a stark contrast to the more relaxed attitude toward time he experienced in the Congo.[3] A whimsical arrangement of symbols, *Doors* reflects on these durational differences while emphasizing the connections between Africa and the world's most economically powerful metropolis.

The drawing pictures a complex system in which energy is transferred between the natural and industrialized worlds, ultimately powering the doors to a New York City subway train car. In this circuitous network, a supersize firefly provides an initial spark whose power is amplified by nuclear and hydropower systems and channeled through popular signifiers of New York City life—rodents, birds, and sneakers—that serve as waystations. Here, the insect is a satirical metaphor. At its subversive scale, the beetle's inherent ability to produce light calls attention to the simple fact that the natural world could sustain itself with its own bounty of resources. This reminder further provokes critical questions regarding equitable access to energy and sustainable practices in securing it. The Congo Basin is known as the "lungs of Africa"—symbolically indexed here by a pair of lungs drawn to the right of the eponymous doors—because of its natural absorption of carbon dioxide and production of oxygen. How can profiteers be so myopic regarding the broader ecological effects of extraction from this region and the unilateral appropriation of its resources? Mukendi's work implies that if imperial extractors have no consideration for the future of the Congo—only a concern with what is to gain in the present—the Congolese must envision their own future.

Another existential issue the Congo contends with is population growth. According to the World Health Organization, the DRC's population has more than doubled since the turn of the century and is projected to increase by another 110 percent in the next two decades.[4] This increase has contributed to a growing waste problem in major cities like Kinshasa, the nation's capital. Mukendi's sculptures and installations reckon with this rapid accumulation; his bricolage constructions of refuse give new

3   Jean Katambayi Mukendi, interview by the author and Ruba Katrib, November 6, 2024.
4   "Democratic Republic of the Congo," World Health Organization Data, accessed January 25, 2025, https://data.who.int/countries/180.

    OPEN-CIRCUIT DREAMING   Sheldon Gooch

life to junked cardboard, wires, and batteries, among other
recurring objects. These works reveal an abiding belief that
runs through the artist's practice: the abundance of natural
and industrially fabricated materials in the Congo presents
the country with the potential to wrest its agency from the
shadows of past colonialism and from the grip of present-
day imperialism. For Mukendi, these materials are the
building blocks of the nation's future, and his assemblages
serve as philosophical blueprints. In *Trash TV* (2022), a
truck windshield is packed to the brim with everyday detritus such as cassette tapes, blister packs, cardboard, and a
toothbrush **(Fig. 3)**. The work's most compelling juxtaposition
is that of a lightbulb and a paintbrush. This intimate duet is
a Duchampian ode to the utopian promise shared between
the available object and radical aesthetic imagination.

Fig. 3   Detail, *Trash TV*, 2022. Photo: Aurélien Mole

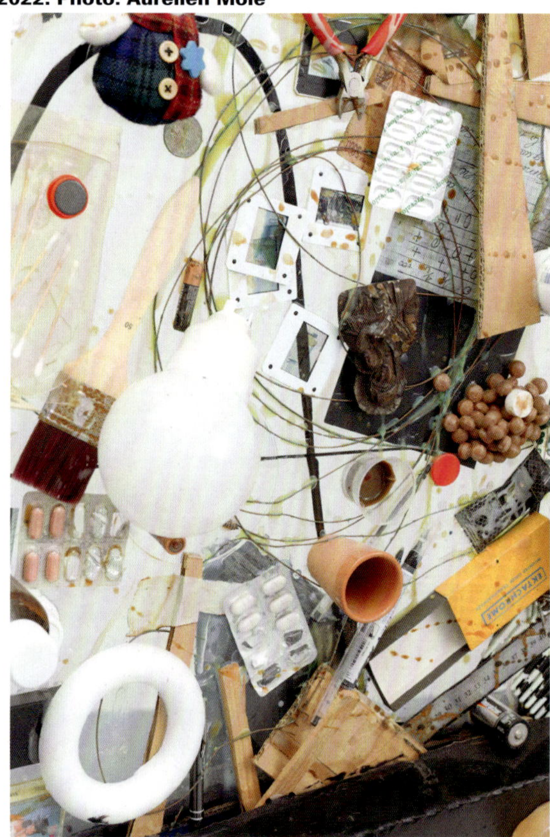

            Jean Katambayi Mukendi

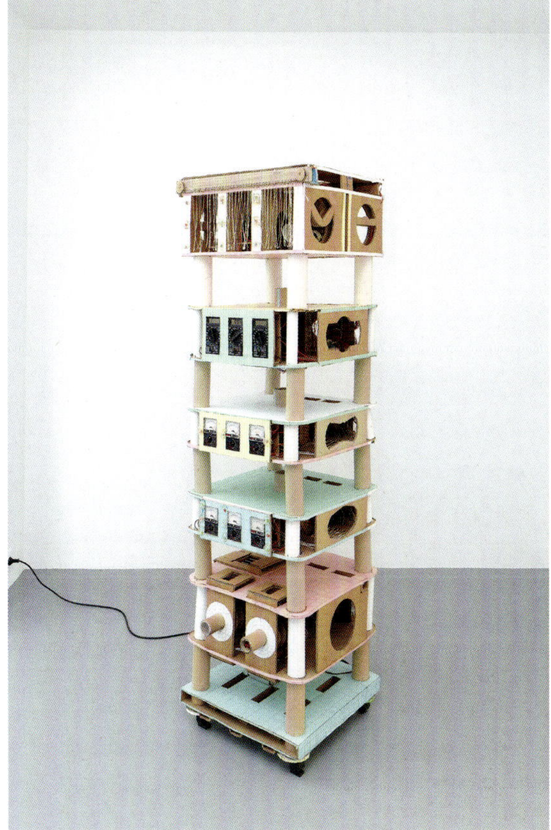

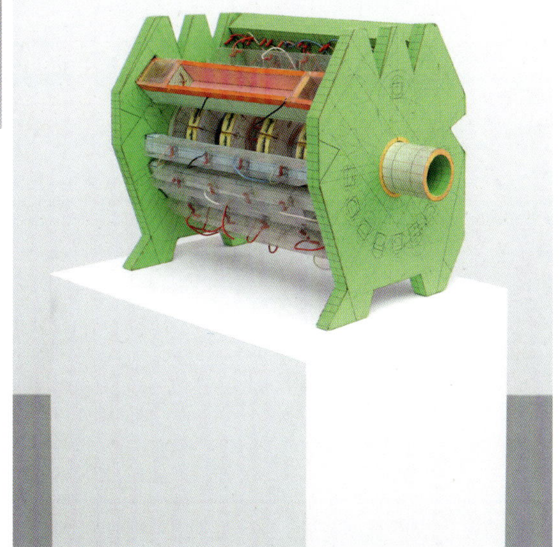

127   OPEN-CIRCUIT DREAMING   Sheldon Gooch

Nick Relph

(British, b. 1979)

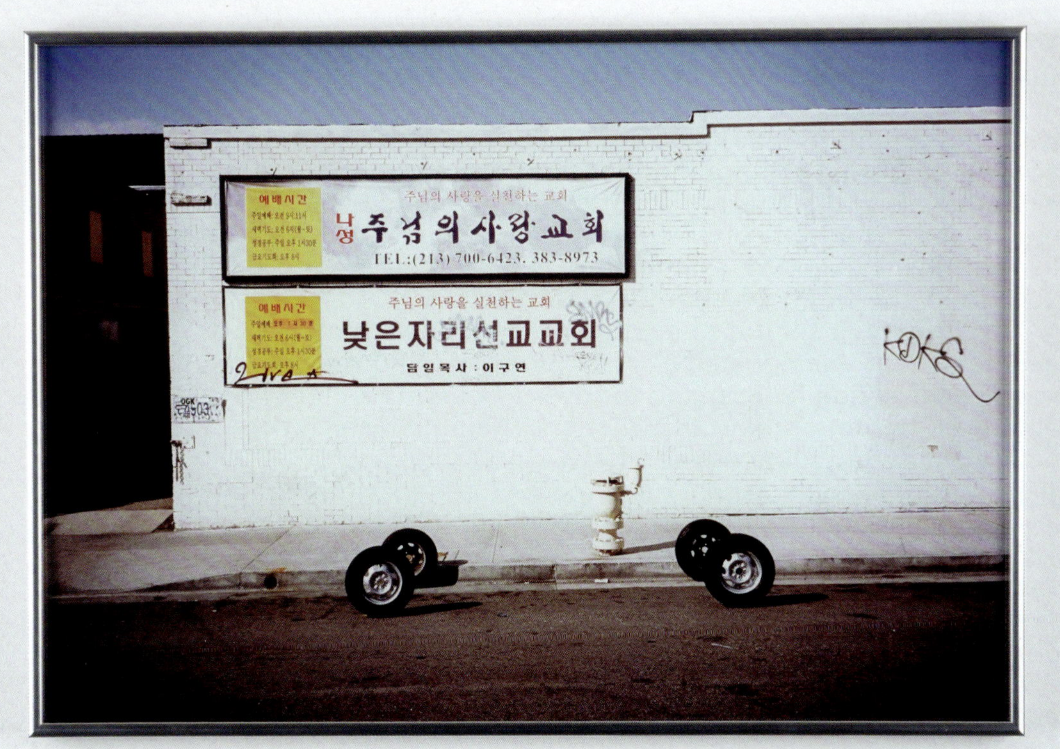
예배시간
주님의 사랑을 실천하는 교회
낮은 주님의 사랑교회
TEL.:(213) 700-6423. 383-8973
주님의 사랑을 실천하는 교회
낮은자리선교교회
담임목사 : 이구연

PATINA OF TIME
Camila Palomino

Guided by an obsessive spirit and archival intuition, Nick Relph documents urban surfaces, mapping erosion and daily archaeologies. Accumulating endless images of worn facades, he gleans new information from the textures and materials that surround us. Often, he presents these reproduced surfaces in book or print form to be read anew. Relph's most exhaustive examination is presented in the 2021 artist's book *Eclipse Body & Soul Syntax* (Figs. 1–2). In 2011, the artist set out to document the architectural renderings that were posted on New York City's hunter green construction fences, and for over a decade he followed a stream of new constructions. Relph conceived of the project during routine walks between Astoria and Long Island City in Queens, where he witnessed the accelerated development and rise of luxury condos that plagued the city in the early 2010s under Mayor Michael Bloomberg. This was on the heels of the 2008 housing market crash and ten short years after much of the industrial area was rezoned for residential housing. Highly reflective steel and glass towers sprang up feverishly over old lots and warehouses, these neighborhoods turning into one giant construction site. Working at night with a handheld scanner, Relph created digital rubbings of the renderings.

Fig. 1   Pages from *Eclipse Body & Soul Syntax*, Pre-Echo Press, 2021.

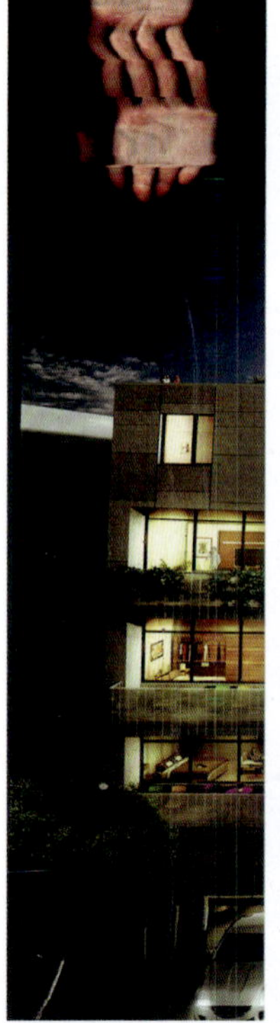
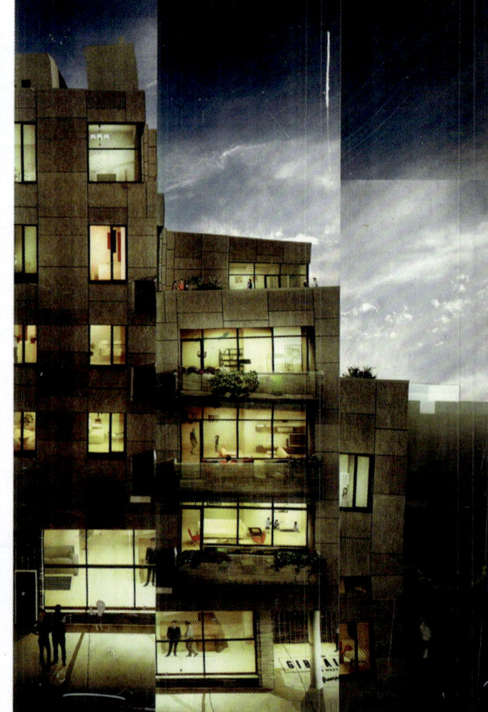

In 2013, amid this era of rapid development, a law was passed in the interest of public transparency mandating that contractors post uniformly designed placards on fencing to inform the public about intended construction. Often, alongside the requisite contact information for contractors and property owners, such signage features images created by architectural firms. These images are legal promises, some more elaborate than others, to city bureaucrats, neighbors, and local passersby alike. As evidenced in *Eclipse Body & Soul Syntax*, their quality varies widely, from grayscale line drawings to hyperreal portals into the future, complete with oversaturated sunsets and ghostly, frenetic people moving about. The shiniest images are clearly marketing gambits to attract tenants and reflect corporate interests, but for most locals, they serve as a reminder that someone else's future started yesterday and their own is farther out of focus. Relph's scans are faithful documents of these promises as they exist in the world, where the placards garner a more immediate and pedestrian kind of public response—graffiti,

Fig. 2   Pages from *Eclipse Body & Soul Syntax*, Pre-Echo Press, 2021.

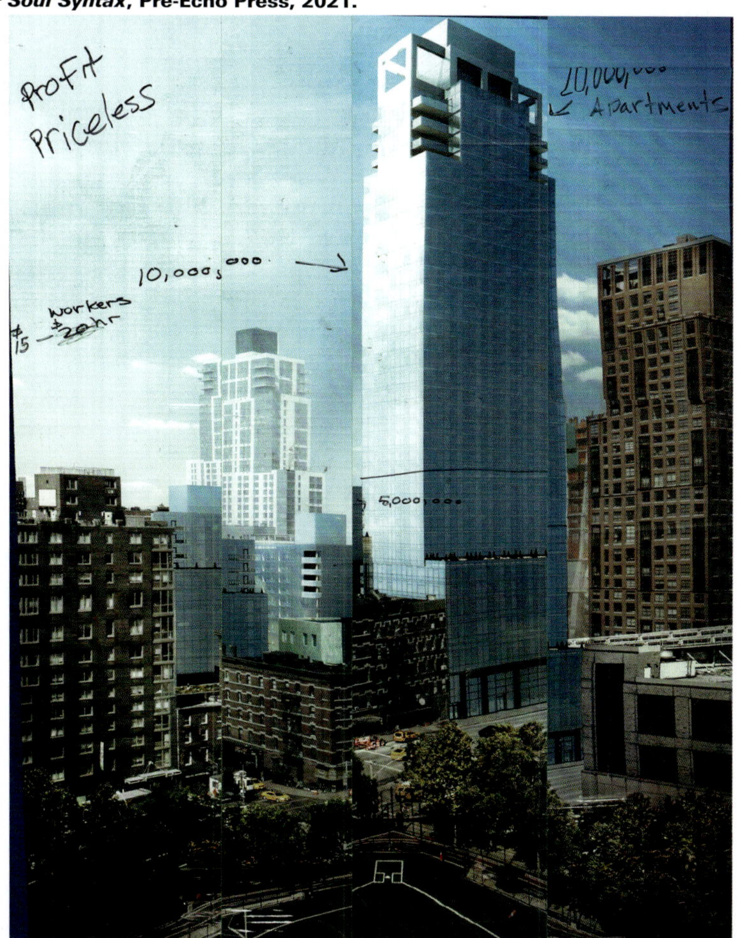

conspiratorial scribbles, and at least two instances of a polite NO THANKS decorate the most extravagant renderings. Relph's scanner processes all of this information equally, capturing precise moments in otherwise convoluted timelines of pedestrian traffic and rapid construction.

The poetry of Relph's work lies in the process of its making. The limitations of his scanning process cause distortions in the images, sharpening the uncanniness of the portrayed fantasies; skylines are fragmented, and buildings open up or undulate. These deformations call to mind Gordon Matta-Clark's "cuttings" of the early 1970s, wherein the artist carved up disused buildings on the Lower Manhattan waterfront and in the South Bronx (among other locations). Matta-Clark's interventions were anarchic gestures of autonomy in a time of "planned shrinkage"—to use a term the city's housing administrator Roger Starr first articulated in the late 1960s, referring to the withdrawal of funds for essential infrastructure from already underserved neighborhoods—a policy that resulted in destroyed communities and urban ruin. Relph's scans capture a different kind of emptiness in a time marked by accelerated speculation and hyperdevelopment in many of the same neighborhoods and waterfront areas that were subjected to neglect decades prior. The jagged metallic structures depicted in his scans seem homogeneously designed, and in these glitchy captures they appear on the brink of collapse—a timely metaphor in an era when architects increasingly design buildings using computers and software, with a dwindling focus on the human scale or psyche. Viewing *Eclipse Body & Soul Syntax*, which contains only a selection from Relph's vast collection of images, one might experience a sense of alienation. While these renderings seem at first to signal civic transparency, their accumulation reveals an architectural typology of the wretched imagination of profit and development, where futures are privatized and "public" spaces are policed by corporations. Perhaps most disconcerting to anyone who has witnessed this immense development and gentrification is the revelation that many of the visions these images projected came to fruition. Relph himself has noted that even the people who mill about the completed buildings resemble the stock-image avatars in the original renderings.[1]

1   Nick Relph, interviewed by the author, October 2024.

During his endless walks, Relph fixates on the materials and encounters within his line of sight. In his latest series, *Chaos* (2025), he continues his inquiry into surfaces, this time scanning the small metal doors that cover gas meters in Rome—trading the collapsing empire of steel for another city of ruins **(Figs. 3–4)**. These miniature doors are installed on building exteriors at the eye level of his young child, with whom he often strolled during an extended stay in the city. Relph's scans reveal distinctions among the coverings, capturing variations in patinas of time and use. Each door is decorated with circular perforations that spell the word GAS, pierced in a playful style that recalls a distinctly Italian reverence for craft and design. As a basic element of industrialization, gas utilities and infrastructures around the world are highly standardized. The word itself reflects this standardization, largely unchanging among world languages—a curious fact, as the word derives from the Greek *chaos*.

Fig. 3   **Sketch for *Chaos*, 2025.**
Fig. 4   **Sketch for *Chaos*, 2025.**

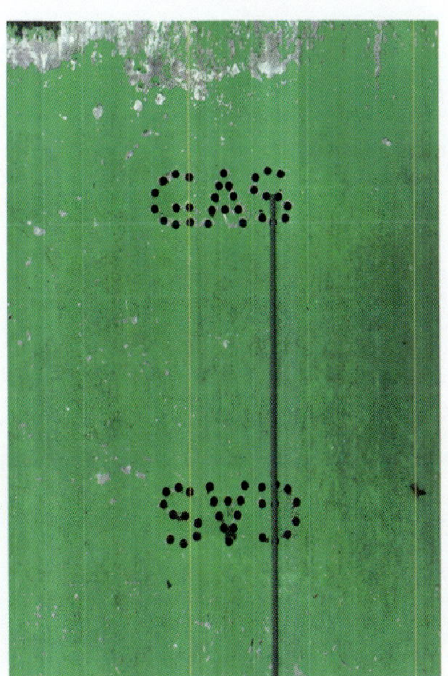
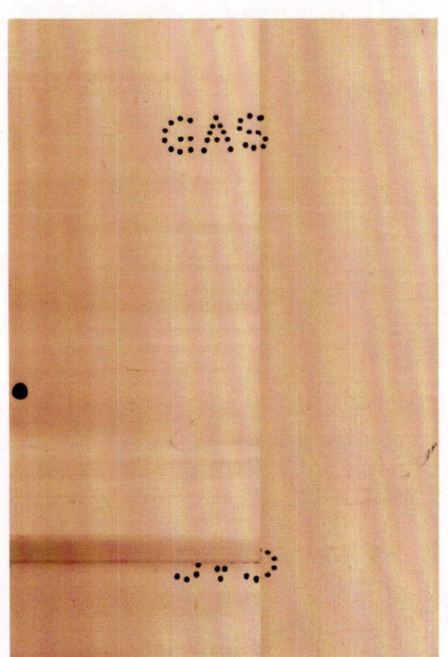

    PATINA OF TIME   Camila Palomino

Chaos is a natural extension of *MONSTERS* (2022), a behemoth book project that pays homage to a fixture of urban nostalgia—the public pay phone (Fig. 5). Presenting 452 scans of different pay phone enclosures in New York City and Los Angeles (out of one thousand images gathered), the book points to the exacting uniformity of the iconic perforated telephone silhouette as it appeared across so many metal booths, even as it was variously abstracted by rust, wear, and posters. New York City allegedly removed the last public phones in 2022—although some remain—replacing them with monoliths clad in high-definition screens and equipped with free public Wi-Fi. This transition marked an effort by Mayor Bill de Blasio, early in his tenure, to ensure New York City's stature as a competitive, highly connected "smart" city. Relph urgently and compulsively documented the obsolete structures at the end of their widespread existence in his matter-of-fact style. His scans emphasize that these relics were also pillars of urban media that answered all sorts of pedestrian needs and facilitated encounters; stuck against the aluminum casings were flyers for jobs, attorneys, quick cash, collective organizing, and finding God. Across these projects, Relph draws attention to the quiet archaeology of the urban surface, unearthing its many layers of memory and communication.

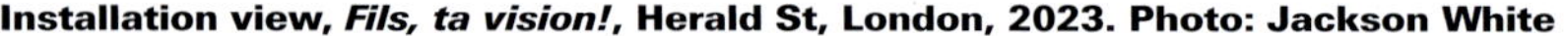

Installation view, *Fils, ta vision!*, Herald St, London, 2023. Photo: Jackson White

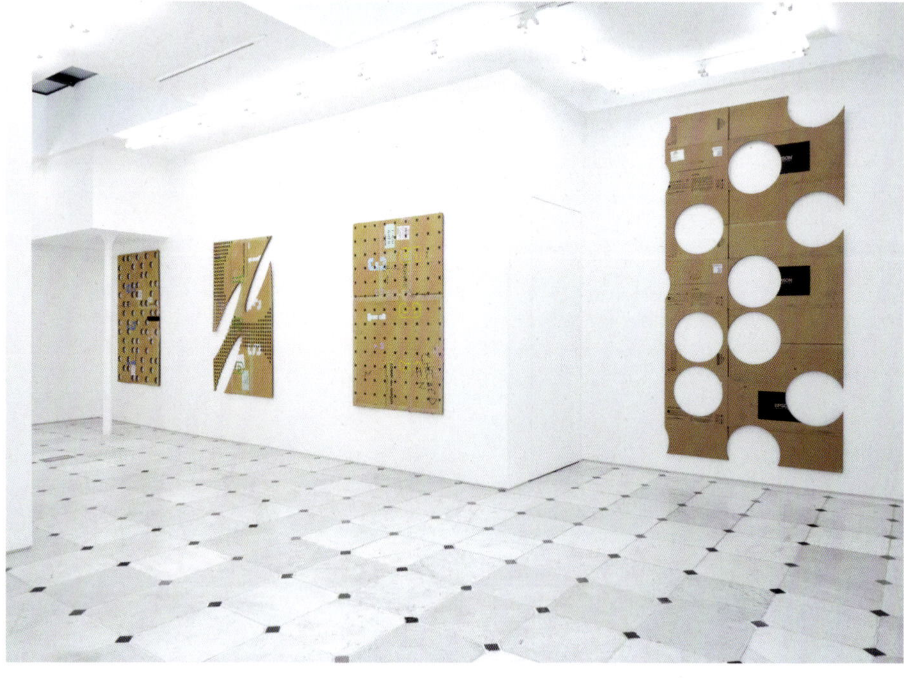

          Nick Relph

Fig. 5   Page from *MONSTERS*, Pre-Echo Press, 2022.

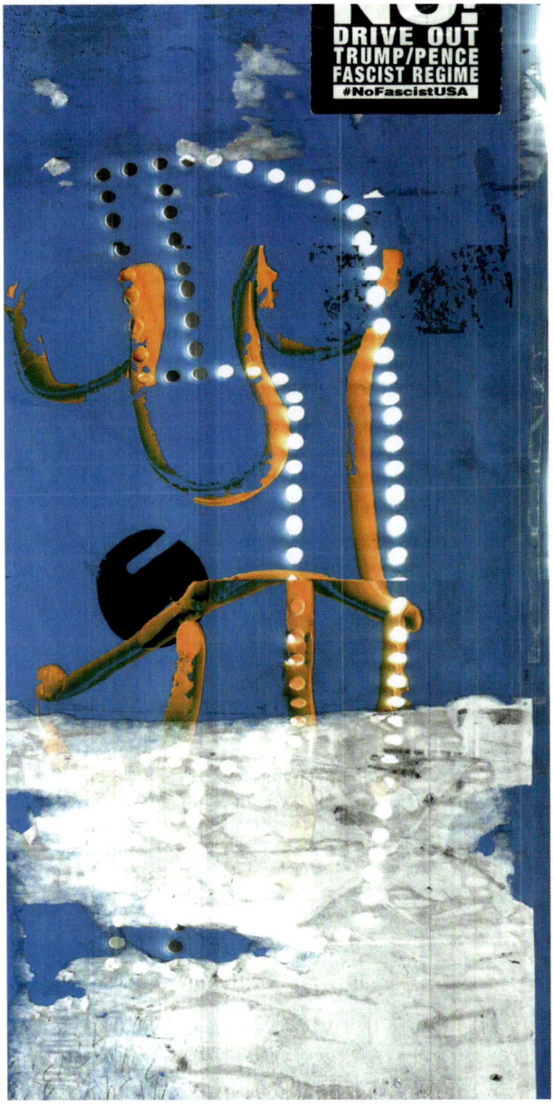

 PATINA OF TIME Camila Palomino

Selma Selman

(Bosnian, b. 1991)

Fig. 1   Installation view, *Flowers of Life*, Schirn Kunsthalle Frankfurt, 2024

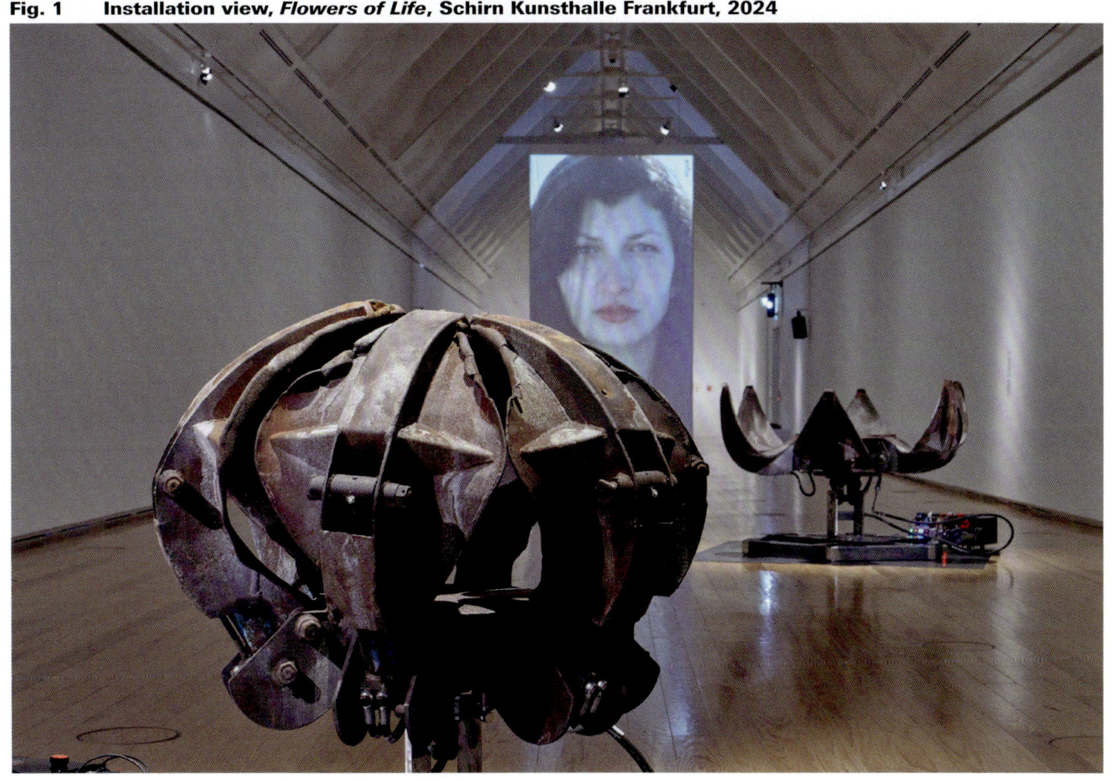

SORT THE WASTE, SALVAGE THE PARTS, AND SURVIVE
Amber Esseiva

Born in 1991, a year before the onset of the Bosnian War, Selma Selman spent her formative years in a Roma community within the volatile landscape of Bihać, Bosnia. Growing up in a historically marginalized population—one that continues to face systemic discrimination—Selman lived by her culture's ingenuity and survival tactics: sorting scrap metal and salvaging parts. Her artistic process embraces these strategies in a multimodal practice that is rooted in resilience, adaptation, and reclamation.

Much of Selman's work, which includes performances, installations, sculptures, and paintings, involves the physical and conceptual transformation of metal waste. Raised to find the value in discarded objects, she learned to strip cars for catalytic converters and dismantle old computers for copper, aluminum, and gold. Integrating such acts of physical labor into her work, she challenges the way cast-off materials, identities, and histories are appraised. In the installation *Flowers of Life* (2024), for example, she transformed grapples salvaged from grab trucks into kinetic sculptures that recall blossoms; the machines' prongs resemble petals that open and close as though responding to their environment **(Fig. 1)**. This is not only a literal act of reclamation, but a metaphorical one. Across her work, Roma history, identity, and experiences are reinterpreted and brought into contemporary discourse. "Over the last one hundred years or so the Roma people were collecting scrap metal, recycling it," Selman has observed. "It's only recently that [modern Western] societies began thinking of recycling as something important."[1] She recasts everyday Roma practices, which are often misunderstood and stigmatized, into potent symbols of cultural resistance and recuperative ingenuity.

In one poignant act of reclamation, part of the project *I Will Buy My Freedom When!* (2014–ongoing), Selman paid her family the lump sum of roughly 11,000 euros as a way to "buy" herself back in an act of self-preservation, highlighting the fact that the societal norms in which she was brought up can change. In many Roma cultures, the family of the groom pays the family of the bride, compensating for the loss of a daughter and her earning power. The money that would have marked Selman

1   Selma Selman, quoted in Krzysztof Kościuczuk, "Selma Selman's Art Is Dirt-Cheap but Worth More Than Gold," *Frieze*, November 28, 2023, https://www.frieze.com/article/selma-selman-her0-profile-2023.

as a commodity was used by her father to purchase a Mercedes-Benz. By reappropriating this transactional tradition, Selman sought to reclaim power and agency from systems that aim to define and control. As part of this project, in 2017 she initiated her foundation Get the Heck to School, which provides Roma girls in Bihać with financial support to complete their primary educations.

In her performances, Selman has frequently collaborated with members of her family, particularly her late father and other male relatives. Here, men labor for a woman they love, undermining the traditional patriarchal roles that both Roma culture and Western society have historically maintained. These performances also elevate forms of labor that are often devalued and ignored. In *Platinum* (2021–23), for example, which was performed at the National Gallery in Sarajevo, Selman and her family members dismantled European cars before an audience; and in her 2023 exhibition *her0* at Berlin's Gropius Bau, they performed *Motherboards* (2023–ongoing), for which they deconstructed disused computers, accompanied by a guitar player and an opera singer (Figs. 2–3). In futuristic protective eyewear, the performers labored with hammers

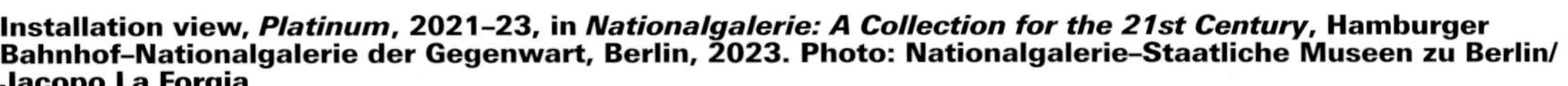

Installation view, *Platinum*, 2021–23, in *Nationalgalerie: A Collection for the 21st Century*, Hamburger Bahnhof–Nationalgalerie der Gegenwart, Berlin, 2023. Photo: Nationalgalerie–Staatliche Museen zu Berlin/ Jacopo La Forgia

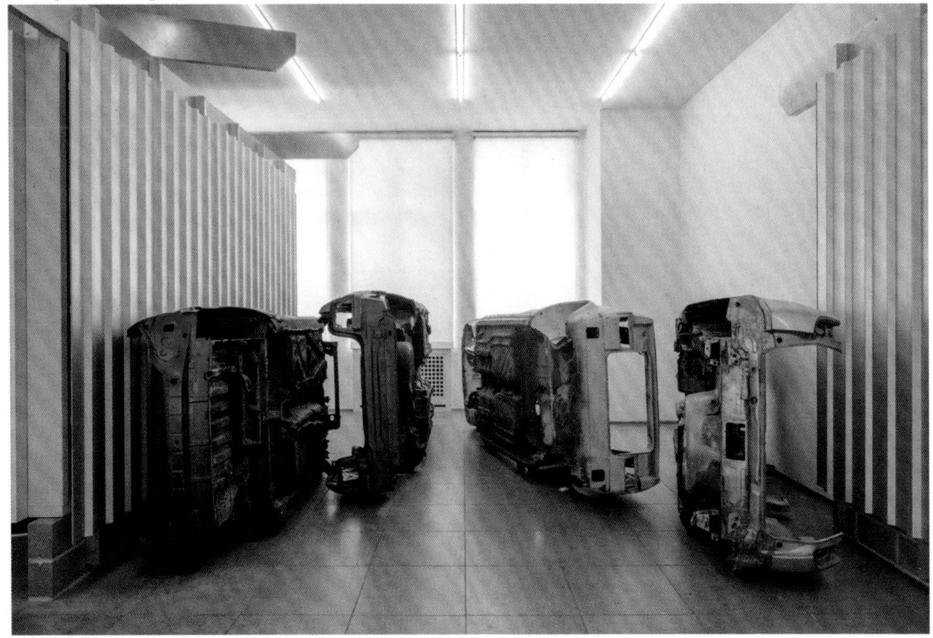

Fig. 2   *Motherboards*, 2023–ongoing, Gropius Bau, Berlin, 2023. Photo: Eike Walkenhorst

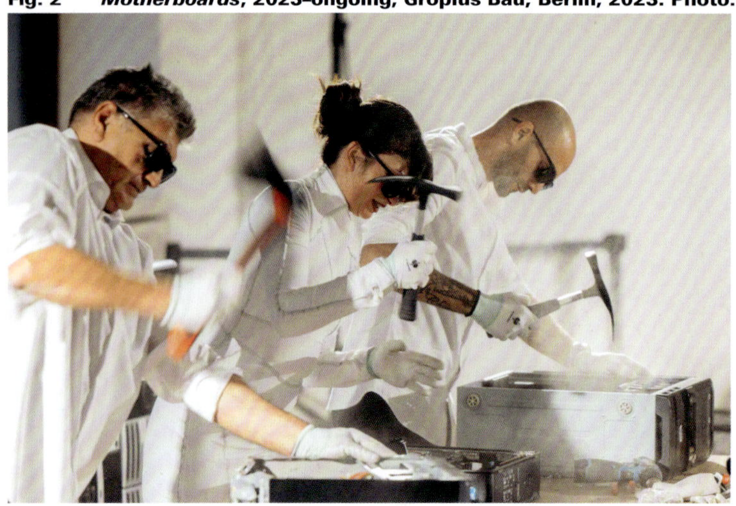

Fig. 3   *Motherboards*, 2023–ongoing, KRASS Festival, Kampnagel, Hamburg, 2023. Photo: Marko Ilić

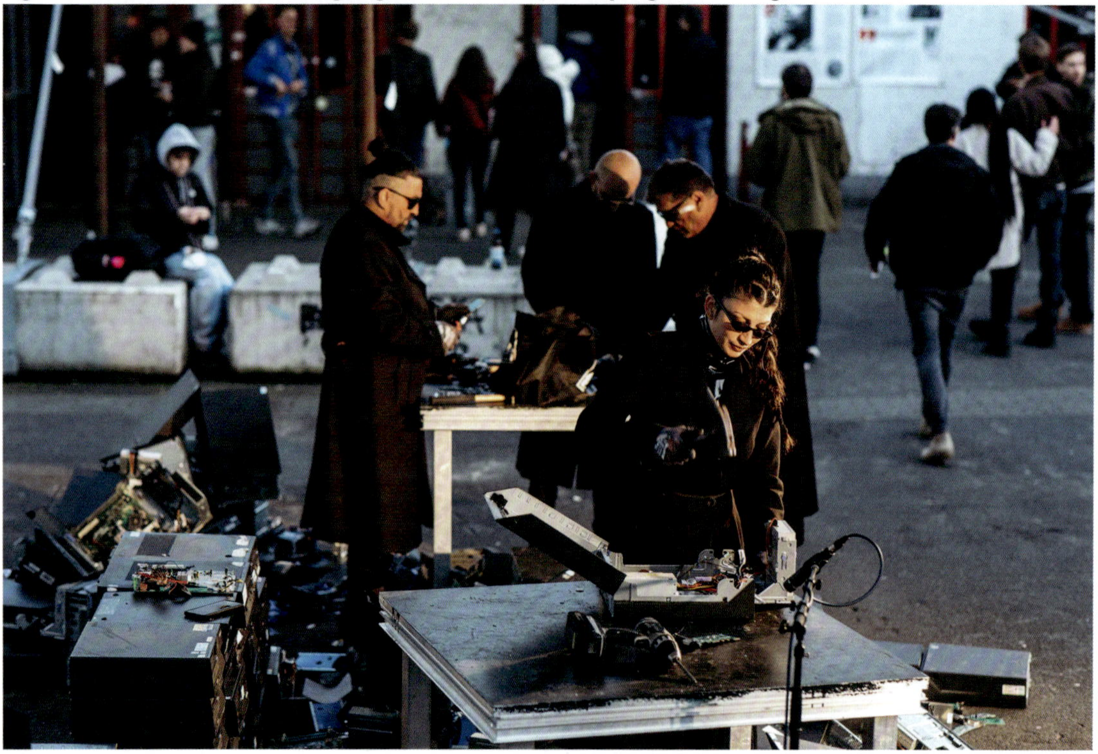

    Selma Selman

and power tools to expose the internal mechanisms of these sleek machines. From the cars, they stripped catalytic converters, and from the computers, they removed motherboards, CPUs, and RAM. After such performances, Selman works with a chemical engineer to extract precious metals from the salvaged parts and, with a goldsmith, transforms the sourced material into sculptures, such as a platinum axe or a golden nail. With these interventions, Selman asks us to reconsider our assumptions about value: What is worth saving, and who gets to decide?

As they scavenge and repurpose materials, Selman's family encounters technological relics, products that were once cutting-edge and essential to modern life but are now obsolete. Cast aside in the ever-accelerating trajectory of technological progress, electronic waste is frequently toxic. Selman draws attention to the ways in which consumer culture creates not only material waste but also social and environmental decay. That decay is often suggested through noxious smells that her sculptures and performances emit.

Fig. 4   *Satellite Dish*, 2023, in *Her0*, Gropius Bau, Berlin, 2023. Photo: Eike Walkenhorst

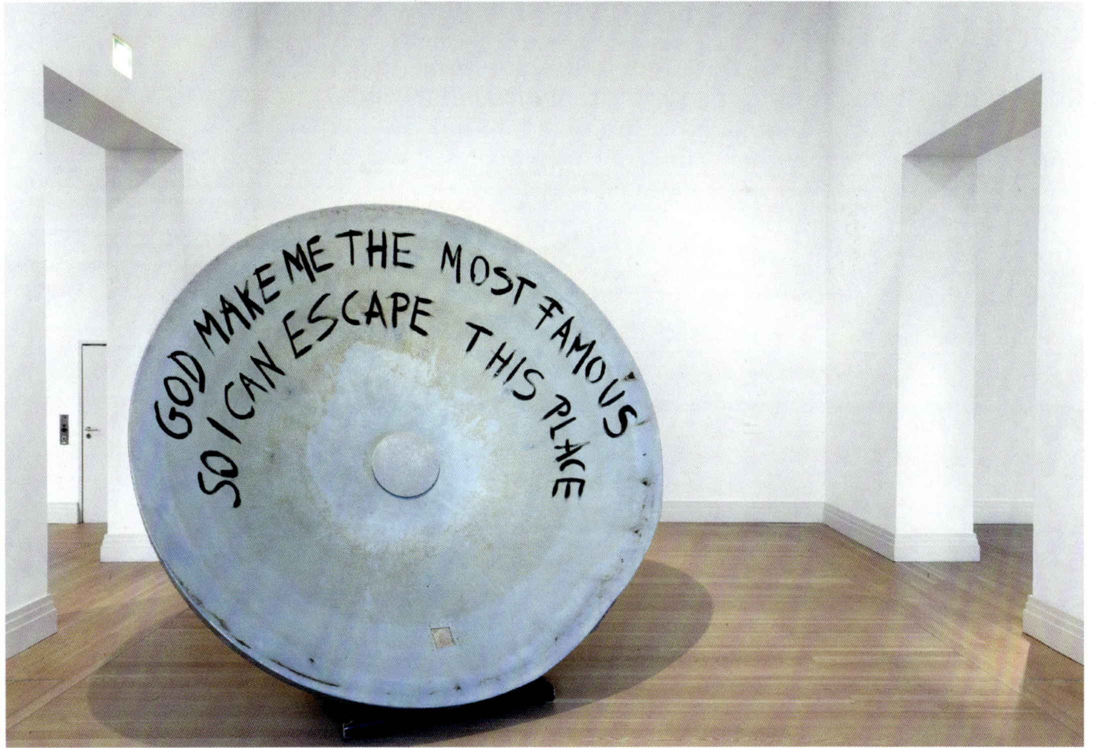

SORT THE WASTE, SALVAGE THE PARTS, AND SURVIVE

Amber Esseiva

The sculpture *Satellite Dish* (2023) encapsulates
Selman's complex relationship with consumerism, fame,
and freedom (Fig. 4). Scrawled across a ten-foot patinated
satellite dish sourced from a scrap yard is a plea: GOD,
MAKE ME THE MOST FAMOUS SO I CAN ESCAPE THIS PLACE.
Contextualized on an object that symbolizes global connec-
tivity, this phrase reflects the flawed notion that one might
escape their circumstances through fame or consumption—by generating an appealing style or look (composed
of consumer objects) for others to consume; through
commodifying herself. For Selman, the desire for fame is
tied to a wish to be liberated from patriarchy, capitalism,
and colonialism. In this context, her message symbolizes
the impossible situation of yearning for both recognition
and freedom from oppressive systems. She has described
that, growing up, "there was an attitude of, 'Is there
something you want? You only have yourself.' ... [*Satellite
Dish* is] about communicating something that I desired
for a long time, but I'm not sure if I want it now. It's about
that paradox. It's kind of making fun of myself, but at
the same time, it speaks to the reality that not only I, but
many of us—especially those who belong to marginalized
communities—experience."[2]

Weaving together personal histories, familial love,
and fierce critique, Selman's work freely traverses the
boundaries of art and activism. She dissects her own life
and the lives of those she cares for, transforming raw
emotion and scrapped materials alike into sharp-edged
commentary. In Selman's hands, heartbreak becomes the
foundation for new forms of truth—truths that rebuild,
reimagine, and reclaim.

2   Selma Selman,
"Transforming Noise and
Holding Space," interview by
Zippora Elders, Gropius Bau
Journal, accessed January 22,
2025, https://www.berliner
festspiele.de/en/bfs-de
/gropius-bau/programm/journal
/2024/transforming-noise
-and-holding-space.

Ser Serpas

(American, b. 1995)

Installation view, *taken through back entrances...*, 2024, in *Even Better Than the Real Thing*, Whitney Biennial, New York, 2024.

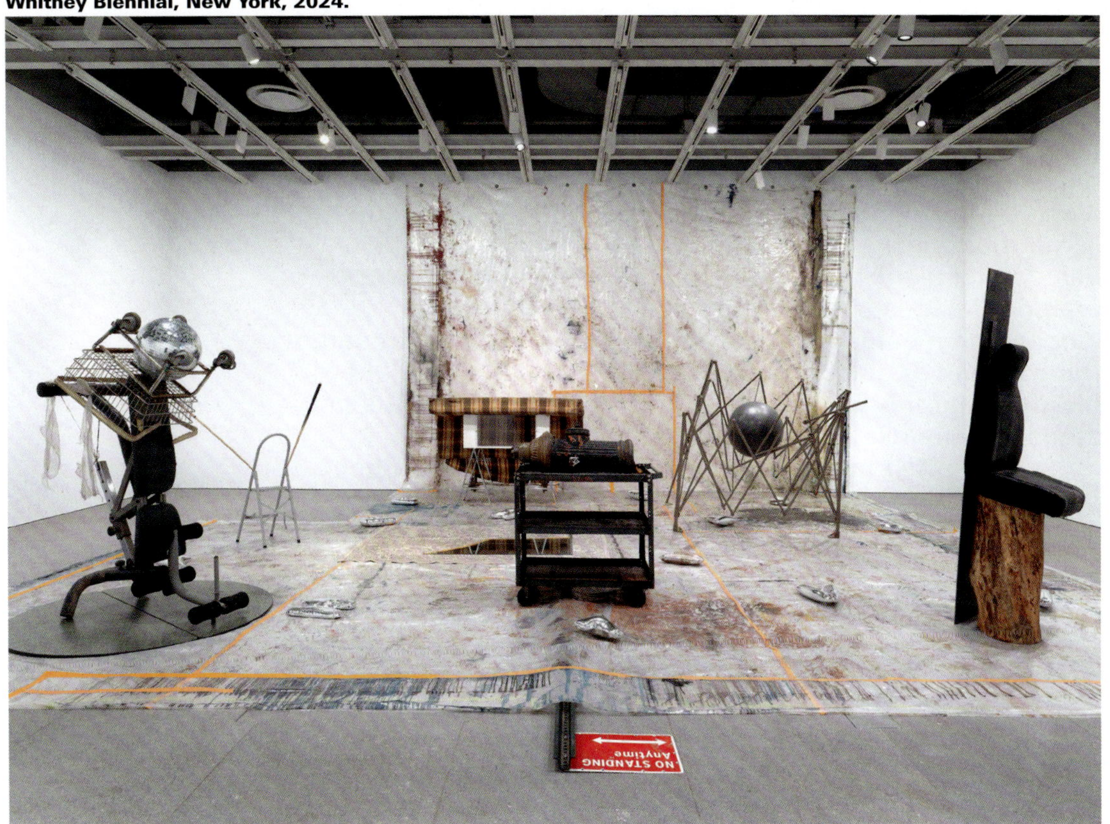

IN THE REMAINS
Quinn Latimer

We glean and we gather; we drag ourselves and the streets
and our memory—for some object or subject, trash that
could be both. By we, I mean Ser Serpas (and perhaps
many of us). Serpas came to be known over the past
decade for found-detritus sculptures that are soaked in
some modernist memory of material and volume, space
and color, balance and precarity. In a sense, these works
are poor images of the modernist sculptural canon from
whose rich meaning-making technologies they exact something potent and new. They are not wet with precedent,
but drily alluring, casual. Their performative and political
ethos, meanwhile, is in their making.

    The artist has long scavenged the streets—of her
native Los Angeles; of New York and Geneva, where she
studied; of Tbilisi, Zurich, and Paris, where she has lived
and exhibited—for cast-off furniture, metal fragments and
plywood planks, plastic tarps and broken umbrellas, all the

Installation view, *Made in L.A. 2020: a version*, Hammer Museum, Los Angeles, 2021.

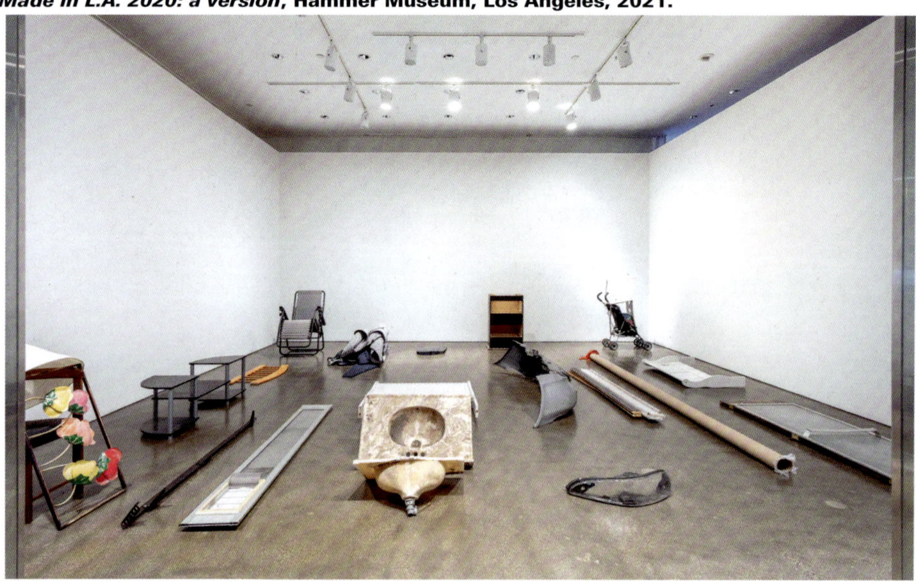

so-called cheap and abandoned materials that script our most banal and ardent grounds and rooms and selves. She then improvises with such materials to create sculptures characterized by intimacy and ingenuity, as well as by some cool remove. She places them across gallery floors in neat grids (as though they are waiting for collection) or weirdly magnetic pairs. Too assured to be accidental, too precarious to be devotional, the sculptures are often attributed to a praxis invested in critiquing late capitalism's globalist waste, full stop.

What waste? Our neoliberal order's excesses and ecocides, its free overnight deliveries and zero-hour contracts, its fast fashions and MDF furniture, littered shores, browning skylines, broken bodies. That is, what is already ruin before its production is finished, before its shipment is processed. That is, what is made only to be thrown away; the abject ruins of material memory and its manufacture; the bodies, shifting through this material, that do not matter, but "without whom the earth would not be the earth."[1]

1   Aimé Césaire, *Cahier d'un retour au pays natal* (Présence Africaine, 1956), 77–78. English translation quoted in Frantz Fanon, *Black Skin, White Masks*, trans. Charles Lam Markmann (Grove Press, 1967), 94.

Installation view, *Head banger boogie*, Galerie Barbara Weiss Trautwein & Herleth, Berlin, 2022.

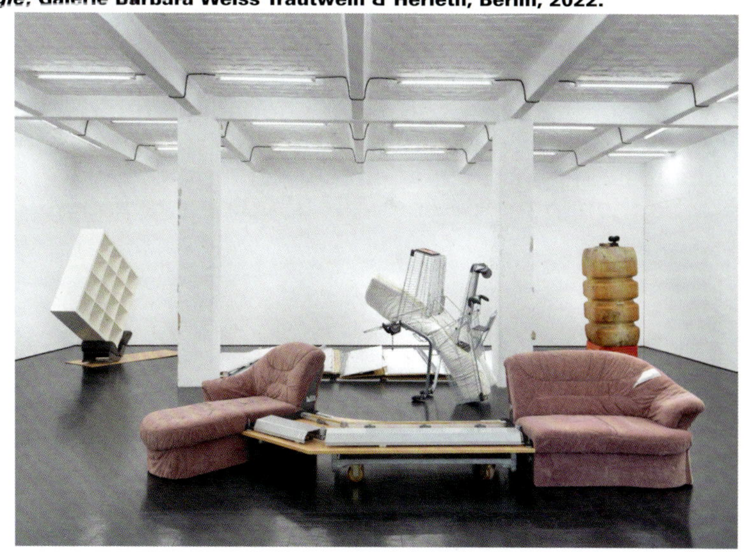

Displacement, dispossession. Césaire and Fanon
as much as Chamberlain and Rauschenberg. The carts
used to collect metal on the streets of Athens, Tbilisi,
East Los Angeles. All rhyme with Serpas's practice.
Indeed, a poignant and desperate sense of passage and
transit—temporal, geographic, corporeal, existential,
economic—marks the artist's works and practices. Their
affect suggests loose ties to a rocky world, where friends
and affection are everywhere, but stable ideas of form and
material, history and ideology, economy and gender, poetics and place, use value and exchange value, are not. *Are
not.* There is also an inclination when writing about work
of such steady accumulation (in an epoch of accumulation)
to try to begin subtracting, clarifying, adding nuance—to
the argument as well as to the form. For this is also a
sculptural tendency: to remove, to refine, to edit, to extract,
to shave down, to delete, to withhold.

Serpas's sculptures of refuse exemplify this
reticence—their balancing act depends on all she leaves
out, narratively as well as materially—but so do her works
in other disciplines. While her large-scale sculptures
have taken most of the space in considerations of her
production, her focus extends to parallel practices of
drawing, poetry, and, most recently, painting. What about
her painting? It seems to gather bodies within the tight
frame of her canvases, then shape and arrange them into
volumes of exposure and concealment, naively overflow-
ing, as though the bodies were simply more sculptural

Installation view, *Hall*, Swiss Institute, New York, 2023.

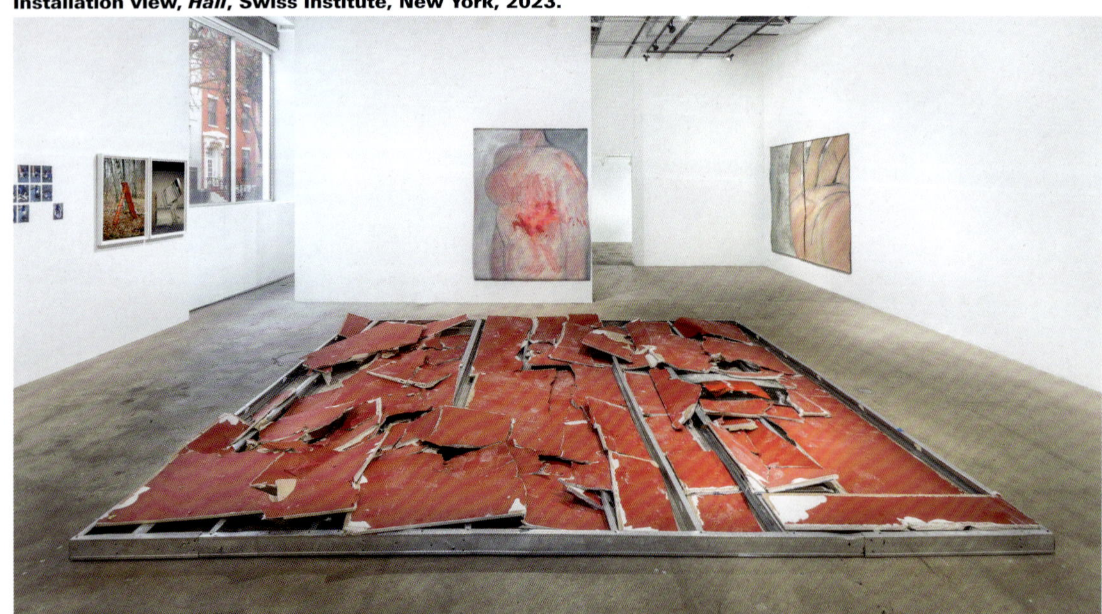

        Ser Serpas

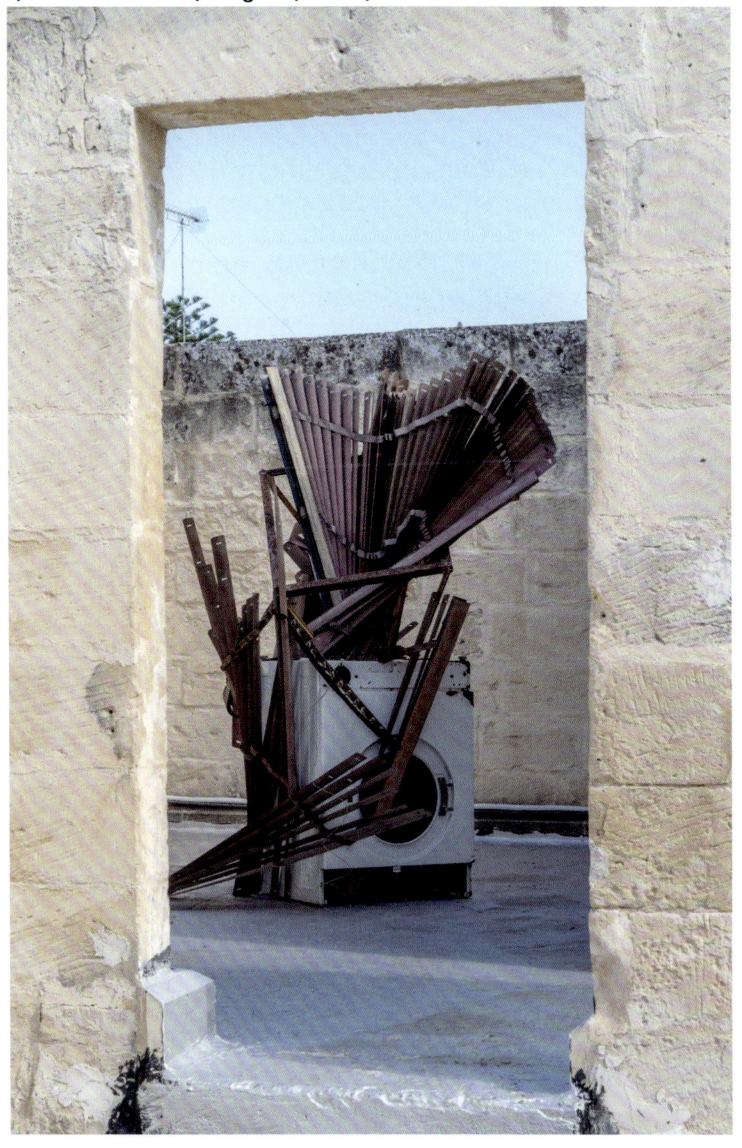

IN THE REMAINS

Quinn Latimer

material to be molded, amended, remade, repositioned.
Is there a practice of repair here? In the sense of what is
overlooked, abandoned, left adrift? Maybe. But the repair
is wildly provisional, not for the long term. These casually
improvised works—whether painting or sculpture, poetry
or drawing—retain their abandon, their fragility, their sense
of time as something acidly, decidedly, in the moment. The
future is not theirs, as it is not ours.

Perhaps this is the wry politics of such a practice:
Serpas mirrors the ideology of accumulation—as it is
mirrored by the rapacious art market (the "world" as
figured by the art world)—and its urge to buy, to own,
to collect, to keep (wealth, material, value, resources,
land, dignity, bodies, language, everything else), and
then upends it, via some casual edit. The disasters of our
vampiric neoliberal orders, the long century's racial capitalism that keeps them coming (every century), the constant
swing toward authoritarianism because everyone loves
a fascist: How to keep up with this trash? In her work—
which is bought, shown, kept, placed in circulation and
in collections—Serpas feeds the cannibalistic mouth that
defines our moment (and the long moment that preceded
it) with that mouth's own trash. I don't know.

What about her poetry, though? To be a poet is
often to proclaim an ethics, to stage the self and its poetics, as much as it is to be someone who produces poems,
moves through their stanzas, their rooms. Serpas has said
that she considers her poems—often written on the move:

Installation view, *I Fear (J'ai peur)*, **Bourse de Commerce Pinault Collection, Paris, 2024.**

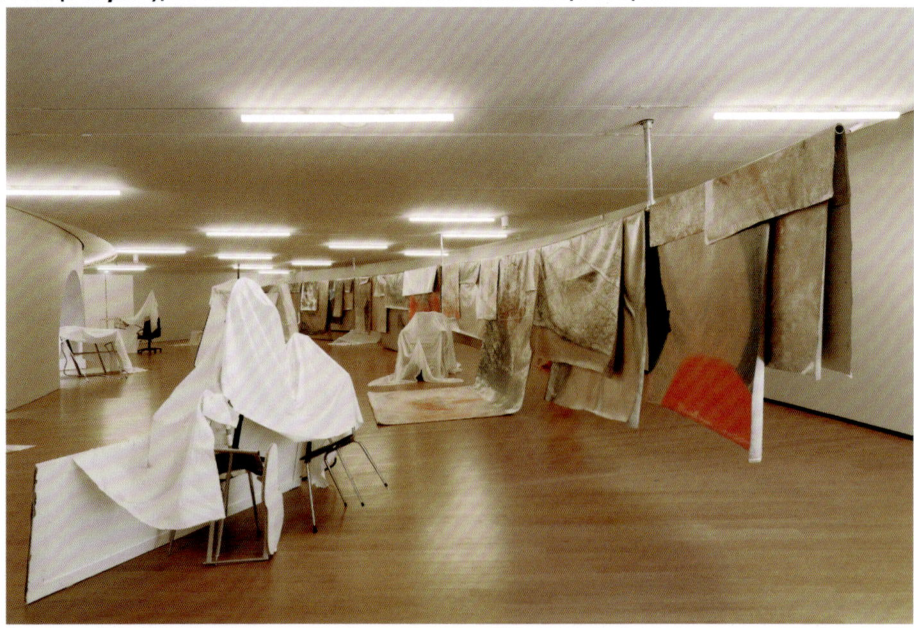

               Ser Serpas

"I always write in transportation"[2]—to be time-sculptures. Of course, she considers most of her practice to be temporal in both its making and its staging, sculptural in its ethos. Her poems, collected in multiple-year cycles and then published alongside a show (or not), speak to the silence of her visual practice. Lines from her poems provide titles for her sculptures, or ideas move back and forth. The quietude of her visual work is in this way given her language's narrative lifts and drips, vernaculars and discards.

A poetry collection, of course, also results from gleaning and gathering material. Bringing poems together into the space of a publication is like bringing sculptures into the space of a gallery or museum, constellating them, placing them into spatial proximity and linguistic and material conversation. A narration of the present through the dialogic documents and refuse of living, Serpas's poetry conjures something both historical and patently contemporaneous in affect and effects. Signs, symbols, significations; transit, transportation, transformation, technology. This excess of material—of language as street detritus, of bodies as their representations and nonrepresentations both—lifted and refashioned as a form of memorialization, gestures to presence, to consciousness, so that life is not left, disappeared, but remains *in the remains*.

"Matter comes to matter," as Karen Barad and others have said.[3] They are speaking to those practices—social as well as technoscientific—that suggest a more performative account of the relationship between the material and the discursive. They are speaking to the nature of materiality itself, where matter is not static but an active participant in the world's becoming. Of power's material constraints and political pressures, Barad notes: "The body reacts to [these] forces, manifest as shifting material alignments and changes in potential, and becomes not simply the receiver but also the transmitter or local source of the signal or sign that operates through it."[4] Watch Serpas, surrounded by her materials—all shifting alignments and changes in potential, all trash and language—becoming both transmitter of their meaning and local source of their signal. See her make a sign, and another, and another. *Read them.*

2   Ser Serpas, "Collecting Time Through Space: A Conversation with Ser Serpas," interview by Ingrid Luquet-Gad, *Flash Art*, February 17, 2022, https://flash---art.com/article/ser-serpas/.
3   Karen Barad, "Posthumanist Performativity: Toward an Understanding of How Matter Comes to Matter," *Signs* 28, no. 3 (2003): 801–31.
4   Karen Barad, "Getting Real: Technoscientific Practices and the Materialization of Reality," *Differences: A Journal of Feminist Cultural Studies* 10, no. 2 (1998), 87.

          IN THE REMAINS   Quinn Latimer

Emilija Škarnulytė

(Lithuanian, b. 1987)

Fig. 1   Installation view, *Sirenomelia*, 2017, Blaffer Art Museum, Houston, 2018. Photo: Peter Molick/
Blaffer Art Museum

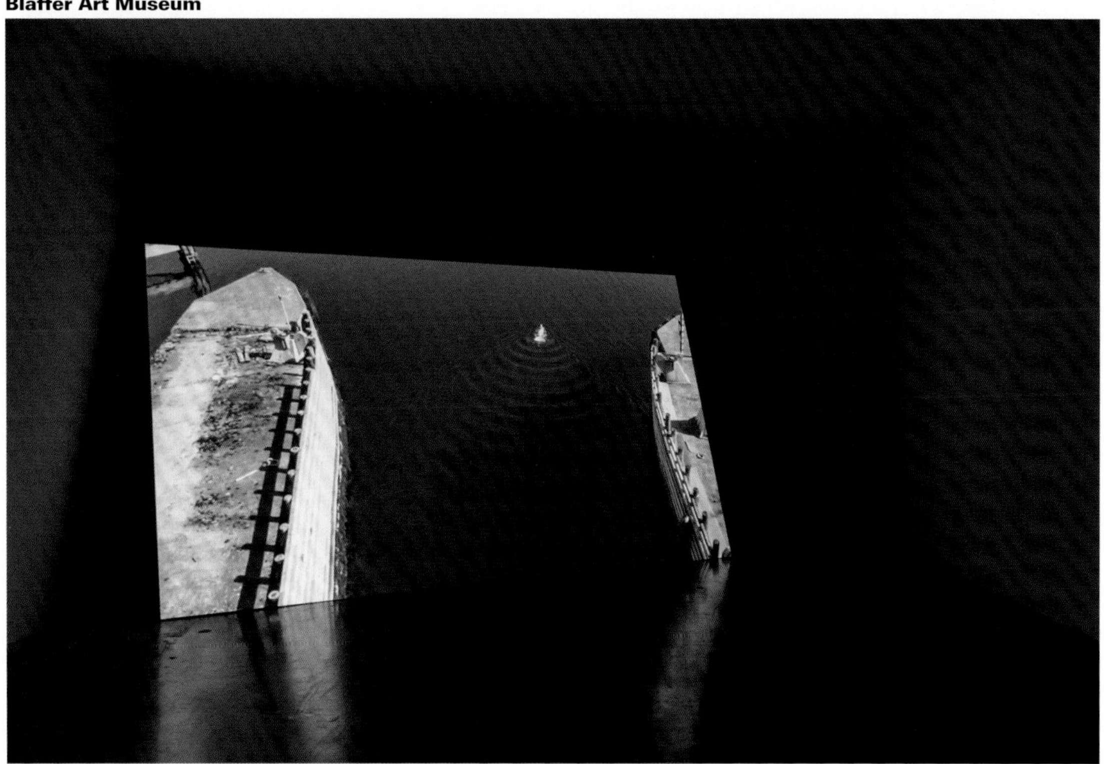

HALF-LIFE
Nadim Samman

> People's thoughts rush noiselessly, in all languages,
> through the serpent of science, for both good and evil.
> —Hans Christian Andersen, *The Great Sea Serpent*

A drone shot, looking down upon the sea below. A figure—
half human, half fish—swims along a boundary where
fresh, muddy water meets that of the dark blue deep. The
swimmer, Emilija Škarnulytė, performing in costume for
her film *Æqualia* (2023), traces the shifting edge of these
two fields. The threshold not a straight line but a shifting,
dissolving limit.

It is common to interpret mermaids as symptomatic
of the male gaze, figuring fascination and fear with
untamed womanhood. Standing for—or, rather, swimming
through—all that is wild. The sailor's attraction to the
mermaid uncovers a moral concerning the profundity of
sexual desire (symbolized by the sea's fathomless depths)
and its apparent danger. And yet, it is worth casting a
wider interpretive net. For mermaids are also a species
of projection in the history of the human imagination,
exploring transcendence of embodied boundaries: that our
lifeworld—requiring air and solid ground, for instance—can
be overcome, or that a powerful desire, manifest as the
siren's call, exists for such. The suggestion that this
fantasy is impotent, leading to death, is a function of
pre-contemporary understanding.[1] In an age of scientific
enterprise, the myth's value stands to be revisited.

Today, technology makes human bodies viable in
unlikely atmospheres—and, accordingly, new prospects
for our species being-in-the-world. We can now inhabit
the subaquatic realm with the help of our tools—via scuba
suit and submarine—as well as volcanic craters, high
altitudes, the poles, and other extreme regions. In turn, the
earth becomes subject to our trans-atmospheric agency:
deep-sea mining companies set their sights on mineral
deposits below the seafloor—a prospect with catastrophic
implications for marine ecology. A corresponding dive into
the abyss has nuclear submarines charting silent courses
throughout the great oceans, conveying the threat of anni-
hilation to every shore. Off world, Martian mineral deposits
come into view. All told, our species' expanded field of
action allows us to shape ecologies on a planetary scale.

1   Indeed, against its seduction would-be sailors must take prophylactic measures. Cf. Odysseus plugging his ears with wax in order not to hear the intoxicating call.

In *Sirenomelia* (2017) Škarnulytė's mermaid swims through the imposing dockyards of a Norwegian nuclear submarine base (Figs. 1–3). Wearing high-tech goggles, this cyber-woman-fish through her radical hybridity speaks to every enterprise that would render the earth—its landscapes, and creatures—a human prosthesis. As the Anthropocene theory maintains, our species signature can be found embedded in the geological record—not least through the atomic contamination we have unleashed. Cast in this light, the mermaid's half-animal status is visible from an obverse perspective, figuring our further intrusions within the domain of biology.

Fig. 2 **Still, *Sirenomelia*, 2017.**
Fig. 3 **Still, *Sirenomelia*, 2017.**

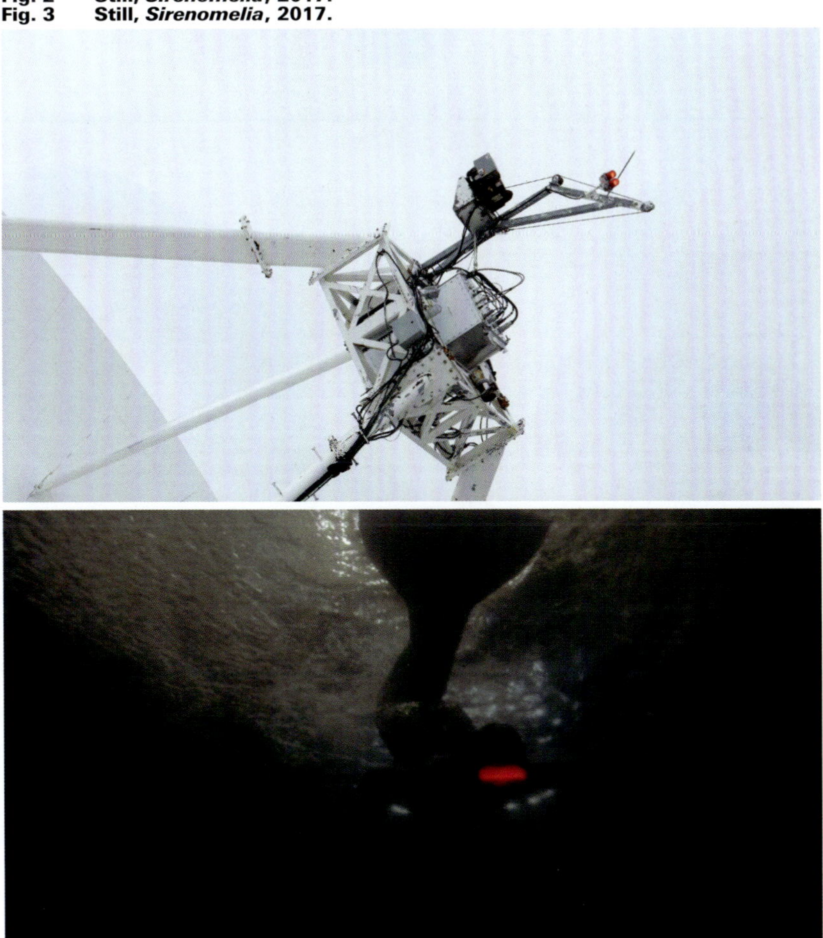

  HALF-LIFE Nadim Samman

In *Burial* (2022), a film partly shot inside the control room of a decommissioned nuclear power station, a large snake sets the blinking lights of this mechanical system into relief (Figs. 4–6). Sliding over buttons and measuring gauges, this lithe constrictor traces out a riddle. Is its presence in a restricted area a sign of foreboding, figuring the latent danger "contained" in the facility; one that threatens to break out? Or, rather, does it suggest that the natural world can return to such a place, able to survive the onslaught of radiation? As the rewilding of the Chernobyl exclusion zone shows, these two options are not mutually exclusive. Tension mounts.

Fig. 4   Still, *Burial*, 2022.
Fig. 5   Still, *Burial*, 2022.

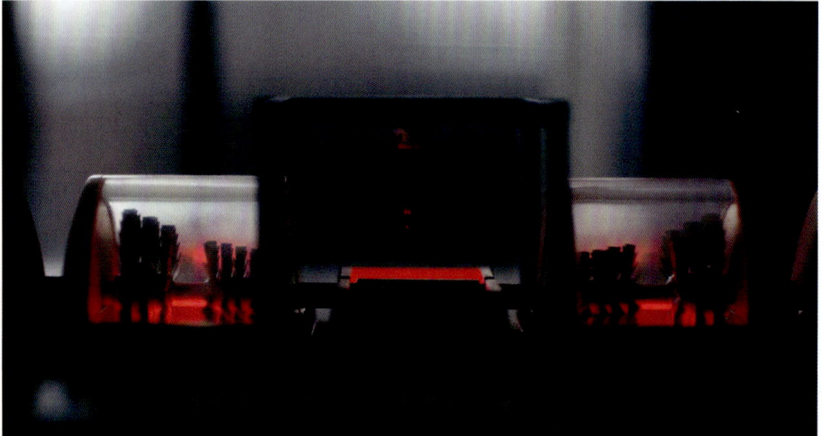

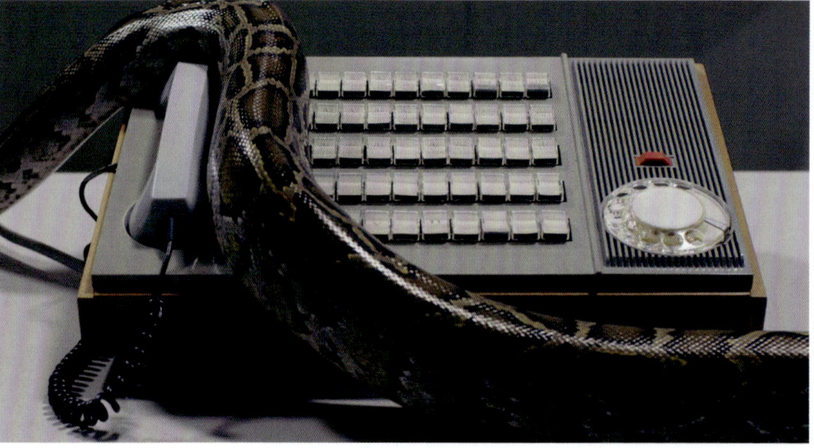

                    Emilija Škarnulytė

The snake extends the iconography present in
Škarnulytė's previous works; its scaly form, lacking legs
(and arms), analogous to the mermaid's bottom half.
And just as mermaid tales speak to temptation, so does
this reptile tail activate a biblical allegory attached to
the serpent, concerning compulsion: that to consume
power—whether in the form of an apple or a split atom.
This power is the fruit of knowledge, revelation and
destruction being two sides of one coin, spinning along
the axis of affordance. When is *knowing more* a problem?
How can one know when this moment occurs?

Fig. 6   Still, *Burial*, 2022.

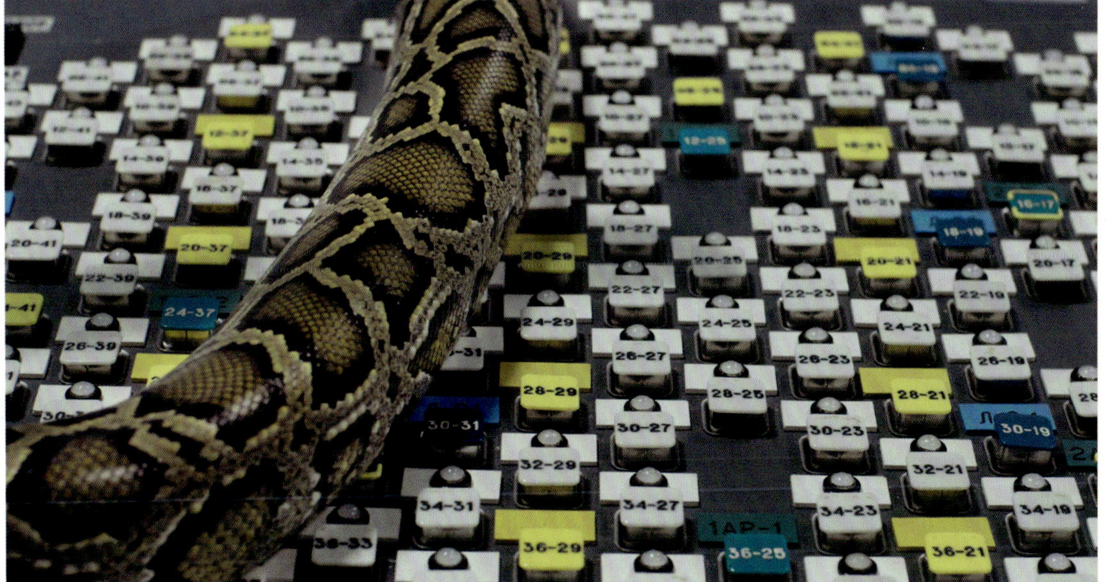

                    HALF-LIFE   Nadim Samman

Even when they are no longer productive, nuclear power stations brim with half-life, their radioactive isotopes still extant, requiring careful management. The work of attending the storage of spent fuel is never truly complete. Atomic waste is undead, full of power. In order for this power to be managed, certain information must be conveyed across generations. Yet information on its own is nothing without the transmission of cultural norms regarding its effective interpretation. These norms survive in certain social and political atmospheres, and die off in others.

Today, we are subject to a surfeit of information. Amid this dense data atmosphere, lack of intellectual synthesis becomes more likely. What signals are lost in the noise? Škarnulytė's atomic poetics appears arrayed against such failure, offering images that work not with facts, per se, but with affect. Here is an artist who understands that imagination is a valuable ecology, in which important knowledge may yet survive.

Installation view, *T 1/2*, 2019, Pinchuk Art Centre, Kyiv, 2019. Photo: Maksym Bilousov/Pinchuk Art Centre

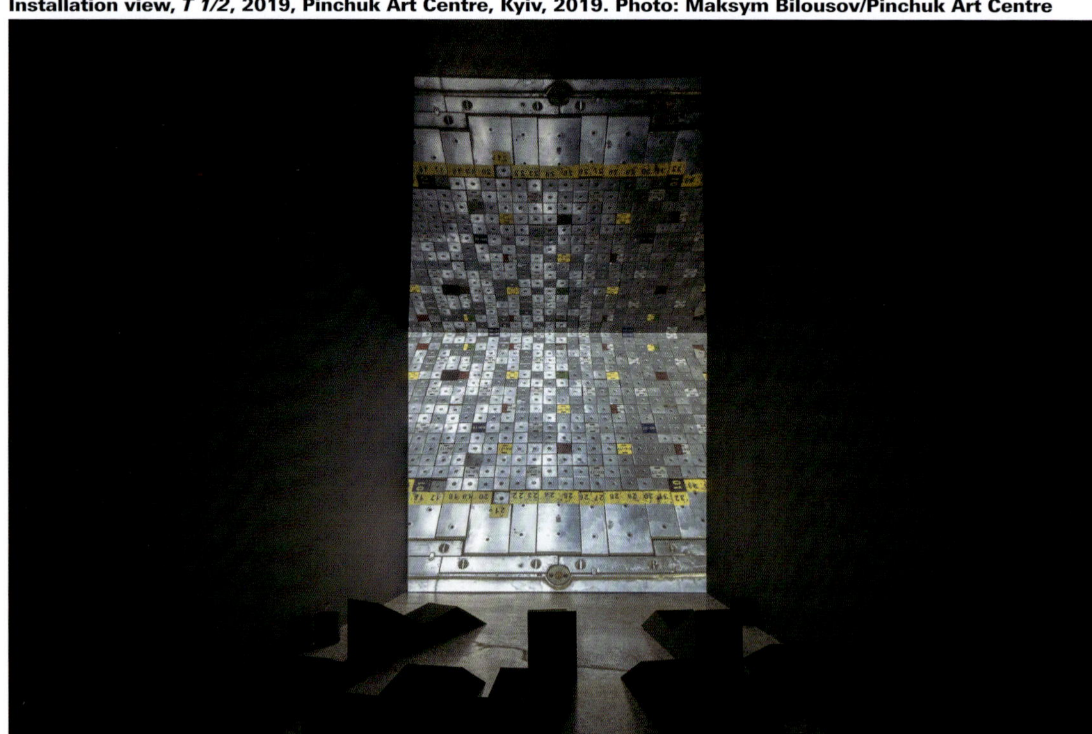

 Emilija Škarnulytė

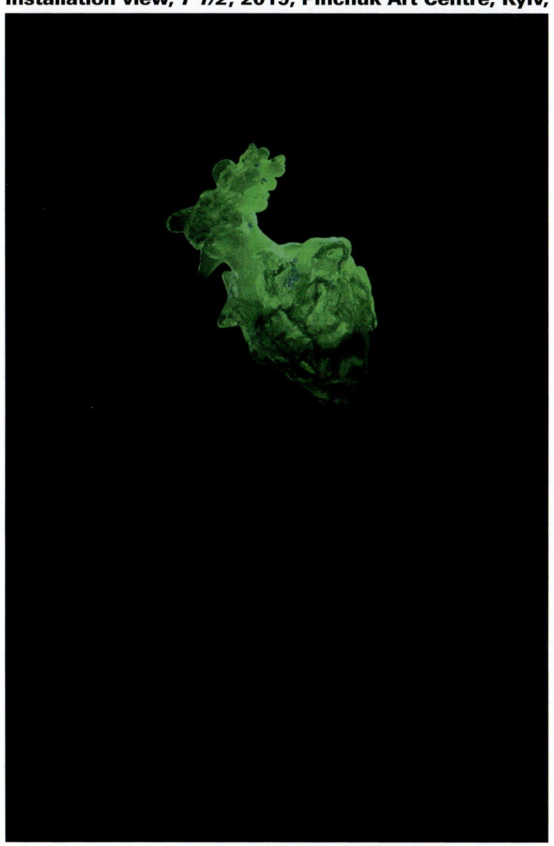

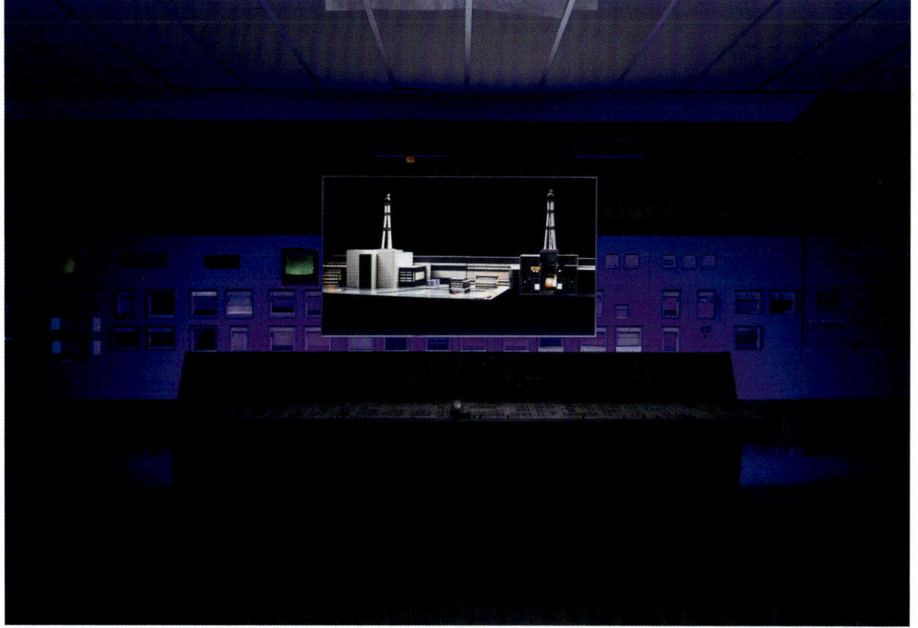

          HALF-LIFE   Nadim Samman

In Hans Christian Andersen's well-known tale, the little mermaid falls in love with a prince of the land. And yet, in his late work *The Great Sea Serpent* (1871), an old "sea cow," who is also described as a mermaid, makes an appearance—offering advice to other creatures.[2] Her discourse concerns a newly laid underwater telegraph cable—confused by many for an eel or serpent. Is it a coincidence that, in this story of human intrusion into a newly mapped undersea space, Andersen's cryptid has evolved into a marine mammal from the realm of zoology? And what does "she" have to say? "They want to catch us," she said; "that's all they live for. [...] Don't touch that junk; in time it will unravel and all turn to dust and mud. Everything that comes from up there cracks and breaks—is good for nothing!" The story announces a sea change concerning who and what carries the mark of fantasy: in a mirrorical inversion, the once godlike mermaid appears adrift in the reality principle, while the cable is elevated to the symbolic lacunae par excellence—the ouroboros, or Midgard snake. Announcing an age in which the power of our tools arrives at planetary scale, Andersen's story has the serpent devouring even our self-regard: "The cable didn't move, but it had its own private thoughts, which it had a right to have, considering that it was filled with other's thoughts."

If you are reading this text online, it is worth recalling a request made by Andersen's last mermaid, in a world disturbed by subsea cables. "Are you seeking knowledge and wisdom? [...] in return I demand that you guarantee safe pasturage on the bottom of the ocean for me and mine." In this "knowledge society," Škarnulytė's works attempt to honor that siren's call.

2   "Presently an old sea cow appeared. People call these mermaids or mermen." See https://andersen.sdu.dk /vaerk/hersholtTheGreat SeaSerpent_e.html.

    Emilija Škarnulytė

Zhou Tao

(Chinese, b. 1976)

Fig. 1   Still, *Blue and Red*, 2014.

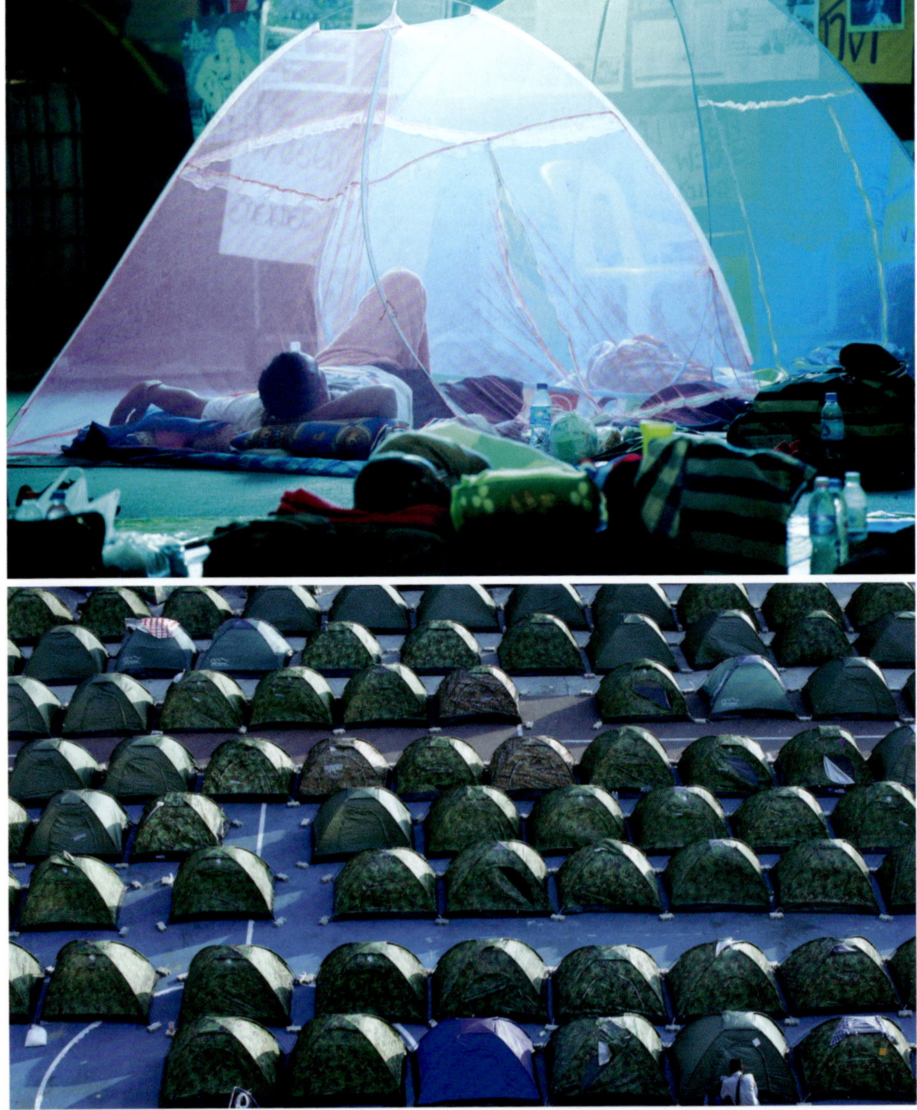

UNDER THE WEIGHT OF THE WORLD
Ruba Katrib

For twenty years, Zhou Tao has produced long-form films that document a world on the brink. His work often centers on artificial and natural structures of seemingly unfathomable scale, following the humans that work in, live near, or even constructed them. With cinematography that foregrounds spatial relationships, Zhou emphasizes the ways in which these structures dwarf the subjects adjacent to them. The grandness of these spaces takes on a vague yet palpable tension, as if one false move would bring it all down. This is both literal and figurative, as his works explore infrastructures and networks as much as discrete architectures. In *Blue and Red* (2014), Zhou seamlessly mixes footage from two cities: Bangkok, where he worked for some time, and Guangzhou, where he is from (Figs. 1–3). Combining abstracted images of protest with those of celebration, Zhou zeros in on details instead of building broader context, producing scenes that are otherworldly. In one, revelers congregate under a gigantic glowing globe that casts a blue light over them. Zhou connects this moment with images of the tents that populated Bangkok's streets during the 2014 anti-government protests in the city; aerial footage scans the demonstrators' informal structures and systems. This work exemplifies Zhou's cinematic language, with static shots, slow pans, and movements through space that mimic a scroll unfurling.

So much of Zhou's work is characterized by ambiguity. His films refuse singular narratives, often melding space and time, as with the unspoken merging of cities in *Red and Blue.* The people he depicts are by turns toiling and at leisure. In his recent film *The Periphery of the Base* (2024), Zhou documents workers who have traveled to the Gobi Desert to construct a major piece of infrastructure that is never named nor identifiable—the film focuses on parts rather than on the whole (Figs. 4–5). What is clear, however, is the immensity of the harsh landscape, the enormity of the structures that need to be assembled, and the stark conditions for the temporary workers. The mystery surrounding the structure is amplified by the vastness of the remote landscape. Zhou's meditation on "peripheral" activities is surreal, even as it is slow and laborious: There are expansive scenes of people walking up a steep sandbank and of two men discussing fishing while sitting on a large concrete slab they presumably will have to move. In this work and others, the artist takes his camera to places that are hard to access; often they are in territories that are between national borders or that exist nearly autonomously because of their location. These sites aren't frequently depicted, and Zhou's images of them are stunning.

Fig. 4   Still, *The Periphery of the Base*, 2024.
Fig. 5   Still, *The Periphery of the Base*, 2024.

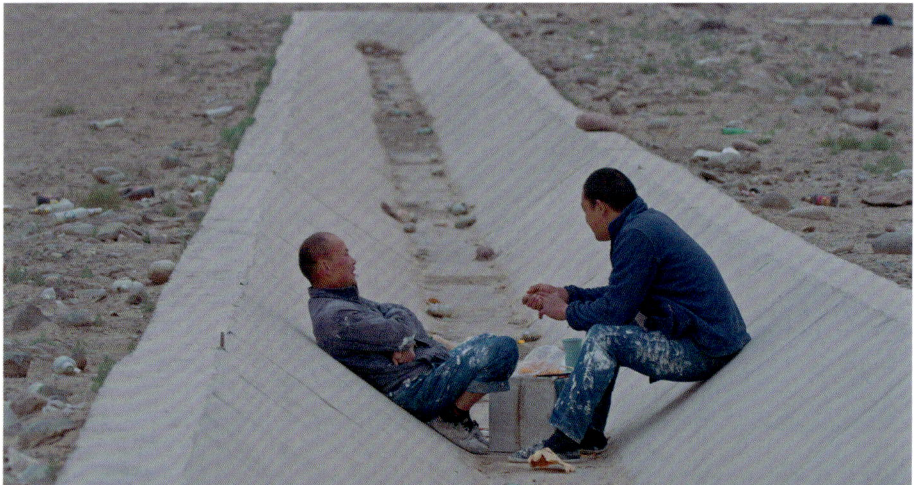

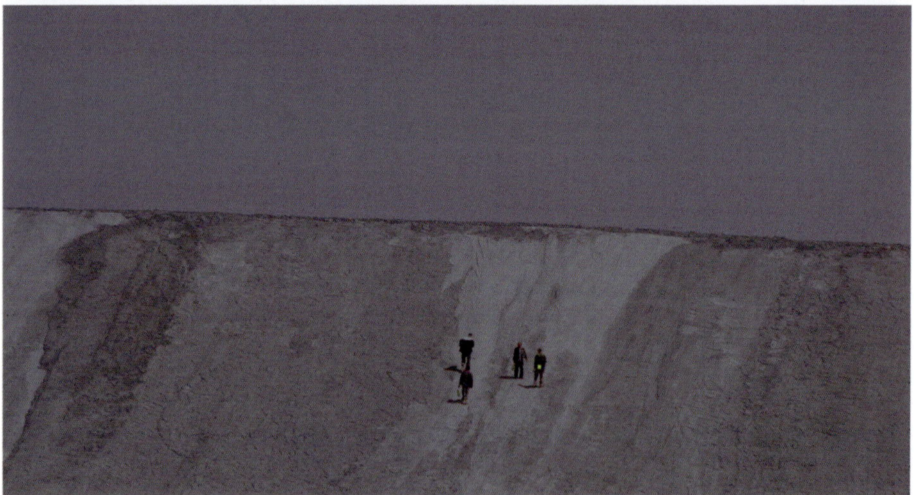

          Zhou Tao

Zhou's film *North of the Mountain* (2019) documents the communities who live close to the land at the base of the Kunlun Mountain range (Fig. 6). His protracted scenes feature people skinning sheep or moving landscapes where ice and greenery converge; he portrays life on the edges of geographies, worldviews, and traditions. With his 2017 film *The Worldly Cave (Fán Dòng)*, Zhou enters even less accessible spaces (Figs. 7–9). He compiles footage of populations living near massive caves in multiple parts of the world, including the Hakka people, who are being pushed out of their ancestral homes in southern China to make way for development. Again, the work shows one way of life tipping into another, framed by the monumentality of the caves. Zhou regularly moves between natural and manufactured landscapes in his works, showing the interrelated ways these realms construct the terms of life that exists around them, sometimes in unexpected ways. His cinematography emphasizes details; he never fully zooms out, but instead moves in and around the contours of the spaces he depicts. Further, Zhou doesn't directly reveal the topics of his films; he captures the tension of each context without offering narration.

Fig. 6   Still, *North of the Mountain*, 2019.

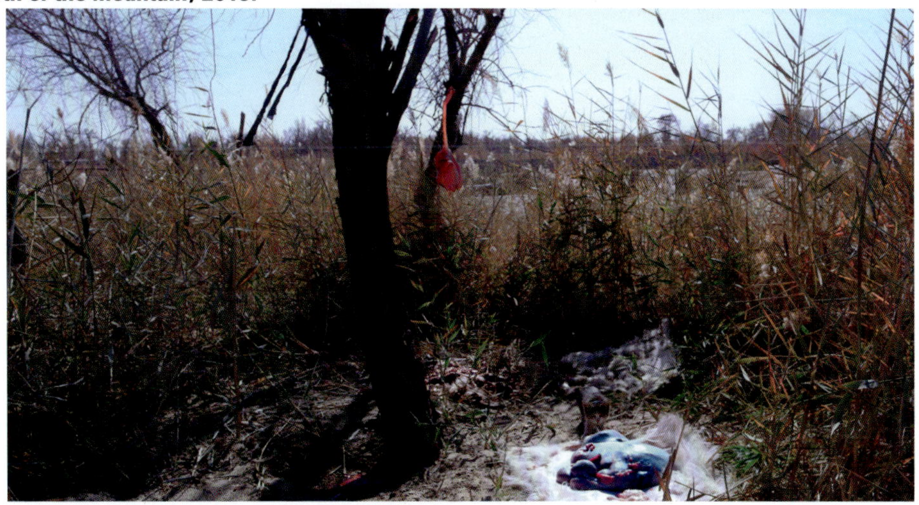

     UNDER THE WEIGHT OF THE WORLD   Ruba Katrib

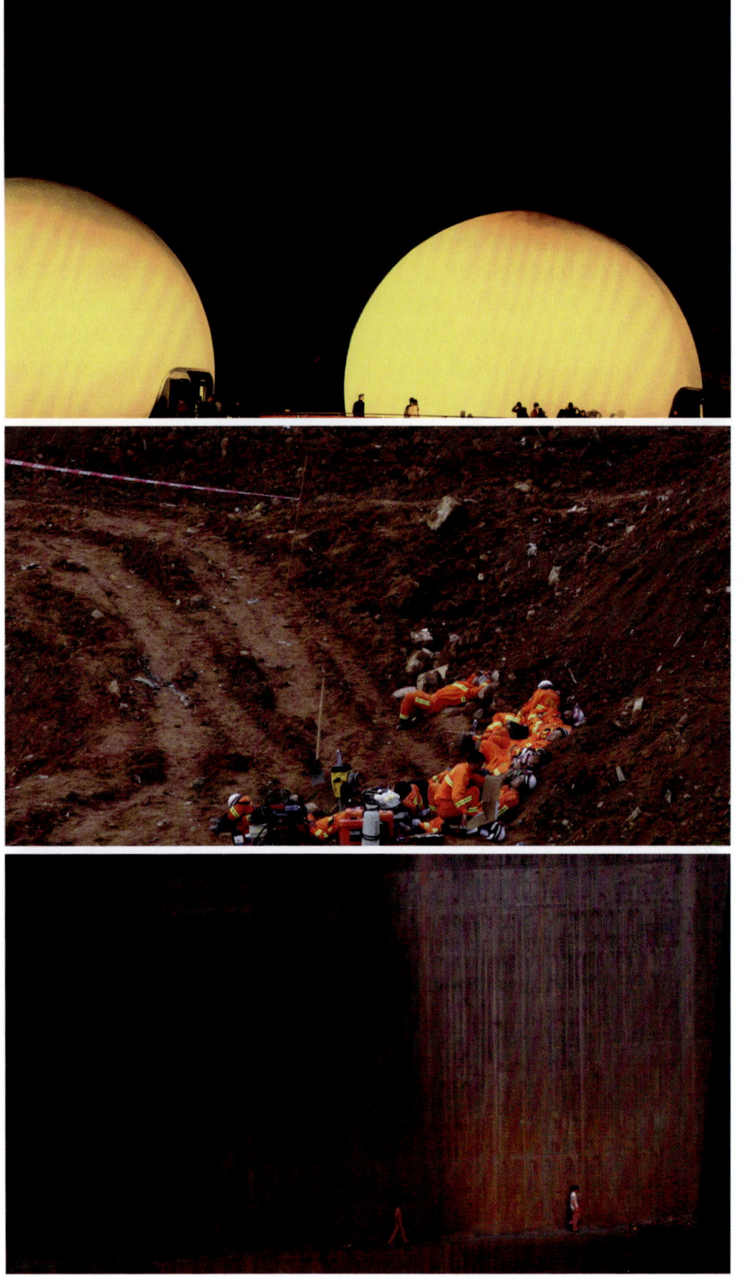

    Zhou Tao

The Axis of Big Data (2024) operates as a sort of companion piece to *The Periphery of the Base*; both feature constantly meandering shots, and the camera is often positioned as if rotating on an axis. This panning movement doesn't allow a subject to fully come into view. Because of this visual strategy, the monumental data center at the heart of *The Axis of Big Data* is obscured. As in *The Periphery of the Base*, we never see the entirety of the portrayed structure, but we understand its scale. The architect Keller Easterling's concept of "extrastatecraft" focuses on the rising prominence of infrastructure projects that transcend national borders to power global networks. Largely out of sight or disguised within urban environments, these physical structures contribute to the convenience of our daily technological behaviors—making phone calls, going online, turning on the lights—just as they facilitate the complex operations and exchanges of financial markets and global trade. The data center is emerging as a central character within what Easterling refers to as "infrastructure space," where "information resides in invisible, powerful activities that determine how objects and content are organized and circulated,"[1] a virtuality that progressively defines our built environment. Of course, large-scale infrastructural projects have been around for hundreds of years or more, but increasingly they belong to sprawling, unlocalized networks—often helmed by ungovernable multinational entities geared toward profit. The data center in Zhou's film is situated in a picturesque rural area of Guizhou, China, surrounded by waterfalls. In recent years, the tech industry has colonized this perhaps unlikely location—Guizhou is currently home to nearly fifty major data centers. The region's hydropower helps to run the many servers, and the cool climate is ideal to offset air-conditioning needs.[2] Built into a mountain and shrouded in greenery, the data center in Zhou's film attempts to blend into its environment. The artist plays with this notion of disguise, scanning the area around the center; he surveils rice farmers walking through fields, tourists on their smartphones, domestic animals, and the strikingly lush features of the mountainous landscape. The resulting documentation stitches together scenes of traditional culture and labor with others that confront the onset of a technological future.

1   Keller Easterling, *Extrastatecraft: The Power of Infrastructure Space* (Verso, 2014), 13.
2   "Guizhou: China's Finest, The Big Data Valley of China," CNN Sponsor Content, accessed February 17, 2025, https://sponsorcontent.cnn.com/edition/2018/guizhou/china-big-data-valley/.

   UNDER THE WEIGHT OF THE WORLD   Ruba Katrib

Zhou has always been preoccupied with scale, with subjects that exceed the confines of the lens and comprehension. In his work exploring the structures that support our digital, "immaterial" lives, he emphasizes the contradiction between the colossal extent of these efforts and their invisibility. He explains that at the "intersection of visible and invisible scales," his camera can serve as "a temporary means of dividing a space."[3] Through his spatial interventions, Zhou reveals the convergence of elements that come to structure a place as well as the lives, big and small, that surround it.

3   Zhou Tao, "The Axis of Big Data," unpublished artist's statement, 2024.

Karimah Ashadu

(pp. 27, 59)
Brown Goods, 2020
Single-channel HD digital video
(color, sound)
12 min.
Courtesy the artist and Sadie Coles
HQ, London

Tolia Astakhishvili

dark days, 2025
Mixed-media installation
Dimensions variable
Courtesy the artist and
LC Queisser, Tbilisi
Adapted from *when the others are
within us*, 2024, commissioned by
SculptureCenter, New York/Valeria
Napoleone XX

Wicked Plans, 2025
Mixed-media installation with
works by Maka Sanadze and Zurab
Astakhishvili
Dimensions variable
Courtesy the artist and LC
Queisser, Tbilisi

Tolia Astakhishvili with Dylan Peirce

(pp. 43, 65)
so many things I'd like to tell you,
2025
Two-channel video (color, sound)
48 min.
Courtesy the artists and
LC Queisser, Tbilisi

Miho Dohi

(pp. 47, 73)
buttai 46, 2018
Wood, brass, paper, cloth, and
plaster
14 × 17 × 15 ⁷/₁₀"
(35.6 × 43.2 × 39.9 cm)
Private collection

(p. 76)
buttai 66, 2019
Brass, copper, cotton, cloth, wood,
and other materials
11 ³/₈ × 7 ⁷/₈ × 15"
(29 × 20 × 38.1 cm)
Courtesy the artist and Gordon
Robichaux, New York

(p. 46)
buttai 75, 2020
Wood, cotton, copper, cloth, yarn,
acrylic, spray, and other materials
18 ¹/₂ × 16 ¹/₈ × 10 ¹/₄"
(47 × 41 × 26 cm)
Courtesy the artist and Gordon
Robichaux, New York

(p. 47)
buttai 89, 2021
Plaster, cloth, thread, brass, wire,
mortar, and acrylic
9 ¹/₁₆ × 13 ³/₄ × 7 ¹/₂"
(23 × 35 × 19 cm)
Collection David Galperin

(p. 76)
buttai 111, 2024
Paper, tape, acrylic, and other
materials
9 ¹/₂ × 6 ³/₄ × 2 ³/₈"
(24.1 × 17.1 × 0.9 cm)
Courtesy the artist and Nonaka-Hill,
Los Angeles and Kyoto

(p. 48)
haha 笑, 2024
Wood, paper, and acrylic
18 ⁷/₈ × 12 ¹/₄ × 1 ⁵/₈"
(47.9 × 31.1 × 4.1 cm)
Courtesy the artist and Nonaka-Hill,
Los Angeles and Kyoto

Andro Eradze

(pp. 52, 81, 85)
Flowering and Fading, 2024
4K video (color, sound)
16 min., 22 sec.
Courtesy the artist, Lo schermo
dell'arte, Firenze, Fondazione
in Between Art Film, Roma, and
SpazioA, Pistoia

He Xiangyu

(p. 91)
Opaque Loop, 2024
Stainless steel, iron, and natural
stones
116 ¹⁵/₁₆ × 18 ⁷/₈ × 52 ³/₄"
(297 × 47.9 × 133.9 cm)
TAO ART Collection, Taipei

(pp. 50, 51)
Rock Tongue, 2024
Stainless steel, iron, and natural
stones
65 ³/₄ × 15 ³/₄ × 42 ¹/₂"
(167 × 40 × 107.9 cm)
Courtesy the artist and Andrew
Kreps Gallery, New York

(pp. 51, 94)
Vessel Project: Yellow Houses, 2024
Saggar clay, bronze, and wood
13 × 16 × 8 ¹/₂"
(33 × 40.6 × 21.5 cm)
Courtesy the artist and Andrew
Kreps Gallery, New York

Samuel Hindolo

(p. 42, 101)
Gare de Bruxelles-Nord, 2024
Oil on paper mounted on fabric
51 ¹/₂ × 24 ¹/₂" (130 × 62.2 cm)
Collection X Museum, Beijing

Galgenberg Hill, 2025
Oil on canvas
24 × 36" (61 × 91.4 cm)
Courtesy the artist and 15 Orient,
New York

Geumhyung Jeong

Removed Parts: Restored, 2025
Mixed media
Dimensions variable
Courtesy the artist

Klara Liden

(p. 33)
Jean, 2021
Junction box and concrete
43 ¹¹/₁₆ × 29 ¹/₂ × 12 ⁵/₈"
(111 × 75 × 32 cm)
Sammlung von Storch

(p. 36)
Untitled (Dunmoore, right), 2023
Metal, wiring, and fluorescent lamp
19 ¹/₄ × 16 ⁷/₈ × 3 ⁷/₈"
(48.8 × 42.8 × 9.8 cm)
Collection Thomas Alexander

(p. 32)
Untitled (Haltestelle), 2024
Metal and plastic
118 ¹/₈ × 23 ⁵/₈ × 23 ⁵/₈"
(300 × 60 × 60 cm)
Sammlung von Storch

(p. 37)
Untitled (Invaliden 2), 2024
Rotating highway sign, spray paint,
poster, and vinyl
77 × 51 × 11"
(195.5 × 129.5 × 27.9 cm)
Courtesy the artist and Sadie Coles
HQ, London

(p. 34)
Untitled (Membrane 5), 2024
Bitumen sheeting (roofing
material), aluminum asphalt paint,
and plywood
52 × 187" (132 × 474.9 cm)
Private collection

Jean Katambayi Mukendi

(p. 22, 23)
Doors, 2023
Acrylic, paint, pen, and marker on
paper
107 × 422" (271.8 × 1071.9 cm)
Courtesy the artist and Ramiken,
New York

(pp. 23, 126)
Trash TV, 2022
Truck windshield, cardboard, found
objects, and marker
51 ¹/₄ × 35 ¹/₂ × 10"
(130.2 × 90.2 × 25.4 cm)
Courtesy the artist; Ramiken,
New York; and Micki Meng, San
Francisco and Paris

Nick Relph

Chaos (29), 2025
Dye sublimation aluminum print
11 ¹/₂ × 17" (29.2 × 43.1 cm)
Courtesy the artist; Herald St,
London; and Gordon Robichaux,
New York

Chaos (31), 2025
Dye sublimation aluminum print
11 ¹/₄ × 17" (28.5 × 43.1 cm)
Courtesy the artist; Herald St,
London; and Gordon Robichaux,
New York

Chaos (41), 2025
Dye sublimation aluminum print
14 × 21" (35.5 × 53.3 cm)
Courtesy the artist; Herald St,
London; and Gordon Robichaux,
New York

Chaos (49), 2025
Dye sublimation aluminum print
10 ¾ × 15 ½" (27.3 × 39.3 cm)
Courtesy the artist; Herald St,
London; and Gordon Robichaux,
New York

Chaos (81), 2025
Dye sublimation aluminum print
15 × 20 ¾" (38.1 × 52.7 cm)
Courtesy the artist; Herald St,
London; and Gordon Robichaux,
New York

Lusty Ghost (51), 2025
Dye sublimation aluminum print
5 ½ × 5 ¼" (13.9 × 13.5 cm)
Courtesy the artist; Herald St,
London; and Gordon Robichaux,
New York

Lusty Ghost (52), 2025
Dye sublimation aluminum print
1 ¼ × 2 ½" (3.1 × 6.3 cm)
Courtesy the artist; Herald St,
London; and Gordon Robichaux,
New York

Lusty Ghost (53), 2025
Dye sublimation aluminum print
11 ¾ × 16 ½" (29.8 × 41.9 cm)
Courtesy the artist; Herald St,
London; and Gordon Robichaux,
New York

Lusty Ghost (54), 2025
Dye sublimation aluminum print
7 × 16" (17.7 × 40.6 cm)
Courtesy the artist; Herald St,
London; and Gordon Robichaux,
New York

Lusty Ghost (55), 2025
Dye sublimation aluminum print
11 ¾ × 17" (29.8 × 43.1 cm)
Courtesy the artist; Herald St,
London; and Gordon Robichaux,
New York

Selma Selman

(pp. 24, 137)
Flowers of Life, 2024
Construction grabs, acrylic on
steel, metal, electric motor, engine
oil, tubes, and cables
47 ⅕ × 47 ⅕" (120 × 120 cm) base
and shovel
10 ⅕ × 19 ⅗ × 23 ⅗"
(26 × 50 × 60 cm) motor
Courtesy the artist; acb Gallery,
Budapest; and ChertLüdde, Berlin
Commissioned by Schirn
Kunsthalle, Frankfurt

Nail, 2025
Nail gilded with gold extracted
from motherboards
3 ½ × ³⁄₁₀" (9 × 0.8 cm)
Courtesy the artist; acb Gallery,
Budapest; and ChertLüdde, Berlin

Ser Serpas

(p. 30–31)
Backdrop, 2025
Oil paint and canvas
120 × 234 ¾" (304.8 × 596.3 cm)
Courtesy the artist and Maxwell
Graham, New York

more dimensional leaning seden-
tary meandering lack of spirit
migrating ellipses catch a glimpse
is of might not be too rough
heeding my brow fodder for the
sacrilegious tube of brief cadavers
made sadder still multiplied empty
sassafras more gently exonerated
trailing talented friend guide me it
festers while it stances up in that
tree find me and surrender cadence
sweet trite maybe lose tinges of
solitude and again acknowledge
me, 2025
Mixed-media sculptures
Dimensions variable
Courtesy the artist and Maxwell
Graham, New York

Emilija Škarnulytė

(pp. 18, 156–57)
Burial, 2022
Single-channel video (color, sound)
60 min.
Courtesy the artist

Zhou Tao

(p. 20)
The Axis of Big Data, 2024
Single-channel video (color, sound)
57 min., 34 sec.
Courtesy the artist and Vitamin
Creative Space, Guangzhou and
Beijing
Co-produced by M Art Foundation,
Hong Kong

Published on the occasion of the exhibition *The Gatherers* at MoMA PS1, Long Island City, NY, April 24–October 6, 2025. Organized by Ruba Katrib Chief Curator and Director of Curatorial Affairs, MoMA PS1, with Sheldon Gooch, Curatorial Assistant, MoMA PS1.

Generous support is provided by the Contemporary Arts Council of The Museum of Modern Art, the International Council of The Museum of Modern Art, and Jamie and Robert Soros. Significant support is provided by The Deborah Buck Foundation. Additional support is provided by George Petrocheilos and Diamantis Xylas, and Eleanor Heyman Propp. Special thanks to the Royal Norwegian Consulate General in New York, Marieluise Hessel, the Lithuanian Culture Institute, the Consulate General of Sweden in New York, Vicky Chen, and Webber Huang.

This publication was made possible with additional support from the MoMA PS1 Publication Fund, with special thanks to Philip Aarons and Shelley Fox Aarons, Elyse Benenson, and Kathy Fuld.

Library of Congress Control Number: 2025903481

ISBN 9780989985994

Published by MoMA PS1
22-25 Jackson Avenue
Long Island City, NY 11101
www.momaps1.org

Available through D.A.P./Distributed Art Publishers
75 Broad Street, Suite 630
New York NY 10004
www.artbook.com

Edited by Ruba Katrib
Editor: Annie Godfrey Larmon
Managing Editors: Sheldon Gooch and Serena Moscardelli
Designer: Alec Mapes-Frances
Proofreader: Polly Watson

This publication is typeset in Univers Next and Ruder Plakat LL

Printed and bound in Turkey by Ofset Yapımevi